THE
ESSENTIAL
TRINITY

THE ESSENTIAL TRINITY

New Testament foundations
and practical relevance

Edited by
BRANDON D. CROWE
and CARL R. TRUEMAN

APOLLOS (an imprint of Inter-Varsity Press)
36 Causton Street, London SW1P 4ST, England
Website: www.ivpbooks.com
Email: ivp@ivpbooks.com

First published 2016

British Library Cataloguing-in-Publication Data
A catalogue record for this book is available from the British Library.

ISBN: 978–1–78359–286–9
eBook ISBN: 978–1–78359–477–1

Set in Monotype Garamond 11/13pt

Inter-Varsity Press publishes Christian books that are true to the Bible and that communicate the gospel, develop discipleship and strengthen the church for its mission in the world.

IVP originated within the Inter-Varsity Fellowship, now the Universities and Colleges Christian Fellowship, a student movement connecting Christian Unions in universities and colleges throughout Great Britain, and a member movement of the International Fellowship of Evangelical Students. Website: www.uccf.org.uk. That historic association is maintained, and all senior IVP staff and committee members subscribe to the UCCF Basis of Faith.

*To all those who have faithfully preached and taught
the trinitarian faith to us and our families*

CONTENTS

CONTRIBUTORS

Richard Bauckham is Emeritus Professor of New Testament studies in the University of St Andrews, Scotland, and Senior Scholar at Ridley Hall, Cambridge, England. A Fellow of the British Academy and the Royal Society of Edinburgh, he is the author and editor of numerous books, including *Jesus and the God of Israel: God Crucified and Other Studies on the New Testament's Christology of Divine Identity*; *The Testimony of the Beloved Disciple: Narrative, History, and Theology in the Gospel of John*; and *Gospel of Glory: Major Themes in Johannine Theology.*

Brandon D. Crowe is Associate Professor of New Testament at Westminster Theological Seminary in Philadelphia, Pennsylvania. He is the author of *The Obedient Son: Deuteronomy and Christology in the Gospel of Matthew* and *The Message of the General Epistles in the History of Redemption: Wisdom from James, Peter, John, and Jude.*

Mark S. Gignilliat is Associate Professor of Divinity at Beeson Divinity School in Birmingham, Alabama. He is the author of *Karl Barth and the Fifth Gospel*; *A Brief History of Old Testament Criticism: From Benedict Spinoza to Brevard Childs*; and *Paul and Isaiah's Servants: Paul's Theological Reading of Isaiah 40–66 in 2 Corinthians 5:14–6:10.*

Benjamin L. Gladd is Assistant Professor of New Testament at Reformed Theological Seminary in Jackson, Mississippi. He is the author of *Hidden but Now Revealed: A Biblical Theology of Mystery* (with G. K. Beale); *Making All Things New: Inaugurated Eschatology for the Life of the Church* (with Matthew S. Harmon); and *Revealing the Mysterion: The Use of Mystery in Daniel and Second Temple Judaism with Its Bearing on 1 Corinthians.*

Jonathan I. Griffiths is a tutor for the Proclamation Trust's Cornhill Training Course, UK. He is the author of *Hebrews and Divine Speech* and the editor of *The Perfect Saviour: Key Themes in Hebrews.*

Daniel Johansson is a lecturer in New Testament studies and Academic Dean at the Lutheran School of Theology, Gothenburg, Sweden. He has authored several scholarly essays in the *Journal for the Study of the New Testament* and *Currents in Biblical Research*, and is a contributor to *Encyclopedia of the Bible and Its Reception*. His PhD thesis is entitled 'Jesus and God in the Gospel of Mark: Unity and Distinction'.

Robert Letham is Professor of Systematic and Historical Theology at Union School of Theology in Bridgend, Wales. He is the author of numerous books, including *The Holy Trinity: In Scripture, History, Theology, and Worship*; *Union with Christ: In Scripture, History, and Theology*; and *The Work of Christ.*

Michael Reeves is President and Professor of Theology at Union School of Theology in Oxford, UK. He is the author of numerous books, including *Delighting in the Trinity: An Introduction to the Christian Faith* and *Rejoicing in Christ*, and the co-editor (with Hans Madueme) of *Adam, the Fall, and Original Sin: Theological, Biblical, and Scientific Perspectives.*

Brian S. Rosner is Principal of Ridley College, Melbourne, Australia. He is the author of numerous books, including *Paul and the Law: Keeping the Commandments of God*; *Greed as Idolatry: The Origin and Meaning of a Pauline Metaphor*; and (with Roy E. Ciampa) *The First Letter to the Corinthians* (Pillar New Testament Commentary).

Scott R. Swain is Professor of Systematic Theology and Academic Dean at Reformed Theological Seminary in Orlando, Florida. He is the author of several books, including *Trinity, Revelation, and Reading: A Theological Introduction to the Bible and Its Interpretation*; *The God of the Gospel: Robert Jenson's Trinitarian Theology*; and *Father, Son and Spirit: The Trinity in John's Gospel* (with Andreas J. Köstenberger).

Alan J. Thompson is a lecturer in New Testament at Sydney Missionary and Bible College in Sydney, Australia. He is the author of *The Acts of the Risen Lord Jesus: Luke's Account of God's Unfolding Plan* and *One Lord, One People: The Unity of the Church in Acts in Its Literary Setting.*

Mark D. Thompson is Principal and the head of the department of Theology, Philosophy and Ethics at Moore Theological College in Sydney, Australia. He is the author of several books, including *A Clear and Present Word: The Clarity of Scripture*; *A Sure Ground on Which to Stand: The Relation of Authority and Interpretive Method in Luther's Approach to Scripture*; and *Too Big for Words? The Transcendence of God and Finite Human Speech*.

Carl R. Trueman is Paul Woolley Professor of Church History at Westminster Theological Seminary in Philadelphia, Pennsylvania, and Pastor of Cornerstone Presbyterian Church. He is the author of several books, including *Luther on the Christian Life: Cross and Freedom*; *John Owen: Reformed Catholic, Renaissance Man*; and *The Creedal Imperative*.

ABBREVIATIONS

General

art.	art.
b.	Babylonian Talmud
col.	column(s)
esp.	especially
EVV	English Versions
Gk.	Greek
lec.	lecture
m.	Mishnah
NT	New Testament
OT	Old Testament
pl.	plural
prol.	prologue
q.	question
tr.	translation, translated
y.	Jerusalem Talmud

Bible versions

AV	Authorized (King James) Version
ESV	English Standard Version, Anglicized
HCSB	Holman Christian Standard Bible
JPS	Jewish Publication Society

LXX	Septuagint
MT	Masoretic Text
NASB	New American Standard Bible
NET	New English Translation
NETS	New English Translation of the Septuagint
NIV	New International Version
NJPS	*Tanakh: The Holy Scriptures: The New JPS Translation According to the Traditional Hebrew Text*
NLT	New Living Translation
NRSV	New Revised Standard Version, Anglicized
OG	Old Greek
RSV	Revised Standard Version
Theo	Theodotion

Apocrypha and Septuagint

1 Macc.	1 Maccabees
2 Macc.	2 Maccabees
Sir.	Sirach/Ecclesiasticus
Wis.	Wisdom of Solomon

Dead Sea Scrolls

1QH[a]	Thanksgiving Hymns[a]
4Q381	Non-canonical Psalms B
4QFlor	*Florilegium*

Mishnah and Talmud tractates

| *B. Meṣ.* | *Baba Meṣiʿa* |
| *Ber.* | *Berakot* |

Old Testament pseudepigrapha

| *1 En.* | *1 Enoch* |
| *2 Bar.* | *2 Baruch* |

2 En.	*2 Enoch*
3 Macc.	*3 Maccabees*
4 Macc.	*4 Maccabees*
Jub.	*Jubilees*
T. Reub.	*Testament of Reuben*
T. Sol.	*Testament of Solomon*

Other Greek works

Diogn.	*Diognetus*

Josephus

Ant.	*Jewish Antiquities*
J. W.	*Jewish War*

Modern works

AB	Anchor Bible
ANRW	*Aufstieg und Niedergang der römischen Welt: Geschichte und Kultur Roms im Spiegel der neueren Forschung*, pt. 2: *Principat*, ed. Hildegard Temporini and Wolfgang Haase (Berlin: de Gruyter, 1972–)
AThR	*Anglican Theological Review*
BBR	*Bulletin for Biblical Research*
BDAG	W. Bauer, F. W. Danker, W. F. Arndt and W. F. Gingrich, *A Greek-English Lexicon of the New Testament and Other Early Christian Literature*, 3rd ed. (Chicago: University of Chicago Press, 2000)
BECNT	Baker Exegetical Commentary on the New Testament
BETL	Bibliotheca ephemeridum theologicarum lovaniensium
Bib	*Biblica*
BibInt	Biblical Interpretation Series
BibSac	*Bibliotheca sacra*
BNTC	Black's New Testament Commentary
BST	The Bible Speaks Today
BZNW	Beihefte zur Zeitschrift für die neutestamentliche Wissenschaft

CBQ	*Catholic Biblical Quarterly*
CBR	*Currents in Biblical Research*
CD	Karl Barth, *Church Dogmatics*, ed. G. W. Bromiley and T. F. Torrance, tr. G. W. Bromiley, 4 vols. (Edinburgh: T&T Clark, 1956–75)
CJT	*Canadian Journal of Theology*
CO	Calvini opera
ConBNT	Coniectanea biblica: New Testament Series
CQR	*Church Quarterly Review*
EBT	Explorations in Biblical Theology
HBT	*Horizons in Biblical Theology*
HTR	*Harvard Theological Review*
ICC	International Critical Commentary
IJST	*International Journal of Systematic Theology*
JBL	*Journal of Biblical Literature*
JETS	*Journal of the Evangelical Theological Society*
JPT	*Journal of Pentecostal Theology*
JSNT	*Journal for the Study of the New Testament*
JSNTSup	Journal for the Study of the New Testament, Supplement Series
JTS	*Journal of Theological Studies*
LCC	Library of Christian Classics
LFC	Library of the Fathers of the Church
LNTS	Library of New Testament Studies
LW	*Luther's Works*, ed. J. Pelikan and H. T. Lehmann, 55 vols. (St. Louis: Concordia; Philadelphia: Fortress, 1955–86)
NAC	New American Commentary
NACSBT	New American Commentary Studies in the Bible and Theology
NICNT	New International Commentary on the New Testament
NIGTC	New International Greek Testament Commentary
NovT	*Novum Testamentum*
NPNF²	*The Nicene and Post-Nicene Fathers*, Series 2, ed. Philip Schaff and Henry Wace, 1890–1900, 14 vols. (repr., Peabody, Mass.: Hendrickson, 1994)
NSBT	New Studies in Biblical Theology
NTS	*New Testament Studies*
OTL	Old Testament Library
PG	Patrologiae, cursus completus, patres ecclesiae, series graeca, ed. J.-P. Migne, 162 vols. (Paris: Cerf, 1857–86)
PL	Patrologiae, cursus completus, patres ecclesiae, series latina, ed. J.-P. Migne, 221 vols. (Paris: Cerf, 1844–64)

PNTC	Pillar New Testament Commentary
PRSt	*Perspectives in Religious Studies*
ProEccl	*Pro ecclesia*
RTR	*Reformed Theological Review*
SBL	Society of Biblical Literature
SBT	Studies in Biblical Theology
SEÅ	*Svensk Exegetisk Årsbok*
SJT	*Scottish Journal of Theology*
SNTSMS	Society for New Testament Studies Monograph Series
SNTW	Studies of the New Testament and its World
ST	*Summa Theologiae*
TNTC	Tyndale New Testament Commentaries
TrinJ	*Trinity Journal*
TTKi	*Tidsskrift for Teologi og Kirke*
TynB	*Tyndale Bulletin*
VTSup	Supplements to Vetus Testamentum
WA	*D. Martin Luthers Werke: Kritische Gesamtausgabe, Schriften*, ed. J. K. F. Knaake, G. Kawerau et al., 66 vols. (Weimar: Böhlaus Nachfolger, 1883–)
WBC	Word Biblical Commentary
WSC	Westminster Shorter Catechism
WTJ	*Westminster Theological Journal*
WUNT	Wissenschaftliche Untersuchungen zum Neuen Testament
ZNW	*Zeitschrift für die neutestamentliche Wissenschaft*

INTRODUCTION

Brandon D. Crowe and Carl R. Trueman

The Trinity is foundational to Christian theology. Indeed, for more than fifty years Christian theological discussion has been increasingly dominated by discussion of the doctrine, in large part due to the provocative move by Karl Barth in making it the every principle of his dogmatic enterprise. Unfortunately, however, it is not uncommon to encounter the view that the Trinity is a non-biblical doctrine (or perhaps one *possible* way of reading biblical texts) that arose only on the basis of later philosophical speculation. Likewise, many consider the Trinity to be a 'take it or leave it doctrine' when it comes to living the Christian life. The Bible – according to many – does not contain the doctrine of the Trinity, and even if it did, that would be something only for theologians to debate. However, historically in the Christian church the Trinity has been understood to be a robustly biblical doctrine with immense relevance for practical living. It is with this in mind that we present this volume, one that eschews overly technical discussion and focuses attention on the importance of the doctrine for every Christian.

The chapters in part 1 consider the trinitarian contours of every corpus of the New Testament, along with a chapter reflecting on the Old Testament roots of trinitarian doctrine. Here we must be clear: the term 'Trinity' and key terminology such as *homoousios* do not appear in Scripture; the technical terminology for trinitarian doctrine comes later, being crystallized in the fourth century. However, this precision of language does not import something foreign into the biblical texts, but faithfully articulates the content of those texts. In other words, it is the presupposition of this volume that trinitarian doctrine legitimately and necessarily follows from the phenomena of Scripture, rightly understood. Therefore, when using the term 'Trinity' or 'trinitarian' throughout this volume in relation to biblical books, we speak of the triadic contours of the text that lead – inexorably – to the doctrine of the Trinity. Stated differently, one of the aims of this volume is to show that faithful exegesis of biblical texts necessitates a trinitarian reading of the biblical texts, especially in the New Testament, where the doctrine is more fully revealed than in the Old Testament. The chapters in part 1 focus primarily on the New Testament witnesses, but also necessarily include reflections on the Old Testament backgrounds for the New Testament theological perspective. Indeed, chapter 8, on Revelation, and chapter 9, the final chapter in part 1, which is devoted to Old Testament revelation, will consider in greater detail how the New Testament's trinitarian witness is rooted in the Old Testament.

In part 2 we will address, at least implicitly, the charge that the Trinity is irrelevant as a practical doctrine. We will begin with a concise definition of the Trinity, followed by several chapters considering topics relevant for Christian life. Some will be more geared to leaders in the church, but we believe that all readers will benefit from the wisdom contained in these chapters.

The contributors to this volume represent a spectrum of theological perspectives, yet all agree that the Trinity is based on Scripture (part 1), and that the Trinity matters for how we live (part 2). This agreement on trinitarian doctrine reflects the agreement of orthodox Christian theology through the centuries. Christian theology has always affirmed the Trinity as a non-negotiable aspect of the one catholic and apostolic faith, even when differences persist over some other theological and ecclesiastical elements. Though one would not expect each contributor to agree with every other in all respects, the scope of the volume provides strong evidence from contributors with various backgrounds that the Trinity is a *necessary* doctrine – necessary both to interpret Scripture faithfully, and necessary for day-to-day living.

The editors would like to acknowledge our gratefulness to Philip Duce and the entire team at Inter-Varsity Press for their support for this volume, along with the contributors for their labours and participation. We would also like to thank the board, faculty and administration of Westminster Theological Seminary for their support in various ways that have helped enable the completion of this project. Special thanks go to our families, especially our wives, Cheryl and Catriona. Finally, we give highest thanks and praise to our triune God, not least because of the grace of the gospel, which bears a trinitarian shape. *Soli Deo gloria.*

PART 1:

NEW TESTAMENT FOUNDATIONS

1. THE TRINITY AND THE GOSPEL OF MATTHEW

Brandon D. Crowe

The Gospel of Matthew provides many insights into the relationship of the Father, the Son and the Holy Spirit. We find that Jesus is the obedient Son of God who enjoys an unparalleled relationship to God the Father. Along with the high Christology of Matthew we also find the presence and activity of the Holy Spirit closely related to both the Father and the Son. We will examine these features in this chapter in the following way. First, we will briefly look at the conception of God the Father in Matthew. Second, we will spend much of the chapter examining the divine Christology of Matthew. Third, we will look at the role of the Holy Spirit in relation to the Father and the Son.

God the Father

We begin with the concept of God as Father.[1] When we read of God as Father in Matthew, we are not encountering a new or previously unknown deity, but are reading about the same God of the Old Testament, the covenantal God of Israel. Therefore, we must understand the foundational self-revelation of God

---

1. In this chapter I will use 'God' and 'Father' virtually interchangeably.

in the Old Testament to understand the context for God in Matthew. It will be helpful to delineate three overarching aspects of the *theology* of Matthew.

First, God is the God of Old Testament Scripture. We can readily see Matthew's indebtedness to the theological outlook of the Old Testament by observing the frequency with which he quotes from and alludes to the Old Testament throughout his Gospel.[2] The number of quotations from the Old Testament is well over fifty (including ten notable fulfilment formula quotations), and allusions and other subtle references are too numerous to count.[3] These quotations often point to the role of Jesus in relation to the Old Testament, but we should also not miss their role in underscoring the theological presuppositions established in the Old Testament.

A brief survey of some of the Old Testament texts that Matthew references will give us a sense of his overall understanding of God. Jesus states that God is in control over the affairs of humanity, and even over the created realm (Matt. 6:25–33; 10:26–33), which echoes the descriptions of God we find in the Old Testament as one who cares for his people (Ps. 37:4, 25). God hears the prayers and knows the needs of his children (Matt. 6:5–13), which is consistent with his responsiveness to prayer in the Old Testament (Gen. 25:21; Exod. 3:7–8; 1 Kgs 9:3; 2 Kgs 19:20; 20:5; 2 Chr. 7:1, 12, 15; Pss 6:9; 65:2; 66:19–20; Prov. 15:8, 29; Dan. 9:21). In Matthew we read that God is good to all, and sends rain on the just and the unjust (Matt. 5:45), which is consistent with the psalmist's poetic reflections on the goodness of God towards all that he has made (Ps. 145:9). Jesus further declares that God resides in the power and holiness of the heavens (Matt. 6:9), which reflects the transcendence of God's power in the Old Testament (Deut. 4:39; 10:14; 1 Kgs 8:23; Ps. 115:3; Dan. 2:28, 44). In sum, to contextualize what we learn about God in Matthew, we must first of all appreciate the continuity of God's character with the Old Testament Scriptures.

Second, building on the previous point, in Matthew's theological outlook God alone is truly God: he has no rivals to his supremacy. God's dwelling in his glorious, heavenly habitation is consistently explained as the unique prerogative of the God of the Bible. Thus Moses proclaims in Deuteronomy 4:39 that the Lord is God in heaven, and there is no other. Additionally, the heavenly God

---

2. I will refer to the author of the first Gospel as 'Matthew', though the Gospel does not explicitly identify its author.

3. For further discussion on the OT in Matthew see Brandon D. Crowe, *The Obedient Son: Deuteronomy and Christology in the Gospel of Matthew*, BZNW 188 (Berlin: de Gruyter, 2012), pp. 6–27.

alone is to be worshipped. We see this explicitly affirmed in Jesus' response to Satan's third temptation (Matt. 4:10). When Satan promises Jesus all the kingdoms of the world if he will worship him, Jesus responds by quoting Deuteronomy 6:13, 'You shall worship the LORD your God and serve him only' (my tr.). Thus we find in Deuteronomy two fundamental tenets of the New Testament's understanding of God: God alone is the supreme Creator, and therefore he alone is to be worshipped. We see this again at Caesarea Philippi in Matthew 16. Here, in the ancient city that was the legendary home of the Greek god Pan, Peter affirms Jesus' identity as the Son of the 'living God' (Matt. 16:16). The phrase 'living God' highlights the reality and the activity of the biblical God in distinction from idolatrous so-called gods who did not intervene because they were not the Creator. Therefore, they were not to be worshipped (Deut. 5:26; Josh. 3:10; 1 Sam. 17:26, 36; 2 Kgs 19:4; Pss 42:2; 84:2 [84:3 EVV]; Jer. 10:10; Hos. 1:10).

It is difficult to overestimate the significance of God's uniqueness as the Creator who is to be worshipped in Jesus' day; this was fundamental to the world view of Jewish monotheism[4] that emphasized the Creator–creature distinction: God alone is the Creator, and all else falls under the category of 'creature' that must not be worshipped. Jesus' response to Satan in the wilderness is therefore consistent with core beliefs about God from the Old Testament. Indeed, in his temptation Jesus quotes Deuteronomy 6 twice, which is the context for one of the most important monotheistic texts in the Bible known as the Shema (Deut. 6:4). The warnings against worshipping a created being in the Old Testament are numerous and clarion (e.g. Deut. 5:6–10; 9:10–21; Num. 25:1–13; Isa. 40:18–23; 43:10–15; 44:6–20; 45:15–23; 46:1–11). What is remarkable in Matthew, as I will argue in the next section, is the attribution of worship to Jesus in a way that does not in any way undermine the monotheism of the Bible.

Third, and also deriving from the Old Testament, we find in Matthew that although God is the creator of all things, he is also known specifically as the covenantal God of Israel. This means that to understand the contours of God in Matthew we must consider the history of Israel in the Old Testament. Matthew 1:1 begins by invoking two leading figures from Israel's history, as Jesus is identified as the Son of David and the Son of Abraham. Matthew then includes a genealogy that gives not only the royal lineage of Jesus, but also traces the history of Israel from the humble beginnings of Abraham to the glories of David, to the nadir of the exile, and concludes with the glorious hope of

---

4. See Richard Bauckham, *God Crucified: Monotheism and Christology in the New Testament* (Grand Rapids: Eerdmans, 1999).

the Messiah. God redeemed his people from Egypt and entered into covenant with them at Mount Sinai (Exod. 19). As the covenant God of Israel, God is known as Father to the nation (e.g. Exod. 4:22–23; Deut. 1:31; 8:5; 14:1–2; 32:4–6, 18–20, 43; Isa. 1:2; Jer. 3 – 4; 31:9, 20; Hos. 11:1). Therefore it is not a completely new development when we find Jesus referring to God as *Father* throughout Matthew. We already find that the Davidic king was known as God's son in the Old Testament (Ps. 2:7; 2 Sam. 7:14), which grew organically out of the sonship of the nation as a whole (and indeed, out of the sonship of Adam). God had always been a Father to Israel, though, to be sure, we find Jesus speaking of God as Father with unparalleled intimacy.

In sum, to understand God in Matthew we must look first of all to the Old Testament, where we find that God is the one true God who had entered into covenant with Israel. At the same time, we learn more about God in Matthew than was revealed in the Old Testament. In particular, we learn that God is pre-eminently the Father of Jesus, who is the Son of God in a unique sense. But how does the distinctive sonship of Jesus relate to the existence and worship of the one true God of the Old Testament? This will be the focus of my next section, where I will examine the high Christology of Matthew.

Jesus, divine Son of God

Though we find in Matthew continuity with the character of God in the Old Testament, we must also note the new revelation we encounter in Matthew, particularly as it pertains to the relationship between the Father and the Son. We will see that Jesus as Son of God stands in clear continuity with Israel, but his sonship surpasses what was true of the nation and the king as son of God. Remarkably, in Matthew Jesus the Son is placed on the Creator side of the Creator–creature distinction.

Jesus and Israel as Son of God

We begin with one of the main Christological concepts in Matthew: Jesus as Son of God. To understand Jesus as Son of God we should again look first of all to the Old Testament. God was Father to Israel, and Israel was God's firstborn son (Exod. 4:22–23), and later this sonship finds particular focus in the Davidic king (2 Sam. 7:14). Thus Jesus' sonship in Matthew is like Israel as son of God, and like David as son of God. So the first clear reference to Jesus as Son of God in Matthew portrays Jesus' sonship in the light of Israel's sonship. In Matthew 2:15 we find Hosea 11:1 applied to Jesus ('out of Egypt I called my son', my tr.), which is an Old Testament text that speaks of God's love for his covenant people. Similarly, Jesus is identified as the beloved Son of God at his baptism (3:17), which may again recall the sonship of Israel, though the filial parallel to Israel is clearer in the temptations of Jesus. In Matthew 4:1–11 Jesus recapitulates the filial temptations of Israel in the wilderness as Jesus' own sonship is tested. Thus Satan explicitly questions the nature of Jesus' sonship in the first two temptations (Matt. 4:3, 6). Additionally, Jesus' first response comes from Deuteronomy 8:3, which derives from a context that underscores God's fatherly discipline of Israel (Deut. 8:5). Therefore it is commonplace to observe that 'Son of God' in Matthew 'must have to do in part with Jesus as the personification or embodiment of true, obedient Israel'.[5]

A comparison with the Gospel of Mark highlights the prominence of the Son of God theme in Matthew, since Jesus is identified as Son of God more frequently in Matthew. For example, in addition to the identification of Jesus as Son of God in Matthew 1 – 4, we find Jesus' sonship confessed by the disciples in Matthew 14:33, it is part of the confession of Peter at Caesarea Philippi (16:16), it is proclaimed by the heavenly voice at both the baptism (3:17) and the transfiguration (17:5), it is part of Caiaphas's question to Jesus at his trial (26:63), and the sonship of Jesus is also the focus of a round of taunts lobbed at him while nailed to the cross (27:39–43). The Son of God title also points to Jesus' kingly status, since Jesus is also the Son of David in Matthew (1:1; 9:27; 15:22; 20:30–31; 21:9; 22:42; cf. 2 Sam. 7:14; Ps. 2:7).

Jesus' privileged relationship with the Father

And yet there is more to the sonship of Jesus than simply recapitulating the history of Israel or fulfilling the hope of the Davidic king. In Matthew we find that Jesus is the Son of God in a way that goes beyond the filial precedents from the Old Testament. Jesus enjoys a unique and privileged relationship with God the Father. This becomes clearer as we move closer to the end of Matthew. Thus we must pay attention to the way that the identity of Jesus is progressively revealed throughout the Gospel, climaxing in the Great Commission (28:18–20).

We begin with the virginal conception and birth of Jesus (1:18–25). We do not find out everything there is to know about Jesus' special relationship to God in this text, but the whole passage is pregnant with significance. First we read that, in distinction from everyone else in Matthew's genealogy, no physical father

---

5. W. D. Davies and Dale C. Allison Jr., *A Critical and Exegetical Commentary on the Gospel According to St. Matthew*, ICC, 3 vols. (Edinburgh: T&T Clark, 1988–97), vol. 1, pp. 263–264.

is attributed to Jesus; we read simply that Jesus *was begotten* (*egennēthē*) of Mary (1:16). Given the cadence of the genealogy to this point in which every king is begotten by a father, this brief statement regarding Jesus' conception stands in sharp relief. Jesus' unique birth receives a bit more explanation in 1:18–25. We read again that Mary was found to be with child (passive voice) before she knew Joseph, her betrothed. At this point Matthew informs us that the child is conceived by the agency of the Holy Spirit (1:18, 20). Nowhere in 1:18–25 do we read explicitly that God is the Father of Jesus, but this reality becomes clearer as Matthew's narrative progresses, and in the light of the whole Gospel we are on firm ground to identify a Son of God Christology in Matthew 1.[6] This Son of God Christology, combined with the role of the (Holy) Spirit in Matthew, indicates that even from the conception of Jesus Matthew is pointing the reader to the remarkable relationship between Jesus and his Father. This special relationship is further underscored with the identification of Jesus as *Immanuel*, which is translated 'God with us' (1:23). I will return to this key theme of Matthew below, but can say by way of introduction that Immanuel is remarkably suggestive nomenclature to use of anyone, especially one who was conceived by the agency of the Holy Spirit in distinction from all other children.

What is introduced in Matthew 1 is therefore clarified as the Gospel progresses. We look next at the baptism of Jesus, which precipitates the opening of heaven, and the divine voice affirming Jesus' sonship (3:16–17). Remarkably, at the baptism of Jesus the Holy Spirit is again mentioned, and rests upon Jesus in the form of a dove. Moreover, the heavenly, fatherly voice identifies Jesus as his Son in whom he is well pleased, utilizing the term *eudokēsa*, which may allude to a pre-temporal choice of the Son of God as Messiah.[7] But regardless of how one interprets this divine good pleasure, the collocation of Father, Son and Spirit in the baptism of Jesus is remarkable.

---

6. See further Brandon D. Crowe, 'The Song of Moses and Divine Begetting in Matt 1,20', *Bib* 90 (2009), p. 52.

7. See Joel Marcus, *The Way of the Lord: Christological Exegesis of the Old Testament in the Gospel of Mark*, SNTW (Edinburgh: T&T Clark, 1992), pp. 73–74; D. A. Carson, 'Matthew', in F. E. Gaebelein (ed.), *The Expositor's Bible Commentary: Matthew, Mark, Luke*, 12 vols. (Grand Rapids: Zondervan, 1984; repr. 1995), vol. 8, p. 109. Thus the language would entail the premise that the Son existed before the incarnation. Cf. Geerhardus Vos, *The Self-Disclosure of Jesus: The Modern Debate About the Messianic Consciousness*, ed. J. G. Vos, 2nd ed. (Grand Rapids: Eerdmans, 1953; repr. Phillipsburg, N.J.: P&R, 2002), p. 186.

We also see Jesus' privileged relationship to God in the way he speaks of God as 'my Father' throughout the Gospel. Jesus speaks about the Father with an intimacy and authority that bespeaks his own privileged relationship to the Father. Thus we read in the Sermon on the Mount that it is only those who do the will of Jesus' Father that enter into the kingdom of heaven, and this is closely linked with hearing and doing the words of Jesus (7:21, 24). Jesus further states that whoever acknowledges or denies him before men, he will acknowledge or deny before his Father in heaven (10:32–33). Here Jesus makes a pronouncement about the heavenly destinies of individuals in a way that invokes his own relationship with his Father. One's relationship to Jesus is determined by doing the will of Jesus' Father (12:50), and one's destiny in relation to Jesus' Father depends on one's relationship to Jesus (25:31–40).

Elsewhere we read that Jesus is privileged to know the mysterious will of his Father. When Peter confesses Jesus as the Christ, the Son of the living God, Jesus affirms Peter and indicates that it was Jesus' own Father who revealed Jesus' true identity to Peter (16:17). Jesus also has the knowledge that the angels of the 'little ones' always see the face of his Father in heaven (18:10 ESV), and where two agree on earth, Jesus states that it will be done for them by his Father in heaven (18:19). Jesus also knows what his Father will do if we do not forgive our brothers from our hearts (18:35), and he knows that it is his Father who grants the privilege to sit at Jesus' right and left hand in the kingdom (20:23). Indeed, Jesus knows that he has but to ask and his Father will send him more than twelve legions of angels (26:53)! Jesus further affirms his own role as the Son of the Most High (26:63–64).

In addition to these profound statements Jesus can make about his Father, we should note how often he speaks of God as '*my* Father'. Even though God was the Father of Israel, it is rare to find individuals addressing God in this way, and certainly not to the extent or with the intimacy with which Jesus addressed God as 'my Father'. It is instructive to observe that Jesus also grants his disciples the privilege of being sons of God, and often refers to God as '*your* Father', but he never uses the phrase '*our* Father' in a way that would imply he and the disciples share an identical sort of sonship. The reason is that Jesus' sonship is qualitatively different from the disciples' sonship. Jesus' sonship is unmediated; the disciples' sonship – though a wonderful blessing and high privilege – is mediated through Jesus as Son of God.[8] Thus Jesus' statements in Matthew not

---

8. See Richard J. Bauckham, 'The Sonship of the Historical Jesus in Christology', *SJT* 31 (1978), pp. 245–260; cf. Geerhardus Vos, *Reformed Dogmatics*, ed. Richard B. Gaffin Jr. et al., 5 vols. (Bellingham, Wash.: Lexham, 2012–), vol. 1, pp. 52–53.

only reveal a deep knowledge about God and his will, but he even determines access to the Father! In sum, we find in Matthew that Jesus possesses an intimacy and knowledge of the deep things of his Father that excels all created beings.

Perhaps the most explicit statement we have about the relationship between Jesus and his Father is found in Jesus' prayer in 11:25–27. Here we are granted a marvellous insight into the depths of the divine unity of the Father and the Son.[9] In this prayer Jesus thanks his Father for his divine good pleasure to hide the realities of eschatological salvation in Christ from the wise and understanding, and reveal them to the childlike. It is crucial to note the balance and mutuality of the statements in this prayer in two ways. First, we see in 11:27 that no one *knows* the Son, but the Father knows him. Perhaps this statement is to be expected since the Father knows all things. But Jesus rounds out this thought in 11:27 by saying no one knows the Father except the Son! The Father's divine knowledge of the Son is thus mirrored by the Son's divine knowledge of the Father. This mutual knowledge denotes the closest possible relationship between the Father and the Son, though they are different persons. Here is an indication that the Son was not created at a moment in time, but he must eternally be the Son to know the Father with the depth that he does; were he ever to have become the Son at some point in history, his knowledge of the Father would be limited.

A second way we see the mutuality of the Father and the Son is in the task of *revealing*. In 11:25 we read that the Father has revealed the knowledge of salvation to the childlike, whereas in 11:27 we read that Jesus has the authority to reveal the Father. In other words, a comparable revealing function is attributed to both the Father and the Son. What is even more remarkable is that Jesus reveals *the Father*. Thus, although no one knows the Father except the Son, Jesus not only knows the Father but has the authority to reveal the Father to whomever (*hō ean*) he (the Son) desires, since all things have been given to him by the Father. Indeed, we also must not miss the parallelism between the Father's lordship of heaven and earth (11:25) and the 'all things' that have been given to Jesus (11:27 ESV), indicating Jesus as the steward of divine authority.[10]

We can say even more about this remarkable prayer. When Jesus speaks of the Father's good pleasure (*eudokia*, 11:26), given the context here and the usage of this term throughout the New Testament, this is most likely a reference to

---

9. In the parallel passage in Luke 10:21 Jesus rejoices *in the Holy Spirit*, bringing the trinitarian aspects even more clearly to the fore.

10. Cf. Joshua E. Leim, *Matthew's Theological Grammar: The Father and the Son*, WUNT 2.402 (Tübingen: Mohr Siebeck, 2015), pp. 83–87.

the Father's divine decree, especially in foreknowledge and election (cf. Luke 2:14; Eph. 1:5, 9; 1 Peter 1:2).[11] It is this divine purpose that Jesus as the Son speaks about with confidence, and the phrasing may even suggest that the Son knew of this plan before his incarnation.[12] Though this aspect may be debated, we must not miss the centrally important role of the Son himself in this prayer. As one scholar has noted:

> Jesus' joy and thanksgiving do not relate to something taking place outside of Himself . . . Jesus thanks God because His own Person is the pivot, the center of the whole transaction. The glory of the Gospel dispensation with its sovereignty and wisdom is focused in His own Person.[13]

In other words, Jesus the Son occupies a central role in the revelation of salvation, even as he is privy to a knowledge of God that is unparalleled among any created being. Jesus' position is squarely on the Creator side of the Creator–creature divide.

The disciples and Jesus' divine sonship

The prayer of Jesus in Matthew 11 provides a window into Jesus' own insight into the Father–Son relationship, and as the Gospel progresses we find that the disciples begin to understand more and more who Jesus really is. The next key text to consider comes in Matthew 14, where Jesus is recognized by the disciples as the Son of God (14:33). Jesus' actions in this context are dripping with divine significance. First, Jesus comes walking on the sea to his disciples in the midst of a raging storm. This action is more than just an impressive feat: it communicates to the disciples (and the reader of Matthew's Gospel) the divine identity of Jesus. For we read in the Old Testament that God alone tramples the waves

---

11. See Herman Bavinck, *Reformed Dogmatics*, ed. John Bolt, tr. John Vriend, 4 vols. (Grand Rapids: Baker Academic, 2003–8), vol. 2, pp. 270, 272; Vos, *Reformed Dogmatics*, vol. 1, p. 80.

12. Note the aorist *egeneto* in Matt. 11:26, combined with a phrase that is not always obvious in English translations (*emprosthen sou*), which seems to denote the immediate presence of God (cf. BDAG, 'ἔμπροσθεν', p. 325, §1.b.β [cf. §1.b.δ]; Matt. 10:32–33). Could we have here an allusion to the eternal, trinitarian plan of salvation often known as the *pactum salutis* or Covenant of Redemption? See also Luke 2:49; 22:29; John 17:4; *Diogn.* 9.1; and historically Zech. 6:13; Vos, *Reformed Dogmatics*, vol. 2, pp. 84–92; Bavinck, *Reformed Dogmatics*, vol. 3, pp. 212–216.

13. Vos, *Self-Disclosure*, p. 147.

of the sea (Job 9:8); it is the Lord alone in Isaiah who makes a way in the sea (Isa. 43:16); and, most impressively, we read in Psalm 77:20 (77:19 EVV; 76:20 LXX) that God made his path in the midst of the chaotic sea. In the same way, Jesus walks confidently upon the sea.

Second, in response to the stupefaction of the disciples (it is no wonder they thought Jesus to be a ghost), Jesus responds with words of comfort and authority that should be read in the light of God's self-revelation in the Old Testament: 'Take heart; it is I [*egō eimi*]; do not be afraid' (14:27, my tr.). The divine presence that should calm our fears is characteristic of God's unique supremacy in Isaiah 40 – 55. Third, not only does Jesus walk on the sea, but in his presence the wind and waves flee (14:32). This further recalls the divine presence in Psalm 77:17, along with texts such as Job 26:11–12,[14] where the waters tremble at the divine presence. Miracles that demonstrate mastery over the natural realm are singularly impressive, and Matthew 14 is arguably even more impressive than Matthew 8:26, where Jesus calms a storm with only his speech. Although one should not underestimate the significance of Jesus' actions in Matthew 8, it appears that the disciples are even more amazed at the silence of the waves without a word in Matthew 14:32.

The disciples' amazement leads to a fourth observation, which is the worship of Jesus in 14:33, in conjunction with the confession that Jesus is the Son of God. Due to a combination of factors, it is best to understand the potentially ambiguous *proskyneō* as 'worship', since Jesus' actions and words are divine – he walks on the sea, calms the storm with his presence and speaks in a way that is proper to God. Thus again we see how greater clarity into Jesus' identity is gained as the Gospel unfolds, here in reference to the worship of him. In Matthew 2 we find the magi worshipping Jesus in his infancy (2:11). Though it is unclear how well the magi understood the significance of their actions, they are portrayed positively in Matthew's narrative. In contrast to King Herod, they have responded appropriately to the birth of Jesus. When Jesus is tempted by the devil in the wilderness, he affirms the teaching of Deuteronomy that only the Lord God should be worshipped and served (Matt. 4:10; cf. Deut. 6:13). The prerogative of God alone to be worshipped was axiomatic in Jesus' Jewish context. Therefore it is most remarkable in Matthew 14 that Jesus himself does not rebuke his disciples when they worship him as Son of God. Indeed, all signs in the narrative, not least of which is the theophanic language, point to the legitimacy and propriety of worshipping Jesus as the Son of God in a

---

14. For other relevant texts see Davies and Allison, *Matthew*, vol. 2, pp. 509–510; Leim, *Matthew's Theological Grammar*, pp. 139–147.

transcendent sense in 14:33.[15] The reader of Matthew is being swept up in the Christological momentum of the Gospel that is leading to the crescendo of the Great Commission.

The disciples' experience in Matthew 14 finds verbal expression in Peter's confession of Jesus as the Christ in Matthew 16:16. As J. P. Meier has observed, 'What 14:22–33 presented by way of dramatic narrative now receives its full explication in the words of Peter and Jesus.'[16] Thus it is important to read Matthew 16:16 in the light of what has come before it, since the Gospel progressively reveals the mystery of the person of Jesus the Son; we know more about who Jesus is the closer we come to the end of the Gospel. Much ink has been spilled on the role of Peter and the church in Matthew 16, but we must not miss the significant Christological point that is foundational to Peter's confession. Particularly noteworthy is the remarkable way that Peter's confession recognizes Jesus' status as uncreated. As noted above, when the Bible refers to God as the *living* God, it underscores the ontological reality that God alone is the true God who really exists. It is also an indication that God is the source of all life, and he is therefore self-sufficient. He is not in need of anything else to be; he simply is. Peter's statement in Matthew 16:16 is thus more than a messianic confession (though it is certainly that); it is also a confession that Jesus is the Son of the Father who shares the quality of *living* and therefore has all life in himself.[17] As the Son of the living God, Peter is pointing to the unique position that Jesus inhabits not only as Messiah, but as the divine Son of God. This is one reason why Jesus blesses Peter's answer and tells him that the Father has revealed this mystery to Peter (16:17). It also helps us understand why Peter would rebuke Jesus for announcing his impending death. How could the Son of the *living* God face *death*? But the cross is at the heart of Jesus' messianic task, and we further learn that as the Son of the living God Jesus will not be bound by death, but will overcome death in the resurrection (16:18, 21). Thus to understand the significance of Peter's confession we may rephrase it by saying Jesus is the *living* Son of God who has all life in himself. Again we see Jesus on the Creator side of the Creator–creature distinction.

---

15. So John P. Meier, *The Vision of Matthew: Christ, Church, and Morality in the First Gospel* (New York: Crossroad, 1991; repr. Eugene, Ore.: Wipf & Stock, 2004), p. 100; Charles L. Quarles, *A Theology of Matthew: Jesus Revealed as Deliverer, King, and Incarnate Creator*, EBT (Phillipsburg, N.J.: P&R, 2013), pp. 169–170.

16. Meier, *Vision*, p. 108.

17. Cf. ibid., p. 109; Vos, *Self-Disclosure*, p. 180.

In Matthew 16 we reach a turning point in the Gospel. From this point Jesus moves deliberately and explicitly towards Jerusalem. From this point the die has been cast, and now we see Jesus speaking with a greater clarity about his person and mission. After Jesus' prediction of his impending death and resurrection, his true glory is revealed on the Mount of Transfiguration (17:2). In the last week of his public ministry Jesus receives the praise of children in the temple (21:9, 14–15; cf. Ps. 8:2),[18] and confounds the Pharisees from Psalm 110:1 by asking how the Messiah can be both David's son (Jesus came from the line of David) and David's Lord (since he has authority over and existed before David).[19] Indeed, Jesus' use of Palm 110 appears to be even more remarkable, since he implies that he himself is 'my Lord' to whom the Lord (YHWH) spoke in David's psalm.[20] After this exchange, no one dared to ask Jesus any more questions (Matt. 22:46).

One of the most climactic moments in the Christological revelation of Matthew comes when Jesus stands trial before the high priest. At this moment Caiaphas adjures Jesus by the living God (!) if Jesus is the Christ, the Son of God. Jesus responds by pointing to Caiaphas's own confession of who he is, and counters with a rebuke of sorts. Jesus quotes Daniel 7:13 in conjunction with his status as Son of Man – the one who is at the right hand of God's majesty and is coming with the clouds of heaven. The title Son of Man is much debated, but it is widely agreed that it is a title used to refer to Jesus' ministry, his passion and his coming again in glory. We therefore must not miss the exalted nature of Jesus that is found in the title Son of Man – though the Son of Man suffers, he will reign and come with the clouds. If we take the cue from Matthew 26:64 and trace the Son of Man back to Daniel 7, which is the most likely option for the imagery of this title, we find that the Son of Man comes to the presence of the Ancient of Days and is given an everlasting kingdom that will never be destroyed.

Jesus as Immanuel
This Son of Man imagery also plays a role in the Great Commission when the resurrected Jesus explains his authority over all things. This brings us to one of

---

18. Cf. Leim, *Matthew's Theological Grammar*, pp. 166–173.

19. On which see Simon J. Gathercole, *The Preexistent Son: Recovering the Christologies of Matthew, Mark, and Luke* (Grand Rapids: Eerdmans, 2006), pp. 236–238.

20. Cf. Matthew W. Bates, *The Birth of the Trinity: Jesus, God, and Spirit in New Testament and Early Christian Interpretations of the Old Testament* (Oxford: Oxford University Press, 2015), pp. 47–54.

the most important Christological themes in all of Matthew: Jesus as Immanuel. This is the theme of the first of Matthew's ten fulfilment formula citations (1:22–23), and serves as an inclusio that bookends Matthew's Gospel. We find the mention of Jesus as 'God with us' in the first episode following the genealogy (1:18–25), and we find it again in the last statement of the Gospel in which Jesus promises to be with his disciples even to the end of the age (28:20). It is important to understand what is entailed by identifying Jesus as 'God with us'. Most simply, it refers to Jesus as the fulfilment of the divine covenant presence, which is the highest covenant blessing imaginable. God's covenant presence was the blessing experienced by Adam and Eve in the Garden of Eden. God's presence was promised to the Israelites as they looked forward to the Promised Land (Lev. 26:12). God's presence filled the tabernacle (Exod. 40:34–35) and later the temple (1 Kgs 8:10–11; Pss 74:2; 76:2; 132:13; etc.). In Matthew Jesus is greater than the temple (12:5–6), greater than Solomon who built the temple (12:42) and greater than the priests who served in the temple (9:1–8). For Matthew, Jesus as Immanuel underscores the Son as God's covenant presence with us in the most profound sense.

Yet we must not neglect to consider the various implications of God's covenant presence. It is indeed the most glorious blessing imaginable that Jesus is God's presence with us, yet this presence is a curse for those who oppose him. Put differently, Jesus is God's presence for blessing or for cursing, depending on one's relationship to Jesus. We can see this by looking to the Old Testament context, where we find Immanuel. In Isaiah 7 King Ahaz of Judah refuses to heed God's command to ask him for a sign, opting instead to trust the Assyrians for protection. In response Isaiah informs Ahaz that the Lord himself will provide a sign to Ahaz – the child who will be called Immanuel. In Isaiah the sign of Immanuel is a curse to Ahaz, who is rebelling against the word of God. However, this same child is a blessing to those whose hope is in the Lord. In the same way, Jesus' presence is a curse for those who, like the Pharisees, reject his word (Matt. 23), but a blessing for those whose trust is in the Son of God (Matt. 14:22–33; 18:20).

In the light of these features of Jesus-as-Immanuel, does this title mean that Jesus is divine? To answer this question, we must again pay careful attention to the way Matthew's Gospel provides more information for the reader as the narrative progresses. That which is introduced suggestively at the beginning of the Gospel is apprehended with greater clarity by the Gospel's conclusion. In Matthew 1 we read of Jesus' lineage deriving from David and Abraham. We read that he is born of Mary, without the agency of a physical father, but conceived by the power of the Holy Spirit. His birth is miraculous, and numerous aspects of his early life are fulfilments of Scripture. We have also traced the intimate relationship Jesus shares with his Father beyond any created being, to which we should add the immense authority of Jesus over sicknesses, the demonic and the natural realm. Later Jesus makes the incredible promise that wherever two or three of his disciples in the church are gathered in his name, there he is with them (18:20). Finally we read in the Great Commission that Jesus is worshipped and all authority in heaven and earth belongs to him,[21] and he will be with his disciples always, even to the end of the age (28:20). Jesus' final promise of his continued presence with his disciples clarifies what is already present in 1:23: he is the fulfilment of God's covenant presence with his people in a way that transcends the presence of any created being. Jesus is the divine Immanuel, who is placed in closest collocation with the Father and the Spirit (28:19). In the light of these textual features we should conclude that Jesus is always with us as the divine Immanuel.

Father, Son and Holy Spirit

Now that we have seen the supremacy of God and the divine nature of the Son of God, we should note the way that Matthew expresses the nature and role of the (Holy) Spirit in relation to the Father and the Son. What we find is a remarkable unity among all three persons in a way that points to the divine role of the Spirit, surpassing any created being.

The Holy Spirit is identified in a number of ways in Matthew. First, Matthew closely associates the Spirit with God the Father. At the baptism in 3:16 it is the Spirit *of God* who rests upon Jesus, and Jesus casts out demons by the Spirit *of God* (12:28), which closely follows the citation of Isaiah 42 that speaks of the Lord's Spirit on the Servant (12:18). The Spirit is elsewhere known as the Spirit of the disciples' Father (10:20).

Second, we also see a close association of the Spirit with Jesus. The Holy Spirit is the creative power behind Jesus' conception (1:18, 20),[22] and it is the Spirit who empowers Jesus for his messianic ministry (3:11, 16; 4:1; 12:18, 28). To blaspheme the Son of Man will be forgiven, but blaspheming the Holy Spirit (who empowers the Son of Man) is blaspheming God and will not be forgiven (12:31–32). Additionally, it is the Spirit who inspired David's prophecy that the Messiah would be both David's son and David's Lord (22:43; cf. Ps. 110:1). In

---

21. Notice the parallels to the authority of the Father in 11:25.

22. Cf. J. Gresham Machen, *The Virgin Birth of Christ* (New York: Harper & Row, 1930; repr. Grand Rapids: Baker, 1985), p. 140.

a few instances we find Jesus speaking of both his Father and the Holy Spirit, in addition to Jesus' own role as Son of Man (10:20–33; 12:28–32). Taken together, these texts reveal the personality of the Spirit, which is a crucial aspect in recognizing his deity. In sum, in Matthew the Spirit of the Father is also known as the Spirit of God, and this is the Spirit who empowers Jesus for his ministry. The role of the Holy Spirit in Matthew underscores the principle that 'all persons of the Trinity share in all the external acts of God (*opera ad extra trinitatis indivisa sunt*)'.[23]

Further supporting this principle, in Matthew we have several texts that present Father, Son and Spirit – sometimes all three present at the same time – in a way that indicates the divine status of each person. At the birth of Jesus we find the Holy Spirit – who, as we have seen, is the Spirit of the Father – is the agent of the conception of Jesus (1:18–20).[24] At the baptism of Jesus we find the voice of the Father, the descent of the dove on Jesus and the sonship of Jesus proclaimed (3:16–17). Here is no modalism, but the simultaneous existence of all three persons of the Godhead at a crucial moment in the history of redemption – the anointing of Jesus for his messianic ministry. In sum, we see the presence of the Father, Son and Spirit throughout the Gospel of Matthew. The Spirit occupies a central role in the work of Jesus the Son in the inauguration and instruction on the kingdom of God the Father.

A similar moment is found on the mount of transfiguration, where the Father, the glory cloud and the Son are all present at the same time as Jesus heads towards the cross (17:5). Though the Spirit is not mentioned explicitly in the way he is at the baptism, one may argue that we have scriptural warrant for connecting the theophanic glory cloud in Matthew 17 with a manifestation of the Holy Spirit, especially since the wording of the divine voice is so similar to the baptism account where the Spirit descends as a dove.[25]

The climax of Matthew's Gospel comes in the Great Commission (28:18–20), and this is also the clearest text in Matthew, and indeed one of the clearest texts in all of the New Testament, that explicitly coordinates the Father, the Son and

---

23. Sinclair B. Ferguson, *The Holy Spirit*, Contours of Christian Theology (Downers Grove: InterVarsity Press, 1996), p. 43.

24. The divine passive is also used in 1:16, 18, 20.

25. On the glory cloud as a manifestation of the Holy Spirit see Meredith M. Kline, 'The Holy Spirit as Covenant Witness' (ThM thesis, Westminster Theological Seminary, 1972), pp. 5–26; Meredith G. Kline, *Images of the Spirit* (Grand Rapids: Baker, 1980), pp. 15, 29; Vern S. Poythress, *The Manifestation of God: A Biblical Theology of God's Presence* (forthcoming), chs. 5, 16–17, 43.

the Spirit. The interrelatedness and distinctions between the persons of the Godhead, which were perhaps more opaque at the beginning of the Gospel, are stated much more forthrightly in Jesus' resurrected state. In Matthew 28 we read that Jesus is the one who has all authority in heaven and on earth, and he commands his disciples to make disciples of all nations, baptizing them in *the name* of *the* Father and of *the* Son and of *the* Holy Spirit. It is significant that the singular *name* encompasses Father, Son and Spirit. Additionally, the definite article is repeated before each person of the Trinity to emphasize the distinctness of each person. The implications seem to be that the Father, the Son and the Spirit are able to be described by one name, yet this does not lead to a conflation of divine persons: Father, Son and Spirit remain distinct persons who share the one name.[26] And as the climax of Matthew's Gospel, we must wrestle with the implications of this statement in the light of the whole Gospel that precedes the final commissioning scene. Put differently, the final words of Jesus sum up his teaching, and our understanding of Jesus in Matthew must be related to the trinitarian directive he gives in his parting words. Therefore it is incumbent upon us to identify and address the trinitarian nature of Matthew's Gospel.

Conclusion

We find in Matthew the good news that is trinitarian in nature. It is good news that comes from Jesus, the resurrected Messiah, the one who has been given all authority in heaven and on earth. Jesus is the Son of God and Mediator who grants us the privilege of becoming sons and daughters of his Father in heaven. Along with this privilege comes the abiding promise that he is Immanuel, who is with us now and will continue to be with us until the end of the age.

© Brandon D. Crowe, 2016

---

26. See Bavinck, *Reformed Dogmatics*, vol. 2, pp. 270, 305–306.

2. THE TRINITY AND THE GOSPEL OF MARK

Daniel Johansson

Given a common opinion that the Gospel of Mark displays a low Christology, it may seem a futile endeavour to take the discussion a step further in exploring whether a trinitarian understanding of God can be traced there.[1] If we assume a 'natural' development from a binitarian (God and Jesus) to a trinitarian view of God (God, Jesus and the Spirit) in the early Christian communities,[2] a view which is often taken for granted but not necessarily demonstrated,[3] it would seem pointless to bring up the question of the Trinity if Jesus is less than divine.

---

1. From the early twentieth century to about 1970 the dominating view was that Mark presented a divine Christ. After that the majority view changed and Mark's Jesus was seen as being merely a human being, albeit an exalted one. It seems, however, that the opinion is about to change again, for several recent studies have argued that Mark portrays a divine Christ. For a survey see Daniel Johansson, 'The Identity of Jesus in the Gospel of Mark: Past and Present Proposals', *CBR* 9 (2011), pp. 364–393.
2. For a survey and critique see J. N. D. Kelly, *Early Christian Creeds*, 3rd ed. (London: Longman, 1972), pp. 13–29.
3. Twofold and threefold patterns may have existed side by side, or, for that matter, a personal understanding of the Spirit could have developed before Jesus was understood in divine terms, a view seldom (if ever) considered.

However, I will argue that the evidence for a uniquely close linking of Jesus to God in Mark is stronger than is often recognized, and, although there are relatively few references to the Holy Spirit, these have some of the characteristics that are normally taken to be evidence for the Spirit's divine and personal status.[4] At the same time, Mark offers strong evidence for the belief in the one, unique God of Israel.

Before turning to the evidence, some words must be said about terminology. From a strictly historical point of view it would be anachronistic to use terms like 'Trinity' and 'trinitarian', since these appeared and were discussed long after Mark was written and involved philosophical categories he does not appear to allude to. For this reason some scholars prefer to speak of a 'proto-Trinitarian' view,[5] a divine triad, a threefold pattern, and so on, when discussing New Testament texts.[6] The present study acknowledges the difficulty in using 'trinitarian' vocabulary. On the other hand, threefold patterns in the New Testament cannot be completely disconnected from the discussions and development of the doctrine of the Trinity in subsequent centuries. The early Christian theologians were in fact among other things also discussing precisely these texts.[7] Thus, while being aware of the difficulties, I nevertheless feel content to ask if a *trinitarian* pattern can be traced in Mark.

The oneness of God

Although some scholars have attributed the ascription of divine status of Christ to the influx of pagans in the Christian communities, who by their blurred concepts of the divine undermined and finally overthrew the solid and strict

---

4. Mark's primary interest appears to lie with Jesus and his relationship to God and less so with the Spirit. But this should not surprise us, as Mark seems to have written a Jesus biography of the ancient type. See Richard A. Burridge, *What Are the Gospels? A Comparison with Graeco-Roman Biography* (Grand Rapids: Eerdmans, 2004). Had Mark written epistles to early churches, more directly addressing the situation after the believers' experience of the Spirit, like Paul did, the evidence might have looked slightly different.

5. Gordon D. Fee, *Pauline Christology: An Exegetical-Theological Study* (Peabody, Mass.: Hendrickson, 2007), pp. 586–593.

6. Cf. Arthur W. Wainwright, *The Trinity in the New Testament* (London: SPCK, 1962); Larry W. Hurtado, *God in New Testament Theology* (Nashville: Abingdon, 2010).

7. See e.g. Novatian, *De Trinitate*.

monotheism of the earliest Jewish believers,[8] the evidence of the New Testament texts points in a different direction, namely that early Christians maintained a monotheistic stance.[9] The Gospel of Mark is no exception in this regard. Even though, or perhaps precisely because, Mark wrote to a primarily Gentile audience,[10] he includes some of the strongest assertions in the New Testament of belief in the one God of Israel.

Mark begins his Gospel by citing the Jewish Scriptures: 'As it is written in Isaiah the prophet . . .' (1:2).[11] This is actually a conflation of three different Old Testament passages (Exod. 23:20; Mal. 3:1; Isa. 40:3), but Mark highlights the Isaiah quotation by explicitly ascribing the entire quotation to Isaiah.[12] By doing this at the outset of his writing[13] Mark connects his own writing both to the Jewish tradition (i.e. their Scriptures) as well as to their God and their monotheism.[14] The very passage Mark cites, Isaiah 40:3, is also the beginning of the most explicitly monotheistic portion of the Old Testament, which combines solemn declarations about Israel's God ('I am YHWH, and there is no other, / besides me there is no God' [45:5]) with hilarious ridiculing of man-made idols. Mark's point, even if implicit, surely is that the one God of Israel, the only creator of everything and the Lord of history, who in ancient days promised

---

8. E.g. Wilhelm Bousset, *Kyrios Christos: Geschichte des Christusglaubens von den Anfängen des Christentums bis Irenaeus* (Göttingen: Vandenhoeck & Ruprecht, 1913; rev. ed. 1921); Maurice Casey, *From Jewish Prophet to Gentile God: The Origins and Development of New Testament Christology* (Cambridge: James Clarke, 1991).

9. E.g. Larry W. Hurtado, 'Devotion to Jesus and Second-Temple Jewish Monotheistic Piety', in idem, *How on Earth Did Jesus Become a God: Historical Questions About Earliest Devotion to Jesus* (Grand Rapids: Eerdmans, 2005), pp. 31–55; Richard Bauckham, *Jesus and the God of Israel: God Crucified and Other Studies on the New Testament's Christology of Divine Identity* (Milton Keynes: Paternoster; Grand Rapids: Eerdmans, 2008), pp. 94–106.

10. Mark 7:3–4 is usually cited as evidence.

11. Translations of Scripture in this chapter are my own.

12. Rikk E. Watts, *Isaiah's New Exodus and Mark*, WUNT 2.88 (Tübingen: Mohr Siebeck, 1997), pp. 57–90.

13. On the importance of the beginning of literature in antiquity see e.g. D. Earl, 'Prologue-Form in Ancient Historiography', *ANRW*, vol. 1.2, pp. 842–856, esp. 856.

14. On the significance of this aspect of the doctrine of the Trinity see Robert W. Jenson, *Systematic Theology*, vol. 1: *The Triune God* (Oxford: Oxford University Press, 1997), pp. 42–60.

to act on behalf of his people, is now about to fulfil his promises.[15] Who this God is, and how he acts, is the story Mark is going to tell.

The most significant passage dealing with the question of God's oneness is found in the theologically dense chapter 12.[16] Asked about the greatest commandment, Jesus responds by citing Deuteronomy 6:4, 'Hear, O Israel: The LORD our God, the LORD is one' (12:29). The scribe is no less emphatic about God's uniqueness in his response: 'You are right, Teacher. You have truly said that *he is one*, and *there is no other except him*' (12:32). This passage is remarkable. Other early Christian writers allude to the first part of the Shema, but this is the only citation of it in the New Testament.[17] Even more surprising is that it is difficult to find any passages in biblical or early Jewish literature rivalling this one when it comes to monotheistic density:[18] Jesus first cites the Shema, and then the scribe adds two monotheistic formulas: 'he is one' and 'there is no other except him'.[19] The monotheistic outlook of Mark's Gospel could hardly have been stated more forcefully. Mark's reason for including it – which is noteworthy in comparison with the omissions in Matthew and Luke – is probably related to the polytheistic environment in which his audience lived, and the Gentile background of many of them. There should be no doubt that the evangelist repudiates the polytheism of the Greco-Roman world. But Mark may have had another reason, namely to avoid misunderstandings about Jesus.[20]

---

15. On the general influence of Isaiah on Mark see Watts, *Isaiah's New Exodus and Mark*.

16. Four highly significant questions for early Christians are raised in dialogues between Jesus and his opponents: the relationship to the emperor (and the state), the question of the bodily resurrection, Jewish monotheism and the identity of Jesus.

17. Deut. 6:4 is omitted from the Synoptic parallels. On allusions to the Shema in the NT see Bauckham, *Jesus*, pp. 94–106. For a recent discussion of Deut. 6:4 see Erik Waaler, *The Shema and the First Commandment in First Corinthians: An Intertextual Approach to Paul's Rereading of Deuteronomy*, WUNT 2.253 (Tübingen: Mohr Siebeck, 2008), pp. 98–114, 123–133.

18. Cf. Waaler's conclusion: 'In Mark, this is given in a purer form than in many earlier Jewish texts' (*Shema*, p. 220). Waaler finds three elements in the scribe's response: (1) confession to God's oneness, (2) denial that there is any other, and (3) the statement of no exceptions.

19. See ibid., pp. 106–114, 154–181, 448–451, and U. W. Mauser, 'Eis Theos und Monos Theos in biblischer Theologie', in I. Baldermann, E. Dassmann and O. Hofius (eds.), *Einheit und Vielfalt biblischer Theologie* (Neukirchen-Vluyn: Neukirchener Verlag, 1986), pp. 71–87.

20. See below.

The keyword 'one' in the Shema appears in two further passages. Both Mark 2:7 and 10:18 include the identical phrase *ei mē heis ho theos*, in both cases probably alluding to the Shema, since in neither case is the word *heis* (one) necessary, and pointing forward to Jesus' quotation of it and the scribe's response in Mark 12.[21] In the first place the words are ascribed to some scribes who object to Jesus' forgiving the sins of the paralytic: 'Who can forgive sins except one, God?' In the second passage Jesus questions the rich man's reason for calling him good: 'Why do you call me good? No one is good except the one God.' The inclusion of the keyword in the Shema, which also was frequently used to stress the uniqueness of Israel's God in the Bible and early Jewish literature, suggests that the monotheistic belief in the one God is the concern in both passages.[22]

Further, God is designated as 'the Most High God' in 5:7. This title often appears in a Gentile context in the early Jewish literature, either when Gentiles are referring to the God of Israel, as is the case in Mark, or when Jews are addressing Gentiles.[23] Although this title could imply an understanding of the divine in which Israel's God is the most powerful among other gods, Bauckham argues that its use in the early Jewish literature rather indicates God's sovereignty over all things, history as well as nations, and for this reason was especially fitting in a Gentile context.[24]

We should also note that Mark identifies God as the creator of all things and the sovereign ruler of history, such that he can shorten the days (13:19–20). Both were central in the Jewish expression of their commitment to God (cf. *3 Macc.* 2.3).[25] The evangelist never elaborates these themes, but appears to take them for granted.

In conclusion, Mark maintains the basic Jewish understanding and belief in one God, which is stressed in particular by the inclusion of the Shema and

21. Joel Marcus, 'Authority to Forgive Sins upon the Earth: The Shema in the Gospel of Mark', in C. A. Evans and W. R. Stegner (eds.), *The Gospels and the Scriptures of Israel*, JSNTSup 104 (Sheffield: Sheffield Academic Press, 1994), pp. 196–211.

22. Joachim Gnilka, 'Zum Gottesgedanken in der Jesusüberlieferung', in H.-J. Klauck (ed.), *Monotheismus und Christologie: Zur Gottesfrage im hellenistischen Judentum und im Urchristentum* (Freiburg im Breisgau: Herder, 1992), pp. 144–162; see p. 151: 'The oneness of God is at stake (Die Einzigkeit Gottes steht auf dem Spiel).'

23. Bauckham, *Jesus*, pp. 107–126. Bauckham includes a table of the occurrences of the terminology in Jewish writings 250 BC – AD 150.

24. Ibid., pp. 116–122.

25. Larry W. Hurtado, *Lord Jesus Christ: Devotion to Jesus in Earliest Christianity* (Grand Rapids: Eerdmans, 2003), p. 36; Bauckham, *Jesus*, pp. 7–11.

repeated allusions to the concept of one God. Mark thus belongs to the group of early Christian writers that provides later theologians with the idea of God's oneness, one of the key elements in the later development of the trinitarian dogma.

God the Father

The word 'God' appears about fifty times in Mark. More than half of these, however, are used in constructions such as the 'kingdom of God', the 'commandment of God', and so on, reducing the number of direct referents to 'God' to about twenty-five. This is significantly fewer than, for example, the name 'Jesus' (which appears about ninety-five times). Statistics can be misused, but these numbers nevertheless indicate some basic features of Mark: the chief character is Jesus, and God has a more concealed role.[26] While Mark continuously relates Jesus' actions, including a number of divine actions that are reserved for God in the Old Testament,[27] God is for the most part referred to either more indirectly or with reference to his actions in the Old Testament. This is not to say that God is absent. His hidden presence is taken for granted throughout the narrative: God forgives sins (2:7; 11:25), is glorified (2:12), joins man and woman in marriage (10:9), makes the impossible possible, that is, for people to enter the kingdom of God (10:27), and has the power to raise people from the dead (12:30). The disciples should have faith that God hears their prayers (11:22); they ought to render to him what is his (12:26) and love him wholeheartedly (12:30).

---

26. This may explain the low number of studies of 'God' in Mark, though more likely it reflects the general neglect in the NT scholarship (see Hurtado, *God in New Testament Theology*, pp. 9–10). The following studies should be mentioned: John R. Donahue, 'A Neglected Factor in the Theology of Mark', *JBL* 101 (1982), pp. 563–594; Gnilka, 'Gottesgedanken'; P. Danove, 'The Narrative Function of Mark's Characterization of God', *NovT* 43 (2001), pp. 12–30; Jack Dean Kingsbury, '"God" Within the Narrative World of Mark', in A. A. Das and F. J. Matera (eds.), *The Forgotten God: Perspectives in Biblical Theology* (Louisville: Westminster John Knox, 2002), pp. 75–89; C. Drew Smith, '"This Is My Beloved Son: Listen to Him": Theology and Christology in the Gospel of Mark', *HBT* 24 (2002), pp. 53–86; Gudrun Guttenberger, *Die Gottesvorstellung im Markusevangelium*, BZNW 123 (Berlin: de Gruyter, 2004); Ira Brent Driggers, *Following God Through Mark: Theological Tension in the Second Gospel* (Louisville: Westminster John Knox, 2007).

27. See the section on Jesus below.

In the light of this it is significant that God enters the scene at three occasions, strategically placed at the beginning, in the middle and at the end of the narrative. First, God's voice, the *Bath Qol* is heard at Jesus' baptism: 'And a voice came from heaven, "You are my beloved Son; with you I am well pleased"' (1:11). For our present purposes we note that God authorizes Jesus and identifies him as his Son, thereby implicitly identifying himself as his Father and introducing another important designation of God in Mark. The next scene, the transfiguration, is with some significant differences a replay of the first. The *Bath Qol* is heard again: 'This is my beloved Son; listen to him' (9:7). While the voice is accompanied by the visible manifestation of the Spirit in the first scene, a cloud appears this time, reminding the disciples and the audience of God's theophany in a cloud at Mount Sinai from which God used to speak. The other difference is that the words are directed to the three disciples present, authorizing Jesus and God's words to him and presenting, for the first time, Jesus as God's Son to human characters in the story.[28] The third scene is the resurrection. Mark never says explicitly that God raised Jesus, but it is implicit in the text. The angel tells the women at the tomb that Jesus has been raised (*ēgerthē*, 16:6). The passive verb almost certainly indicates that *God* has raised Jesus, especially in the light of the discussion in 12:19–27, which identifies God as the one who raises the dead. Thus Jesus has not been forsaken (cf. 15:34), but has finally been vindicated and authorized by God.

It follows then that, although God at first glance seems to take the back seat in Mark, he enters the story and acts in a profound way in three crucial and strategically placed scenes. In this way God's essential function becomes 'to identify and endorse Jesus', but thereby God also shows himself to be 'the origin and ultimate meaning for Jesus' activities'.[29]

But it also follows that the title 'Father', which plays an important, even if implicit, role in two of these scenes, is significant in Mark's presentation of God. The *Bath Qol* is identified not as 'God' but in relation to Jesus ('my Son'), that is, the one who speaks stands in a familial relationship to the one spoken to or about. In terms of the sheer number of occurrences 'Father' is not particularly prominent.[30] The title appears only four times. In three of these cases 'Father' is related to Jesus (8:38; 13:32; 14:36), and in one case God is the Father

---

28. Jack Dean Kingsbury, *The Christology of Mark's Gospel* (Philadelphia: Fortress, 1989), pp. 80–85.

29. Hurtado, *God in New Testament Theology*, p. 19, summarizing Kingsbury's conclusion in 'Narrative World'.

30. Cf. Matthew (forty-four times).

of the disciples (11:25). To these we could add those instances where Jesus is presented as Son of God, which implicitly makes God the Father of Jesus (1:1, 11; 3:11; 5:7; 9:7; 12:6; 13:32; 14:61; 15:39). Thus God is primarily 'Father' in relation to Jesus.[31]

This brings us to the third important designation of God in Mark: *kyrios* (Lord). God is the one Lord and God of the Shema (12:29). This title appears sixteen times in Mark. It is, however, a designation also shared by Jesus and it is often very difficult to determine whether God or Jesus is the referent. God is clearly one of the *kyrioi* in 12:36 and also the referent in the Scripture citation in 12:11. But in the remaining cases the title seems to create an overlap between God and Jesus. Before we look at this in some detail, however, we turn our attention to Jesus and the Spirit.

Jesus Christ, the Son of God

The protagonist of Mark's Gospel is presented with several different titles, among these Messiah/Christ and Son of God, which appear in the opening line.[32] For a long time research of Mark's Christology focused solely on the study of Christological titles.[33] Although such studies can be helpful in delineating Mark's presentation of Jesus, a full understanding of Jesus can by no means be restricted to such a study. The designation 'Son of God' is a good example of this. It is without doubt important, since it appears in three pivotal passages, at the beginning, in the middle and towards the end of the Gospel (1:11; 9:7; 15:39).[34] Nevertheless, the title as such can evoke various meanings. For non-Jewish Hellenistic readers it would certainly imply that

---

31. The heading of this section, 'God the Father', is thus not primarily prompted by the topic under discussion, but by the evidence in Mark.

32. *Huios theou* is missing in some early manuscripts (e.g. ℵ, *, Θ). The view that they were inserted at a later stage, defended by e.g. Peter M. Head, 'A Text-Critical Study of Mark 1:1', *NTS* 37 (1991), pp. 621–629, has recently been challenged by Tommy Wasserman, 'The "Son of God" Was in the Beginning (Mark 1:1)', *JTS* 62 (2011), pp. 20–51.

33. See e.g. the survey in Jacob Chacko Naluparayil, 'Jesus of the Gospel of Mark: Present State of Research', *CBR* 8 (2000), pp. 191–226.

34. On the importance of the title see Kingsbury, *Christology*, pp. 173–176; Edwin K. Broadhead, *Naming Jesus: Titular Christology in the Gospel of Mark*, JSNTSup 175 (Sheffield: Sheffield Academic Press, 1999), p. 123.

Jesus is a divine figure, but in the biblical literature it is variously used of angelic beings (Gen. 6:2; Job 1:6), Israel (Exod. 4:22; Hos. 11:1), the king (Ps. 2:7) and the righteous individual (Wis. 2.16–20), and in Qumran it had possibly become a messianic title (4QFlor [4Q174]).[35] Which of these did Mark intend? Or, did he intend a new meaning, perhaps even one that is close to the meaning most readers informed by the doctrine of the Trinity would believe it has? Only a careful study of the overall presentation of Jesus can help us in this regard.

In the following I restrict myself to the question of the divinity of Jesus and look particularly at three individual passages and the phenomenon that all, in their particular ways, present Jesus as if he in some mysterious way is the God of Israel.[36]

As already noted, Mark opens his Gospel by quoting three Scripture passages: Exodus 23:20; Malachi 3:1; and Isaiah 40:3. In the first of these God addresses Israel and promises to send his angel before them. This text is conflated with Malachi 3:1, where YHWH promises to send a messenger or an angel before himself: 'Behold, I send my messenger, and he will prepare the way before me.' In Mark, however, 'the way before me' becomes 'your way' (1:2). The next verse is a verbatim citation of the LXX, except that 'paths of our God' in the LXX is changed to 'his paths'. In its original context the text refers to a manifestation of YHWH, resulting in salvation for God's people. Mark's identification of Isaiah as the source of the citation makes it clear that he sees the Isaiah text as the most important one. As for the conflation in 1:2, Malachi 3:1 takes precedence over Exodus 23:20.[37] Accordingly, the original contexts of the primary Old Testament texts Mark cites both refer to the preparation of a way before the God of Israel. In Malachi a promised messenger prepares the way of YHWH; in Isaiah a voice cries out to prepare the way of YHWH.

In Mark, however, these texts are applied to John the Baptist and Jesus. John the Baptist wears clothes like Elijah's (1:6; cf. 2 Kgs 1:8); he prepares the people

---

35. Cf. e.g. Broadhead, *Naming Jesus*, pp. 116–120.

36. For a full study of all the significant passages that present Jesus in the role of Israel's God see Daniel Johansson, 'Jesus and God in the Gospel of Mark: Unity and Distinction' (PhD diss., University of Edinburgh, 2012).

37. Mal. 3:1 addresses a similar situation to that of Isa. 40:3, focusing on the event the messenger prepares. The messenger is also identified as Elijah in Malachi (4:5), and Mark makes it clear that John the Baptist fulfils the promise of his coming (cf. Mark 1:6 with 2 Kgs 1:8; Mark 9:12–13). Cf. Watts, *New Exodus*, pp. 86–87.

for the coming Lord by 'proclaiming a baptism of repentance for the forgiveness of sins' (1:4; cf. Mal. 3:2–4; 4:5–6); he proclaims the one who will come *after* him (1:7–8). If we were to isolate 1:2–8 from what follows, we would expect a great theophany in which YHWH appeared! But that is not the case. Instead, Jesus appears on the banks of Jordan, and becomes the object of John's expectation and Mark's Old Testament texts (1:9).[38]

By introducing Jesus in this way Mark applies to him two Old Testament texts that have YHWH as their subject. Isaiah 40:3 is particularly significant since this also includes the divine name, YHWH. This verse belongs to a group of similar passages in the New Testament where Jesus is made the subject of an Old Testament text that has YHWH as its subject.[39] In the case of Mark this means not only that another important title alongside 'Christ' and 'Son of God' is given to Jesus, namely 'Lord'; it also means that Jesus and God by means of this citation are linked in the closest possible way to each other.[40] That Mark's citation appears as part of the opening sentence makes it programmatic for the whole Gospel, and the reader is provided with a hermeneutical key to the Christology of Mark. This is confirmed in the following passages.

In Mark 2:1–12 Jesus forgives the sins of a man who is brought to him: 'Child, your sins are forgiven' (*teknon aphientai sou hai hamartiai*, 2:5b). Mark narrates the response of some scribes: 'Why does this man speak like that? He is blaspheming. Who can forgive sins except one, God?' (*tis dynatai aphienai hamartias ei mē*

---

38. See further Daniel Johansson, '*Kyrios* in the Gospel of Mark', *JSNT* 33 (2010), pp. 101–124.

39. These texts are listed in Bauckham, *Jesus*, pp. 186–188, 219–221. On this phenomenon in Paul see David B. Capes, *Old Testament Yahweh Texts in Paul's Christology*, WUNT 2.47 (Tübingen: Mohr Siebeck, 1992).

40. William Horbury, *Jewish Messianism and the Cult of Christ* (London: SCM, 1998), pp. 103–104, has suggested that this Christian phenomenon has an antecedent in Jewish messianism. Horbury refers to *1 En.* 52.6 and *4 Ezra* 13.3–4, which use language from biblical theophany passages (Pss 97:5; 104:32; Mic. 1:3–4) to describe a reaction to the presence of the messianic agent. However, unlike Mark, these are not introduced by a citation formula and neither passage includes the divine name YHWH or any of its substitutes and applies this to the messianic figure. These passages merely use images and language that the biblical literature uses for YHWH, whereas Mark explicitly cites passages about YHWH with reference to Jesus, seeing the fulfilment of these in Jesus and applying the divine name to Jesus.

heis ho theos, 2:7). The response is significant in two ways. First, it clarifies that Jesus himself forgives the sins of the paralytic,[41] and second, that Jesus acts in a role that belongs exclusively to God and thereby, in the eyes of his audience, commits the worst sin possible against God – blasphemy. Nothing seems to suggest that Jesus or Mark disagree with the scribes' interpretation, apart from the blasphemy accusation. Jesus confirms in 2:10 (*exousian echei aphienai hamartias*) that he has this right in words that in both form and content correspond to the pronouncement of the scribes in 2:7 (*dynatai aphienai amartias*). Thus what is said of God in 2:7 is said of the Son of Man (Jesus) in 2:10. The evangelist maintains both that God alone has the authority to forgive sins and that Jesus has authority to forgive sins. Mark thereby, so it seems, places Jesus on the divine side.[42]

If Mark helps the reader to understand the significance of Jesus' forgiving the paralytic's sins, he offers more of a challenge in the next significant episode. Having seen Jesus' stilling of wind and water (4:36–41), the terrified disciples[43] ask each other, 'Who then is this, that even the wind and the sea obey?' (4:41). The audience must supply the answer. So what would this be if we look at the Jewish and Greco-Roman cultural background of Mark's audience?

The Old Testament is unambiguous. There is only one whom sea and wind obey: the God of Israel. Numerous passages attest to the sovereign lordship

---

41. Some scholars argue that the passive form of the verb implies a *passivum divinum* (divine passive), which would mean Jesus is announcing *God's* forgiveness. Apart from the fact that the context ascribes the forgiveness to Jesus, there are several Hebrew/Aramaic texts that use the passive expression in an active sense, including texts with God as speaker. See Otfried Hofius, 'Jesu Zuspruch der Sündenvergebung: Exegetische Erwägungen zu Mk 2,5 b', in *Neutestamentliche Studien*, WUNT 132 (Tübingen: Mohr Siebeck, 2000), pp. 38–56, esp. 50–52.

42. Despite the Marcan text's stating unambiguously that God alone forgives sins, several scholars have contested this, instead suggesting that Jesus acts in the capacity of priest, prophet, Messiah or the angels. With the exception of the Angel of YHWH, the biblical and early Jewish literature, however, ascribes forgiveness to God alone. See Daniel Johansson, '"Who Can Forgive Sins but God Alone?" Human and Angelic Agents, and Divine Forgiveness in Early Judaism', *JSNT* 33 (2011), pp. 351–374.

43. Note that Mark seems to ascribe a greater fear to the disciples after than before the storm (4:41; cf. Jon. 1:5, 10).

of YHWH over water and storms.[44] The same is true of the early Jewish literature.[45] In fact, God's sovereignty over the sea is sometimes used to demonstrate
that the God of Israel is the one true God.[46] A passage of particular relevance
for Mark 4 is 2 Maccabees 9.8, where Antiochus Epiphanes is described in this
way: 'Thus he who had just been thinking that he could command the waves
of the sea, in his superhuman arrogance, [. . .], was brought down to earth and
carried in a litter, making the power of God manifest to all' (RSV). Accordingly,
shortly afterwards Antiochus is called a blasphemer (9.28). 2 Maccabees thus
provides evidence that the Jews regarded the claim to have ability to command
the waves of the sea as a claim to divinity, which in their view was to make
oneself equal to God.

The Greco-Roman thinking about power over sea and wind does not differ
from the Jewish view to any significant degree. Authority over wind and water was
of course attributed to those gods of the Olympic pantheon particularly associated
with the sea (Poseidon/Neptune and Aphrodite/Venus), but also a number of
other divine (e.g. the Dioscuri; cf. Acts 28:11) or semi-divine beings.[47] When
human beings, such as Apollonius of Tyana, were associated with this power, the
motif was used to demonstrate that they were divine. The difference from Judaism
is thus merely a less strict concept of the divine and the number of deities.

Thus whether a reader or hearer of Mark's Gospel was a Jew or a pagan, the
same conclusion would be drawn. Jesus acts as a divine being when he calms
the storm, and appears to share another divine prerogative, indeed an attribute
that demonstrates YHWH's absolute sovereignty over all creation. To ascribe
such powers to Jesus is to equate him with God himself.[48]

Finally, I would like to draw attention to what kind of a relation Jesus expects
the believer to have with him, namely readiness both to live and die for him.

---

44. E.g. Gen. 1:1–10; Exod. 14:21–31; Pss 77:15–16; 106:9; 107:23–32; Isa. 50:2;
    Jon. 1. For a survey see e.g. Reinhard Kratz, *Rettungswunder: Motiv-, traditions- und
    formkritische Aufarbeitung einer biblischen Gattung* (Frankfurt am Main: Lang, 1979),
    pp. 27–78; Wendy Cotter, *Miracles in Greco-Roman Antiquity: A Sourcebook* (London:
    Routledge, 1999), pp. 138–142.

45. E.g. Sir. 43.23–26; *1 En.* 101.4–9; 1QH^a XI, 1–18; XIV, 22–24; *b. B. Meṣ.* 59b; *y.
    Ber.* 9.13b.

46. Jon. 1; *y. Ber.* 9.13b.

47. See texts in Kratz, *Rettungswunder*, pp. 79–94; Cotter, *Miracles in Greco-Roman
    Antiquity*, pp. 132–137.

48. Thus clearly in 2 Maccabees, but also implied in passages where this attribute
    is used to demonstrate YHWH's superiority over other gods.

We therefore again turn to the Shema, but this time to its second part: 'And you shall love the Lord your God with all your heart [*kardia*] and with all your soul [*psychē*] and with all your mind [*dianoia*] and with all your strength [*ischys*]' (12:30). In the later rabbinic exposition of Deuteronomy 6:5 each element of the love command was assigned specific meaning: 'with all your heart' referred both to the good and the evil inclinations of a human being, that is, an undivided heart; 'with all your soul' meant 'even if he takes your soul', that is, even at the cost of one's life; 'with all your strength' referred to one's whole property.[49]

What is striking about the Gospel of Mark, however, is Jesus' requirement of such loyalty to *his own person*: Jesus demands undivided attention to his word (4:1–20; 7:1–23) and the kingdom of God (9:43–48); the disciples should be ready to suffer and die for the sake of him and the gospel (8:34–35); the disciples have left everything to follow Jesus (10:28–30).[50] Mark apparently includes Jesus in the devotion that, according to the Shema, should be offered to God alone. Or, to put it differently, the Christian reader of Mark's Gospel must, in order to fulfil the Shema, include Jesus in the devotion directed to God.

Whether or not this rabbinic interpretation of the love command goes back to the first century,[51] there is nonetheless abundant evidence that the Marcan Jesus in more than one way expected or was given the loyalty by his followers that God alone could demand.

Persecution even unto death for the sake of Jesus is one important example.[52] The biblical and, to a greater extent, the early Jewish literature attest to many

---

49. See e.g. *m. Ber.* 9.5; *Sipre Deut.* 31 – 32. Cf. Rikk E. Watts, 'Mark', in G. K. Beale and D. A. Carson (eds.), *Commentary on the New Testament Use of the Old Testament* (Grand Rapids: Baker Academic, 2007), p. 217.

50. Birger Gerhardsson has traced this phenomenon in Matthew. See 'Monoteism och högkristologi i Matteusevangeliet', *SEÅ* 37–38 (1972–3), pp. 125–144, esp. 135–141. For an earlier discussion of this kind of devotion to Jesus in all three Synoptic Gospels see S. Aalen, 'Jesu kristologiske selvbevisshet: Et utkast til "jahvistisk kristologi"', *TTKi* 40 (1969), pp. 1–18.

51. Gerhardsson has, in a number of studies now collected in *The Shema in the New Testament* (Lund: Novapress, 1996), tried to demonstrate that the rabbinic interpretation of Deut. 6:5 went back to the first century AD and was known at least to Matthew. The interpretation of 'all your strength' as referring to all one's property is attested already in Sir. 7.30–31. This kind of piety is illustrated by the poor widow (Mark 12:42–44), who gives her whole life (*ton bion autēs*) to the temple.

52. Mark 4:17; 8:34–35, 38; 13:9, 13.

examples where the Jews are expected to die for God and the law.[53] Josephus, for example, mentions that Jewish captives after the war, adults and children alike, accepted torture rather than confess that 'Caesar was lord' (*J. W.* 7.417–19), for God alone was their Lord (*J. W.* 7.410). However, in Mark the absolute commitment shown to YHWH and the law in the Jewish tradition has become complete loyalty to Jesus and the gospel (8:35, 38; 10:29). Furthermore, the warning against denial of Jesus and his words (8:38) seems to have a parallel in *3 Maccabees* 7.10, where transgression against 'the holy God and his Law' is denounced. Loyalty to Jesus is thus a presupposition for faithful devotion to Israel's God. In this context the relationship to Jesus appears to be motivated by his sharing the very glory of his Father (8:38). The reason why Jesus can be the object of ultimate devotion is, thus, his close association with the one God of Israel.

These and several other passages or features in Mark portray Jesus as a divine being.[54] Were it not for the firm stance on monotheism and consistent linking of Jesus to God, Jesus could easily be conceived as a second deity alongside God. Instead, Jesus is somehow closely identified with God himself, in a unique way placed with God on the God–creation divide.

The Holy Spirit

The Greek word *pneuma* (spirit) appears twenty-three times in Mark, but only six of these are references to the Holy Spirit.[55] Of the remaining seventeen, fourteen refer to unclean spirits,[56] and three appear to refer to the spirit of a human being.[57] In comparison with the large number of references to God and Jesus, these are few and, with the exception of 1:8–12, appear only to be mentioned more or less in passing. Such evidence should not be disregarded, though, since this may give us hints of what the author believed and took for granted.

---

53. Ps. 44:22; Dan. 3, 6; LXX Dan. 3:41; 1 Macc. 1.63; 2.50; 2 Macc. 6.30; 7.9, 23, 30; *3 Macc.* 7.16; *4 Macc.* 9.8; 10.20; 12.14; 16.18–21, 25; 17.20.

54. E.g. his raising of the dead, walking on water, the transfiguration, his return on the day of YHWH, the healing miracles and his acting in divine roles in parables.

55. Mark 1:8, 10, 12; 3:29; 12:36; 13:11.

56. Mark 1:23, 26–27; 3:11, 30; 5:2, 8, 13; 6:7; 7:25; 9:17, 20, 25 (twice).

57. Mark 14:38 refers to humanity (or Christians) in general, whereas 2:8 and 8:12 refer to Jesus' spirit. However, it cannot be excluded that the latter two are references to the Holy Spirit, with whom Jesus has been endowed in a special way.

I will not discuss these passages in detail, but instead focus on two issues: the question whether the Spirit is presented as a person or an impersonal power, and the Spirit's relation to God and Jesus.

We begin with the three references to the Spirit in the prologue.[58] In a crucial statement John the Baptist states that the one who will come after him will baptize 'with holy Spirit' (*en pneumati hagiō*, Mark 1:8). The comparison to and contrast with water (John's baptism) and the lack of the definite article suggest that the Spirit is here primarily conceived of as an impersonal power rather than a person.[59] In the next reference (1:10) the Spirit has a more personal character when in the form of a dove[60] he descends upon or into[61] Jesus. In the final reference in the prologue the Spirit is the subject of an action. Jesus is driven out into the wilderness by the Spirit (1:12). The latter could be either the action of a person or an impersonal power. However, the next reference can be taken only personally.

In 3:29 Jesus states that his opponents' accusation of his being possessed and doing the works of Satan is sin against the Holy Spirit (*to pneuma to hagion*), and as such an unforgivable sin. In this case the Spirit is clearly described as a personal being. One does not commit sins against an impersonal power or force.[62] The same must be said about 13:11, where Jesus promises that his disciples need not worry beforehand about what they are to say when they face trials, 'but say whatever is given you at that time, for it is not you who speak, but the Holy Spirit [*to pneuma to hagion*]'. The Spirit is more than a mere power

---

58. The placing of three references in the introduction may suggest that the Spirit has a more prominent role in Mark than is otherwise suggested by the remaining three references. See e.g. Morna D. Hooker, *The Gospel According to Saint Mark* (Peabody, Mass.: Hendrickson, 1991), pp. 51–52; Emerson B. Powery: 'The Spirit, the Scripture(s), and the Gospel of Mark: Pneumatology and Hermeneutics in a Narrative Perspective', *JPT* (2003), pp. 184–198, esp. 187.

59. Wainwright, *Trinity*, p. 202. Mark does not tell us about the fulfilment of this promise, although a passage such as 13:11 seems to suggest that all believers will have the Spirit in the future. This should further warn us against pressing the impersonal character of the Spirit in 1:8 too stridently. For in 13:11 what has been given to the disciples through baptism now *speaks* (a personal quality) through them.

60. I take *hōs peristeran* adjectivally, referring to the Spirit rather than the descent.

61. The preposition is *eis*, and may in this context mean both *upon* and *into*.

62. This statement is similar to passages such as Acts 5:3 and Eph. 4:30, where the Spirit is lied to and caused to grieve.

here, a personal being speaking and putting the right words in the mouths of the disciples.[63] A similar line of thought is probably behind the brief observation in 12:36 that David spoke the words of Psalm 110 'by the Holy Spirit' (*en tō pneumati tō hagiō*). Though this could refer to divine inspiration, it should probably be understood that the Spirit gave the words to David just as the Spirit is going to give words to persecuted followers of Jesus.[64]

Mark offers references to the Holy Spirit, which, if interpreted in the light of their immediate contexts, in some cases seem to describe the Spirit as an impersonal power and in other places as a personal being.[65] In this Mark reflects a general tendency in the New Testament.[66] Personal and seemingly impersonal descriptions could stand side by side.[67]

The Spirit is never called God in Mark,[68] and no passages are used from the Scriptures that, in their Old Testament contexts, with God as their subject are applied to the Spirit (cf. 1:2–3). There is on the whole little direct evidence for the Spirit's taking on divine prerogatives. But there is plenty of evidence for a close association of the Spirit with both God and Jesus.

The promise of a baptism with the Holy Spirit is generally agreed to allude to the Old Testament promise of an eschatological outpouring of the Spirit of God,[69] an event that is not fulfilled within the narrative of Mark.[70] For our purposes it is significant that the gift is God's Spirit and that God is the dispenser: '*I* will pour out *my* Spirit' (Isa. 44:3). Thus even if not made explicit in the

---

63. Wainwright, *Trinity*, p. 200.

64. Powery, 'Spirit', p. 190, argues for a connection between 12:36 and 13:11.

65. A further argument for the personal being of the Holy Spirit may be offered by Mark's numerous references to evil spirits. These undoubtedly seem to have a personal character (e.g. Mark 5:1–20), and it is reasonable to see an analogy between these and the Holy Spirit. See Wainwright, *Trinity*, p. 30, with reference to Kenneth E. Kirk, 'The Evolution of the Doctrine of the Trinity', in A. E. J. Rawlinson (ed.), *Essays on the Trinity and the Incarnation* (London: Longmans, Green, 1928), p. 187.

66. Wainwright, *Trinity*, pp. 200–204.

67. Cf. e.g. Acts 2:4; 11:12–16.

68. Just as in the other NT writings.

69. Isa. 32:15; 44:3; Ezek. 36:26–27; 37:14; Joel 2:28–32.

70. An exception is Robert H. Gundry, *Mark: A Commentary on His Apology for the Cross* (Grand Rapids: Eerdmans, 1993), pp. 38–39, 45, who argues that the fulfilment takes place in Mark's narrative world in Jesus' teaching and mighty works.

narrative, it is implied that John is referring to the Spirit of *God*. However, the Spirit is not only linked to God but also to the coming one, Jesus, who will baptize with the Holy Spirit.[71]

In 1:10–11 God, Jesus and the Spirit are linked by the narrative. Jesus, coming out of the water, sees the Spirit descending upon him and hears a voice from heaven (God's voice) saying, 'You are my beloved Son.'

In the next passage the Spirit acts on Jesus, driving him into the wilderness (1:12). This is perhaps less significant for the relationship between the Spirit and Jesus in terms of a uniquely divine relation, since similar activities by the Spirit on other human beings are recounted in Scripture (1 Kgs 18:12; Ezek. 8:3; Acts 8:39).

More important in this regard is Mark 3:29. Sin against the Holy Spirit is deemed unforgivable by Jesus. Important to note about this passage is not only that Jesus can define what is forgivable, but that sin or blasphemy against the Holy Spirit is the accusation that Jesus is demon possessed and his activities are of Satan. That is, total opposition to Jesus is also at the same time committing of the unforgivable sin against the Holy Spirit.[72] If anything, this demonstrates a close linking of the Holy Spirit to Jesus.

Jesus' statement that David spoke through the Holy Spirit (12:36) when composing Psalm 110 also brings together the Spirit, Jesus and God. The Spirit appears as a witness to a dialogue in heaven in which the one *kyrios*, God, addresses the other *kyrios*, Jesus:

Sit at my right hand,
    until I put your enemies under your feet.[73]

We will presently look more closely at the significance of this passage. For now it is sufficient to observe that the Holy Spirit also in this connection is associated with both God and Jesus.

The final reference to the Spirit has more to say about relationship between the Spirit and Jesus' disciples (13:11). The disciples must not worry even when they face trials, as the Holy Spirit will be speaking. Nevertheless, it is significant that Jesus has the most intimate knowledge of the Spirit's future activities

---

71. This is similar e.g. to Acts 2:33.

72. Cf. Joel Marcus, *Mark 1–8: A New Translation with Introduction and Commentary*, AB 27 (New York: Doubleday, 2000), p. 284.

73. Though Jesus never explicitly identifies himself with the second lord, this is clear from the context in Mark.

so that he can make a promise on the part of the Holy Spirit. Jesus' promise is similar to the one given by God to Moses (Exod. 4:10–17) and Jeremiah (Jer. 1:6–10),[74] with the one difference that God himself promises to put his own words in their mouths.[75]

Isolated from the overall context of Mark, the close relationship between the Spirit and Jesus may not need to indicate more than that Jesus is a human prophet led by God's Spirit. However, once the extent to which Jesus acts in uniquely divine roles, unprecedented in the Old Testament and early Judaism, becomes clear, it is evident that there is more to this relationship than merely the authorization of a prophet. Indeed, Jesus himself stands 'above' the Spirit in one of these passages, as he is portrayed as the dispenser of the promised Spirit of God (1:8). This leads us to consider the overall relationship between God, Jesus and the Spirit.

The relationship between God, Jesus and the Holy Spirit

The Gospel of Mark does not include any threefold formulas such as the baptismal formula in Matthew 28:19, the benediction in 2 Corinthians 13:13 or the greeting in Revelation (1:4–5). Nor do we find passages with dense triadic patterns in which the author frequently and in varying ways refers to God, Jesus and the Spirit (e.g. Rom. 5:1–8; 8; Gal. 4:4–6; Eph. 1:3–14). In this way the triadic pattern in Mark is far less intensive. Nevertheless, we have found that while Mark maintains monotheism, he presents Jesus as belonging to the divine side of the God–creation divide and furthermore portrays the Holy Spirit in personal terms, linking the Spirit both to God and Jesus. Before finally considering the Marcan passages where the three appear together (1:9–11; 12:36), I would like to draw attention to two larger patterns in Mark and the transfiguration scene.

First, we should look more closely at the overlap between God and Jesus created by the *kyrios* title, mentioned above. I have developed this argument elsewhere and will here briefly summarize only the most important points.[76] The designation *kyrios* appears sixteen times rather uniformly spread throughout

74. Craig A. Evans, *Mark 8:27–16:20*, WBC 34B (Nashville: Nelson, 2001), p. 311.

75. Jesus' promise appears in a number of variants in the Synoptic Gospels. Luke records both this (Luke 12:12) and one in which Jesus himself promises to give the proper words to the disciples (Luke 21:15; cf. Matt. 10:19).

76. Johansson, '*Kyrios*', pp. 101–124.

the Gospel.[77] Upon a closer examination of the referent of each of these, it appears that it is extremely difficult to decide whether God or Jesus is the referent. For example, when the Gerasene demoniac has been healed, Jesus sends him away with the words

> 'Go home to your friends and tell them how much the Lord has done for you
> [*hosa ho kyrios soi pepoiken*] . . .' And he went away and began to proclaim in
> the Decapolis how much Jesus had done for him [*hosa epoiēsen autō ho Iēsous*].
> (5:19–20)

Is Jesus speaking of himself or God? The best solution is probably to distinguish between what the characters in the story would perceive and what the audience is supposed to understand. Regarding the former, Jesus may be understood as speaking of the work of the Lord God, in which case Jesus, who has healed the man, identifies his own work with that of God. But Mark's audience hears not only that there is a unity of act between God and Jesus (i.e. what Jesus does, God does), but also that Jesus is linked to the title *kyrios* (i.e. what the *kyrios* did, Jesus did). God and Jesus thus become united under the designation *kyrios*. Now, this could be a coincidence were it not for the observation that this pattern is found elsewhere, particularly when *kyrios* appears for the first time in 1:3. Mark cites Isaiah 40:3, where in the original context the Lord God is the referent. However, as Mark moves the reader from 1:3 to 1:9 the referent of *kyrios* moves from God to Jesus. Therefore to ask whether *kyrios* refers to Jesus *or* God in 1:3 is simply wrong. It refers to *both* and, consequently, links Jesus to God. The question becomes how the relationship between God and Jesus should be understood if they share the designation *kyrios*. This question becomes particularly pressing in 12:28–37, where two Old Testament *kyrios* passages are juxtaposed: the Shema and Psalm 110:1. How can the insistence that there is only one *kyrios* be reconciled with the statement about the presence of two *kyrioi* on the divine throne? I suggest that Psalm 110:1 *defines* the correct understanding of the Shema and reinterprets monotheism so that there is one *kyrios*, and yet two figures – God and Jesus – share this name and title. The one designation *kyrios* guarantees the oneness of the *kyrios*. It follows then that God and Jesus are united and inseparable by means of this shared title. At the same time, Mark maintains a clear distinction in that *two* figures are linked to *kyrios*, and Jesus is never called God and/or Father.

---

77. Mark 1:3; 2:28; 5:19; 7:28; 11:3, 9; 12:9, 11, 29 (twice), 30, 36 (twice), 37; 13:20, 35.

A somewhat similar pattern also appears in the transfiguration narrative. There is general agreement that the most important background of this passage is found in Exodus 24 and 34, where Moses encounters God on Mount Sinai.[78] Furthermore, Mark seems to present us with two divine manifestations, one of Jesus (9:2–3) and one of God (9:7).[79] Prior to the transfiguration Jesus claimed that he one day would come back 'in the glory of his Father' (8:38). A preview of this glory Jesus shares with the father is now given to Moses, Elijah and the three disciples present with Jesus on the mountain. God, on the other hand, is manifested in the cloud in a manner similar to the Exodus account. The crucial difference between this and the Exodus account is that the glory earlier present in the cloud (cf. Exod. 24:16–17; 40:34–35) is now separated from the cloud and present in Jesus prior to the arrival of the cloud. The divine manifestations of the transfiguration narrative, I suggest, in significant ways repeat the Sinai theophany, but with the fundamental difference that what is said of the God of Israel *alone* in the Exodus account is split between Jesus and God in the present narrative: God appears in the cloud and speaks from the cloud (Exod. 24:16–17); Jesus manifests the glory of YHWH, and Moses and Elijah see and speak to him (cf. Exod. 33 – 34 and 1 Kgs 19:8–18). In the light of this, God's declaration that Jesus is his Son takes on a new meaning. The two divine manifestations, so to speak, relate to each other as a father to a son. This use of language from familial relationships is rooted in the Old Testament; the king (Ps. 2:7) and the people (Exod. 4:22) can be designated 'sons' of Israel's God. While this language is used of Jesus, Mark here seems to go beyond Old Testament usage, for Jesus is not only fully human, but is also found on the divine side of the God–creation divide to be participating in his father's divine reality.[80]

While the previous two patterns could be termed 'binitarian', we turn to one that also includes the Spirit. Four times in Mark a blasphemy accusation is raised. This has led some scholars to speak of a 'battle of blasphemies' in

---

78. See e.g. W. R. Stegner, 'The Use of Scripture in Two Narratives of Early Jewish Christianity (Matthew 4.1–11; Mark 9.2–8', in C. A. Evans and J. A. Sanders (eds.), *Early Christian Interpretation of the Scriptures of Israel: Investigations and Proposals*, JSNTSup 148 (Sheffield: Sheffield Academic Press, 1997), pp. 98–120.

79. H.-P. Müller, 'Die Verklärung Jesu', *ZNW* 51 (1960), pp. 56–64; Simon S. Lee, *Jesus' Transfiguration and the Believers' Transformation: A Study of the Transfiguration and Its Development in Early Christian Writings*, WUNT 2.265 (Tübingen: Mohr Siebeck, 2009), p. 14.

80. Cf. Lee, *Transfiguration*, pp. 34–35.

Mark.[81] Jesus is twice accused of blasphemy (2:7; 14:64). Shortly afterwards a description of how his opponents blaspheme or risk blaspheming follows (3:28–29; 15:29). In the first battle Jesus is accused of blasphemy for violating the prerogatives of God, that is, by putting himself in the place of God (2:7). In the next passages the tables are turned. Jesus accuses his opponents of blasphemy of *the Holy Spirit*, on the ground that they do not receive him, and accuse him of being in alliance with Satan (3:28–29). The third blasphemy accusation reflects the first in that Jesus is again accused of blasphemy against God by claiming the place at the right hand of God on his throne (14:62–64). In the view of Jesus' opponents he again blasphemes *God*. In the fourth passage Jesus himself becomes the object of blasphemy when Mark describes his opponents as committing blasphemy against *Jesus* (15:29).[82] The 'battle of blasphemies' thus involves God, the Holy Spirit and Jesus. In two cases it is clear that the blasphemy is related to the first commandment: it is a threat to the oneness of YHWH, the unique status of the God of Israel (2:7; 14:62–64). Is it then mere coincidence that the opponents of Jesus are accused of blasphemy for not responding properly to the Spirit and Jesus, particularly as this is related to eternal salvation?[83] Is it merely coincidence that this looks like a trinitarian pattern?

We finally turn to two direct references to 'the divine triad': 1:9–11 and 12:36.[84] Jesus' baptism has been considered as one of the chief texts for trinitarianism.[85] In a canonical reading of the Old and New Testaments this status seems well founded, but the question is whether this is the case if we limit the context to Mark or the passage itself. Wainwright questions that this is 'trinitarianism', on the grounds that 'nothing is said about the divinity of Son and Spirit, and there is no question of interaction between Father and Spirit or even between Son and Spirit'.[86] But, he goes on, 'the event itself is one which has

81. Darrell L. Bock, *Blasphemy and Exaltation in Judaism and the Final Examination of Jesus*, WUNT 2.106 (Tübingen: Mohr Siebeck, 1998), pp. 188–189.

82. The parallel usage of the verbs *empaizein* and *oneidizein* in the immediate context (15:29–32) suggests that the primary meaning of *blasphēmein* is 'insult', but Mark probably also wished to signal to his readers that the one who was accused of blasphemy is in reality the one who is blasphemed.

83. Blasphemy against the Holy Spirit cannot be forgiven; following after the one on the cross is necessary for salvation (8:34–38; 10:45).

84. The latter is overlooked by Wainwright (*Trinity*, p. 251).

85. Jenson, *Systematic Theology*, p. 111.

86. Wainwright, *Trinity*, p. 251.

the threefold pattern'. The baptismal account is, as can be seen by a survey of the commentaries, open to different interpretations. Nevertheless, in the light of Mark's overall presentation of God, Jesus and the Spirit, we must say that a threefold divine pattern is present in this strategically placed passage. The same can be said about 12:36, where *Jesus* cites Psalm 110:1. In Mark's version the words of Scripture are revealed by the Holy Spirit and refer to the Lord Jesus and the Lord God. The Spirit is thus the one who guarantees and explains how Jesus and God as *kyrioi* relate to each other.

Concluding observations

Mark's primary focus is on Jesus. Therefore Jesus' relationship to God stands in the foreground. This relationship is such that we can speak of a binitarian pattern, a Christological monotheism that includes Jesus in the divine identity of God.[87] But the question remains whether Mark is also conscious of the Holy Spirit's inclusion in this identity. My survey of the passages that deal with the Spirit demonstrates that the Gospel of Mark follows the same pattern we find elsewhere in the New Testament. There are passages where the Spirit seems to be described more as an impersonal power than a person, but also passages where the Spirit undoubtedly appears as a personal being. Furthermore, there are a number of passages in which the Spirit is implicitly or explicitly juxtaposed with both God and Jesus (e.g. 1:8, 10–11; 12:36) and 'the battle of blasphemies' could very well be another instance where the triad is intentionally linked. Thus, although the evidence is slim in comparison to many other New Testament writings, it seems that the author of the Gospel of Mark nevertheless was aware of and to some extent communicated what

---

87. For this terminology see Bauckham, *Jesus*, pp. 18–59. Smith, 'Beloved Son', p. 86, speaks of a 'christological theology' and a 'theological Christology' in Mark. Cf. Gnilka, 'Gottesgedanken', p. 152: 'We are in the early stages of a christological-theological process of reflection [Wir stehen an den Anfängen eines christologisch-theologischen Reflexionsprozesses].' Jesus 'determines . . . the concept of God in the Gospel in a unique way. One could even say – and this anticipates Johannine thought – that for Mark Jesus in a certain sense is the revealed God [bestimmt . . . das Gottesbild des Evangeliums auf unverwechselbare Weise. In einem bestimmten Sinn wird man sogar sagen können – und das bereitet johanneisches Gedankengut vor –, dass für Markus Jesus der Offenbarer Gottes ist]' (p. 154).

may be described as a proto-trinitarian view, even to the extent that he placed the most important trinitarian passage (1:9–11) at the beginning of the Gospel.[88]

---

88. Thus I think the evidence is somewhat stronger than did Wainwright, who nevertheless judged that Mark was aware of 'the threefold nature of the divine revelation' (*Trinity*, pp. 251, 266).

3. THE TRINITY AND LUKE-ACTS

Alan J. Thompson

How is the doctrine of the Trinity related to Christian life and ministry? One of the aims of Luke in his two-volume work Luke-Acts is to provide assurance for believers such as Theophilus (Luke 1:1–4). To provide this assurance Luke outlines evidence that Jesus is the incarnate Lord who accomplishes the saving purposes of his Father by the power of the Spirit. Furthermore, the risen Lord Jesus continues to administer the Father's saving rule by the Spirit, who empowers God's people to bear witness to the Lord Jesus and his salvation. Thus the triune God – and what he has done – is at the heart of Luke's pastoral project to provide assurance.

I will devote the bulk of my discussion of Luke's Gospel, in keeping with the emphasis of the narrative, to Jesus as Lord and Son and his relation to the God of Israel. Then I will turn to the Holy Spirit's relationship to the Father and Son.[1] I will focus primarily on how themes introduced in the opening

---

1. I will focus on the narrative and its emphases as a complete unit rather than attempt to determine possible sources or developments, and will not be investigating any perceived differences between the theological outlook of Luke and the historical Jesus. See Simon Gathercole, 'The Trinity in the Synoptic Gospels and Acts', in G. Emery and M. Levering (eds.), *The Oxford Handbook of the Trinity* (Oxford: Oxford University Press, 2011), p. 55. (I would like to thank Merryn Weaver,

chapters of Luke's Gospel prepare for the narrative development that follows and also return with a resounding crescendo in the concluding chapter. When I come to Acts, I will again begin with Luke's focus on the lordship of Jesus, before turning to expressions of the triunity of Father, Son and Holy Spirit in Acts.

The Trinity in Luke's Gospel

The God who keeps his promises
In both the introduction and conclusion of his Gospel account Luke makes clear that he is describing the fulfilment of God's saving purposes as anticipated in the promises and expectations found in the Old Testament (Luke 1:1). Thus Luke is describing the continuation of God's saving purposes for his people and as such is assuming a continuation from the Old Testament in the identity and nature of God.[2] Thus 'God' (*theos*) is introduced in the narrative without any explanation of who he is. Zechariah and Elizabeth observe God's commands (1:6), Zechariah serves God in the temple (1:8) and God is the one who announces his saving purposes in the world by sending an angel to Zechariah (1:19), Mary (1:26) and the shepherds (2:9–15). God is Saviour (1:47), Lord (1:6, 16, 46, 68), mighty (1:37, 49), holy (1:49), merciful (1:50, 72, 78) and sovereign (2:29). The overwhelming emphasis in the opening chapters of Luke's Gospel is that the one God of Israel is keeping his promises (to Abraham, 1:55, 73, and David, 1:32–33, 69; 2:4, 11), and is to be praised (1:42–45, 46–47, 58, 64, 68; 2:13–14, 20, 28, 38) for the joyful arrival of his long-hoped-for salvation (1:47, 71, 77; 2:30), the forgiveness of sins (1:77), the 'consolation of Israel' (2:25), the 'redemption of Jerusalem' (2:38), as well as his 'revelation to the Gentiles' (2:32)[3].

At the conclusion to his Gospel there are again references to people who had been 'waiting for the kingdom of God' (23:51 NIV) or hoping that Jesus had been the prophet to 'redeem Israel' (24:21). Likewise, explanations of the 'necessity' of God's saving plan (24:7, 26, 44; cf. 22:22) and an emphasis on the fulfilment of the Scriptures (24:25–27, 44–47) dominate the narrative and Luke's readers are prepared for the proclamation of the 'forgiveness of sins' to

---

Rob Smith, Brian Tabb, Andy Naselli, Stephen Wellum and my wife, Alayne Thompson, for feedback on an earlier draft of this chapter.)

2. Ibid., p. 56. Note also the reference to only one God in 5:21.
3. Unless stated otherwise, Bible quotes in this chapter are from the ESV.

be announced in Jerusalem and to all nations (24:47). In the last verse Luke returns to the themes of the opening scenes of his account (e.g. the temple) with the disciples continually 'praising God' (24:53 NIV). Between these 'bookends' Luke regularly draws attention to the praise given to God (5:25–26; 7:16; 9:43; 13:13; 17:15; 18:43; 19:37) because God has 'visited' or 'come to help' (NIV) his people (7:16; cf. 1:68, 78; 19:44).

The Lord and Son: Jesus' relation to the Lord and Father

Of course, it is obvious that people praise God in Luke's Gospel because of the arrival and actions of Jesus. Does this mean, however, that Jesus should be understood as merely a human 'agent' of God? The identity of Jesus is a prominent theme with questions about who he is appearing regularly in the first half of Luke's Gospel.[4] Many have noted the multifaceted Christological themes in Luke's Gospel: Jesus is the royal Messiah (e.g. 1:32; 24:26, 46), the 'rejected prophet' (e.g. 4:24; 13:33; 24:19) and Isaianic Servant (e.g. 2:32; 3:22; 4:16–21; 22:37). Luke's multifaceted Christology is due in part to his conviction that Jesus fulfils *all* of the Scriptures (e.g. 24:44). Yet Jesus also transcends these categories: he is 'more than' a son of David, prophet and servant; he is 'the Lord' and the unique 'Son of God'. We will first note the important ways in which Jesus is introduced in Luke's narrative as 'Lord'. This is foundational for understanding who Jesus is in his identification with the God of Israel. Then we will note the further nuance to this identity with the Father–Son relationship in Luke's Gospel.

Jesus as Lord

As noted above, from the first mention of God in the narrative it is clear that 'God' (*theos*) is 'the Lord' (*kyrios*, 1:6), and this designation continues throughout these chapters. Sometimes these two terms are used together (e.g. 'the Lord their God', 1:16; 'the Lord God', 1:32; 'the Lord God of Israel', 1:68), sometimes the terms are used interchangeably in the immediate context, where it is clear that 'Lord' refers to 'God' (e.g. 1:6, 8–9, 11, 19, 26, 28, 37–38, 46–47), and sometimes 'God' is simply referred to as 'Lord' (e.g. 1:25, 45, 58; 2:9, 22; cf. also the 'Law of the Lord', 2:23–24, 39).[5]

Since the term 'Lord' is used predominantly to refer to Yahweh, the God of Israel, it is stunning to find in these same narrative contexts references to Jesus

---

4. Luke 4:22, 36; 5:21; 7:19–20, 39, 49; 8:25; 9:18, 20.

5. Robert L. Mowery, 'Lord, God, and Father: Theological Language in Luke-Acts', in *SBL 1995 Seminar Papers* 34 (Atlanta: Scholars Press, 1995), p. 85.

that identify him with this Lord.[6] Thus Zechariah is told that not only will his son John (the Baptist) bring many back to 'the Lord their God' (1:16); he will actually 'go before him [the Lord]' and 'make ready for the Lord a people prepared' (1:17). Similarly, when Zechariah himself praises 'the Lord God of Israel' (1:68), he declares that John will be a prophet of the Most High who will 'go before the Lord to prepare his ways' (1:76).

In the narrative context, given the consistent use of *kyrios* (Lord) to this point, it could be assumed that the 'Lord' whom John will go before is Yahweh, the Lord God of Israel. Between these statements to and by Zechariah, however, Elizabeth, empowered by the Holy Spirit, calls Mary 'the mother of my Lord' (1:43)![7] In the immediate context of references to Yahweh as 'Lord' (1:38, 45–46) this exclamation of Elizabeth exalts the one her husband, Zechariah, had been told their son would go before!

When John begins his public ministry calling for repentance and announcing the arrival of one 'mightier' than him (3:16), he begins with the words of Isaiah that describe his ministry as one that prepares the way for 'the Lord' and makes straight paths for him (3:4). In the context of the quotation from Isaiah it is obvious that this is a reference to the Lord, the God of Israel. In the context of Luke's Gospel, however, with the role of John as the prophet who goes before Jesus, it is Jesus who is the Lord (2:11) whom John goes before.

Parallel to these references that identify Jesus with the Lord God of Israel are references that also identify Jesus as the 'Saviour'. In the Old Testament Yahweh was the only God and 'Saviour' (*sōtēr*) of his people.[8] Similarly, in Luke's Gospel Mary begins her praise by glorifying 'the Lord' and rejoicing in 'God my Saviour' (1:47). The only other use of the title 'Saviour' in Luke's Gospel comes with the announcement from the 'angel of the Lord' that the one born in the town of David is both 'Saviour' and 'Christ the Lord' (2:11).

---

6. Of course not every use of the term 'lord' (*kyrios*) refers to God (e.g. 19:33, 'owners'). It is the context that helps us determine the meaning of a term. Cf. C. Kavin Rowe, *Early Narrative Christology: The Lord in the Gospel of Luke* (Grand Rapids: Baker Academic, 2009), pp. 31–77. Rowe's work is a healthy corrective to a supposedly 'low' Lucan Christology (and a supposedly 'low' use of the vocative 'Lord' in Luke). See now also Richard B. Hays, *Reading Backwards: Figural Christology and the Fourfold Gospel Witness* (Waco, Tex.: Baylor University Press, 2014), pp. 55–74.

7. Mary is still in need of a Saviour (1:47).

8. Cf. Ps. 65:5 (LXX 64:6); Isa. 12:2; 45:21.

So, when John announces that he is calling people to be prepared for 'the Lord', in Luke's Gospel the quotation from Isaiah 40 extends to the statement that everyone will see 'the salvation of God' (3:6; citing Isa. 40:5). Jesus, therefore, is the Isaianic 'Lord' and 'Saviour' as well as the 'servant of the Lord'.

Thus in the narrative flow of Luke 1 – 3, with statements about Jesus in 1:43 ('my Lord'), 2:11 ('the Lord') and 3:16 (the 'mightier' one coming after John), the references to the 'Lord' in 1:17, 76 and 3:4 as the one whom John will go before should not be reduced to the false dichotomy of a reference either to Yahweh or to Jesus; Jesus is the incarnation of Yahweh.[9] See below, however, that the description of Jesus as 'Son' indicates there is a duality of Father and Son within the unity of the one Lord. In Luke's narrative 'both the Father and the Son bear the divine name *kyrios*'.[10]

As we glance further ahead in Luke's Gospel we find, in keeping with these early chapters, that Jesus the Lord is not merely an agent of the God of Israel, but is identified with this God. So, at the beginning of Jesus' ministry, when Simon Peter sees the sovereign power of Jesus' word (5:5) over the fish in the depths of the lake, he responds, like Isaiah (Isa. 6:5), with fear because he recognizes that he, as a 'sinful man' is in the presence of someone who is 'Lord' (Luke 5:8–10).[11] In this context Jesus' assurance to Peter that he should not be afraid (5:10) implies that Jesus is the Lord whom John was to go before, the one who would come to bring forgiveness of sins (1:77). This implication is made clear for us later in this same chapter when Jesus declares forgiven the sins of the paralytic (5:20). The Pharisees and teachers of the law recognize this as not merely a statement that God will forgive sins, but that Jesus himself is doing the forgiving, as they think to themselves, 'Who is this who speaks blasphemies? Who can forgive sins but God alone?' (5:21).[12] In this context Jesus, the knower of thoughts and hearts (5:22; as in 7:39–40; 9:47; 11:17; cf. 16:15) and the forgiver of sins (as also in 7:48–49), is doing what only God does (cf. 2 Chr. 6:30).

---

9. C. Kavin Rowe, 'Luke and the Trinity: An Essay in Ecclesial Biblical Theology', *SJT* 56 (2003), pp. 1–26.

10. Ibid., pp. 21–22.

11. In this context Simon moves from calling Jesus 'master' before the miraculous catch to 'Lord' after the display of Jesus' sovereign power (5:5, 8).

12. In the historical context clearly Peter and the disciples had a way to go before they grasped the full implications of this. Nevertheless, grappling with the significance of these actions and declarations of Jesus formed part of their struggle to answer the question 'Who is this?' (8:25).

Later Jesus states that John is a prophet, indeed 'more than a prophet' (7:26), and in fact greater than anyone born of a woman (i.e. everyone!). Why was John so great? Because, although the Old Testament prophets told of the coming messianic age, John was the messenger of Malachi 3:1 who would go before the Lord to prepare the way for him (7:27). Other prophets pointed ahead to the one to come; John was privileged to point to that One himself. In other words, Jesus essentially says that John is greater than anyone else who was ever born, because he points to me, the Lord of Malachi 3!

Throughout the narrative of his Gospel Luke regularly designates Jesus as 'the Lord' (7:13, 19; 10:1, 39; 11:39; 13:15; 17:5–6; 18:6; 22:61). In the dramatic conclusion to the challenges to his authority from the Jerusalem leadership Jesus ends with a question of his own. Without denying the Davidic descent of the Messiah, Jesus asks why David himself calls his descendant not his 'son' but his 'Lord' who will sit in the presence of 'the Lord' at his right hand (Luke 20:41–44, citing Ps. 110:1). Jesus, as 'the Christ', is of course a descendant of David; but is also more than a descendant of David: he is 'Lord'. Before leaving the subject of Jesus as 'Lord' in Luke's Gospel, let us reflect a little further on the significance of this for Luke's intriguing placement of references to Jesus and 'God'.

Jesus and 'God'

This identification of Jesus as 'the Lord' (*kyrios*), the incarnation of Yahweh, may also help to shed light on the frequent juxtaposition of references to Jesus and 'God' (*theos*) in Luke's Gospel. Thus whereas Jesus tells the man who has demons cast out of him to return home and tell what '*God* has done for you', Luke immediately adds that the man goes and tells what '*Jesus* has done for him' (8:39)![13] After Jesus heals a boy and gives him back to his father, the crowd are all 'astonished at the majesty of *God*'. Then Luke says, everyone was 'marvelling at everything he [*Jesus*] was doing' (9:43). The Samaritan who has been healed of leprosy returns to Jesus 'glorifying *God*' (17:15; cf. also 17:18) and falls on his face at Jesus' feet 'thanking *Jesus*' (17:16).[14]

Similarly, there are close links between the activity of Jesus and praise to God. After the Pharisees correctly ask, 'Who can forgive sins but *God* alone?' (5:21), Jesus demonstrates that *he* has 'authority on earth to forgive

---

13. Cf. Mark 5:19, where 'Lord' is used. The following parallels are unique to Luke's Gospel.

14. My translations. The words 'glorifying' and 'thanking' as present tense participles are paralleled in 17:15–16.

sins' (v. 24) by healing the paralytic instantaneously with just his word. At this display of the sovereign power of *Jesus* the man gets up and goes home 'glorifying *God*' (v. 25), and the crowd are also amazed and 'glorified *God*' at what they have seen *Jesus* do (v. 26). Similarly, the blind beggar, after receiving his sight, 'followed him [*Jesus*], glorifying *God*' (18:43), and the crowd also give praise to God for what they have seen Jesus do. At the triumphal entry the disciples who rejoice and 'praise *God*' for the miracles they have seen (19:37) then say, 'Blessed is *the King* who comes in the name of the Lord' (19:38).[15]

It is of course possible that these parallel statements may be read as simple expressions of praise to God without making any further claims about Jesus' identity with God. The concluding words of Luke's Gospel, however, add one more final and significant parallel. Following the ascension of Jesus, the disciples 'worshipped him' (i.e. Jesus) and returned to the temple in Jerusalem 'praising God' (24:52–53 NIV), deliberately recalling the opening scenes of Luke's Gospel. Not only does this closing scene include another of these parallels between Jesus and God, but we also have the remarkable statement that the disciples worship Jesus! That this action indicates a recognition of the divinity of Jesus is easily recognized in the context of Luke's Gospel, as it is Jesus himself who says at the beginning of his public ministry that worship belongs to 'the Lord your God' alone (Luke 4:8, quoting Deut. 6:13).[16] The significance of this worship of Jesus is further highlighted when the distinctions between 'God' and 'humanity' in Luke-Acts are recalled. In Acts Peter, Paul and Barnabas refuse worship because they 'are men', just like the potential worshippers (Acts 10:26; 14:15). Herod, however, is struck dead at his acceptance of the crowd's acclamation that his voice is that 'of a god, and not of a man' (Acts 12:22–23). This worship of Jesus at the conclusion of Luke's Gospel culminates Luke's entire Gospel account of Jesus.

Thus throughout Luke's Gospel Jesus is identified with God and does what God does. He forgives sins (5:20–21; 7:48–49), is sovereign over creation (5:4–7; 8:25), knows people's hearts and thoughts (5:22; 7:39–40; 9:47; 11:17; cf. 16:15), brings divine judgment (12:49) and salvation (19:10), and, climactically, receives

---

15. Jesus' teaching on the kingdom of God may be added here too, but space does not allow for detailed treatment of this major theme. E.g. the kingdom is Jesus' (22:30) and conferred by him (22:29), yet is God's kingdom (22:16, 18; and throughout Luke) and conferred by the Father (12:32).

16. The word used here for 'worship' (*proskyneō*) occurs only in these two locations in Luke's Gospel.

worship (24:52). The notes of hope sounded at the outset of Luke's Gospel (Luke 1:17, 76) and reverberating throughout the Gospel, rise to a resounding crescendo in the concluding chapter: the Lord himself has come to save his people and is to be worshipped!

Jesus as the unique Son of God

The Father–Son relationship further contributes to our understanding of Jesus' identification with God in Luke's Gospel. On the one hand, he is 'the Lord', the incarnation of Yahweh. On the other hand, he is not the Father; he is the Son. This combination of 'Lord' and 'Son' in the narrative of Luke's Gospel is determinative for our understanding of the trinitarian nature of God. As Rowe observes, 'The Lukan narrative assumes the differentiation of the Father and Son, but nonetheless gives the divine name both to the Father and to Jesus . . . The duality of Father and Son in the Lukan narrative is no threat to the unitive identity of the one Lord.'[17]

As with the term 'lord', the designation 'son of God' need not imply a unique identification with the nature of God. After all, Adam is called the son of God in Luke 3:38, and those who love enemies are called sons of the Most High in Luke 6:35–36. Elsewhere in the Bible, Israel, Solomon, peacemakers and angels are called God's sons.[18] In Luke's Gospel the designation 'Son of God' can be understood as synonymous (though not completely interchangeable)[19] with 'Christ' (4:41), reflecting 2 Samuel 7:14 and Psalm 2:7. These different referents of the designation 'son of God' reflect the various ways in which God may be imitated and his likeness seen.[20] However, Jesus is also the 'Son of God' in a unique sense. The announcement to Mary that her child will be called the 'Son of the Most High' (1:32; in contrast to John the Baptist, who will be called a 'prophet of the Most High', 1:76) is linked in the first instance to Jesus' reign on 'the throne of his father David' (1:32–33). As the narrative proceeds, however, it is clear that Jesus is the 'Son of God' in a unique sense. On the one hand, he has an everlasting life and an indestructible reign that will have 'no end' (1:33). On the other hand, his conception is supernatural, something not said of any other Davidic king! Mary, who is explicitly identified as a virgin (1:27 [twice],

---

17. Rowe, 'Luke and the Trinity', p. 22.
18. Cf. D. A. Carson, *Jesus the Son of God: A Christological Title Often Overlooked, Sometimes Misunderstood, and Currently Disputed* (Nottingham: Inter-Varsity Press; Wheaton: Crossway, 2012), p. 13.
19. Ibid., p. 95.
20. Cf. ibid., passim.

34, lit. 'I know no man'), will be overshadowed by the power of the Most High and this supernatural virginal conception is given as the reason why Jesus, the Son of God, will be called holy (1:35).[21] Although the full significance of this is not developed here in the narrative, these are the beginnings of a picture of Jesus as 'Son of God' in a unique rather than a merely human messianic sense.[22]

This account of Jesus' supernatural birth is in keeping with indications of his pre-existence in Luke's Gospel.[23] In the same chapter as the announcement of this supernatural birth Zechariah refers to the 'sunrise' that will 'visit us from on high' (i.e. heaven, 1:78).[24] The virgin birth, therefore, is the beginning of Jesus' humanity, not the beginning of his existence. Jesus himself claims divine prerogatives and assumes pre-existence in the 'I have come' sayings. He 'came to cast fire' (i.e. divine judgment) on 'the earth' (12:49; cf. Gen. 19:24). The demons, with supernatural insight, fear that he has come to destroy the demonic realm (4:34). Jesus also says he was 'sent' to preach the good news of the kingdom of God (4:43; cf. also 9:48; 10:16). Reflecting the same language as Ezekiel 34:16, Jesus does what only God does: he 'came to seek and to save the lost' (19:10).[25] Jesus' parable of the tenants describes the history of Israel as one in which God, as owner of the vineyard, repeatedly sends his servants to the nation, alluding to the long line of persecuted prophets (cf. Jer. 7:25–26). Finally, God sends not another servant-prophet, but his own beloved son (Luke 20:13). Jesus is qualitatively different and therefore is not the last prophet: he is the unique Son.

The unique relationship Jesus has with God the Father is a prominent emphasis in Luke's Gospel. Although, as we have seen, there are a variety of

---

21. Cf. Robert H. Stein, *Luke*, NAC (Nashville: B&H, 1992), pp. 85–86, for a brief summary of the exegetical issues involved in 1:35. Cf. a similar construction in 2:23. Note that Luke's historical account (1:1–4) is nothing like later Greco-Roman biographies with legends of gods having sex, etc.

22. Though, as noted above regarding Jesus' use of Ps. 110, the OT also anticipated more than a merely human messiah.

23. Simon J. Gathercole, *The Preexistent Son: Recovering the Christologies of Matthew, Mark, and Luke* (Grand Rapids: Eerdmans, 2006), p. 285.

24. Cf. ibid. pp. 238–242, and the references above to God's 'visitation' in Luke's Gospel.

25. The combination of *zēteō* (seek) and *to apolōlos* (the lost) reflects the description in Ezek. 34:16 LXX of the divine mission to seek the lost (cf. also Ezek. 34:4, 11, 22; Luke 15:4, 6).

ways of referring to God in the opening chapters (e.g. 'Lord', 'God', 'Most High'), a reference to God as 'Father' comes with Jesus' own opening words in this Gospel. In an account given only in Luke's Gospel Luke provides a deliberate contrast between the words of Mary and the words of Jesus in 2:48–49 concerning his 'father'. Upon finding him in the temple courts, Mary says that 'your father and I' had been searching anxiously (2:48). Jesus replies, however, that they should have known that he would be in 'my Father's house' (2:49), indicating an awareness at age 12 of his unique relationship with God as his Father.[26]

Indeed, throughout Luke 3 – 24 references to God as 'Father' occur sixteen times and all of these references are in Jesus' words. Most striking are his words in 10:21–22 (and most concentrated, with five references to 'Father' in these two verses), where Jesus speaks of his relationship to the Father as something unique and exclusive.[27] To say 'no one knows . . . who the Father is except the Son' is staggering! This kind of reciprocal knowledge cannot refer to something Jesus gained as part of his messiahship! Rather this points to an intimacy of a Father–Son relationship that precedes messiahship. It is the Son's unique knowledge of the Father that enables him to reveal the Father in his sovereignty. Included among Jesus' references to the Father in Luke's Gospel are phrases such as 'my Father' (10:22a; 22:29; 24:49) and 'your [pl.] Father' (6:36; 12:30, 32). This phraseology, along with the large amount of Jesus' teaching about the character of God the Father,[28] 'represents a narrative portrayal of Jesus' claim that he alone knows "who the Father is" (10:22c) and reveals the Father to whom he chooses (10:22c)'.[29] Interestingly, in

---

26. See also qualifications regarding Jesus' 'father' in 3:23 (Jesus was the son, 'as was supposed', of Joseph), and in the inadequate observation of 4:22 ('Is not this Joseph's son?'). Thus 2:48 is not an unguarded contradiction in Luke's infancy narrative but is a deliberate indicator of Jesus' unique relationship with God, his Father.

27. See Stephen J. Wellum, 'The Deity of Christ in the Synoptic Gospels', in C. W. Morgan and R. A. Peterson (eds.), *The Deity of Christ* (Wheaton: Crossway, 2011), p. 82, for the following discussion (though Wellum is referring to the parallel in Matt. 11:27). See also the studies of Brandon Crowe (on Matthew) and Scott Swain in this volume.

28. Cf. Luke 6:36; 11:13; 12:30; esp. 15:11–32 (not included in the list of sixteen references to God as Father), which is dominated by references to the character of the forgiving Father in the parable.

29. Mowery, 'Lord, God, and Father', p. 87.

the narrative of Luke's Gospel not only are Jesus' *first* words a reference to his Father, but his *final* words in Luke's Gospel also speak of 'my Father' (24:49).

This unique knowledge of and revelation of the Father that the Son has provides insight into the differentiation of Father and Son within the one Lord. Thus, while the Son is sovereign in election (10:22), it is the Father who has delegated 'all things' to the Son (10:22a), things that in the context of Luke 10:21–22 include the revelation of a saving knowledge of the Father.[30] It is the Father who sends his beloved Son (20:13), and so it is the Son, not the Father, who comes as the incarnate Lord. The Son rightly rules the kingdom because his Father has granted this to him (22:29; cf. 12:32). The Holy Spirit, whom the Son will send, is the promise of the Father (24:49). There is both unity of sovereign power and purpose between Father and Son as well as a distinction in person and order. As the last reference has indicated, this combination of unity and distinction is further seen in the description of the Holy Spirit in Luke's Gospel.

Father, Son and Spirit in Luke's Gospel

In keeping with the focus of Luke's Gospel I have concentrated primarily on Jesus as Lord and Son. Hence the following discussion of the Spirit in Luke's Gospel will be brief. Within the narrative of Luke's Gospel it is clear that the Holy Spirit is fully God. The Holy Spirit is spoken of in terms of God's power as the 'power of the Most High' (1:35) and 'power from on high' (24:49). He is 'the Spirit of the Lord' (4:18; i.e. 'of Yahweh', citing Isa. 61:1).[31] Yet the Spirit is not the Father. The Spirit comes upon Jesus at his baptism, whereas the voice of the Father speaks from heaven (3:22). The Spirit is also given by the Father who is in heaven (11:13), and is the promise of the Father (24:49). Interestingly, denying Jesus will result in being denied by God, just as blaspheming against

---

30. Scott Harrower neglects 10:22a in his attempt to claim that 10:22 teaches that the Father is subordinate to the will of the Son (Scott Harrower, *Trinitarian Self and Salvation: An Evangelical Engagement with Rahner's Rule* [Eugene, Ore.: Pickwick, 2012], pp. 109–114).

31. On the 'Spirit of the Lord' see below on Acts 16:7. The 'power of God' in 22:69 is a circumlocution for God. On the 'power of the Lord' (5:17) as Christological see Rowe, *Early Narrative Christology*, pp. 92–98. Luke 11:20 has 'the finger of God' (reflecting God's power in Exod. 8:19) where Matt. 12:28 has 'the Spirit of God'. See also Acts 10:38.

the Holy Spirit results in no forgiveness from God (12:9–10).[32] The three are one, yet distinguishable.

In Luke's Gospel the Spirit is most often involved in empowering God's people to speak. They are 'filled' with the Holy Spirit and enabled to proclaim and praise God for the arrival of the Lord Jesus (1:41–45, 67–79; 2:25–32), or empowered to speak for Jesus under pressure (12:12). It is also in an empowering capacity that the Holy Spirit is most prominently involved in the life of Jesus. There is no question of course that Jesus, as the incarnation of Yahweh, is human. The placement of the genealogy in descending order through to Adam immediately next to the account of Jesus' temptation by the devil deliberately shows Jesus to be the new Adam who will not succumb to temptation (3:37 – 4:13). The humanity of Jesus then is clear, as he is born like any other human baby (2:7), 'grew and became strong' from child to adult (2:40, 52; cf. 1:80), is submissive to his parents (2:51), experiences hunger (4:1), sleeps (8:23) and dies (23:46). His human body, which goes into the tomb (23:52–53), is also his after his resurrection (24:3, 39–43).[33]

The Spirit's relationship with Jesus appears to be primarily in empowering and sustaining the human life of Jesus.[34] This is seen from the first announcement of the birth of Jesus. As noted above, the virgin Mary will conceive and give birth because of the creative 'overshadowing' (cf. Gen. 1:2) power of the Holy Spirit in the womb of Mary generating the humanity of Jesus (1:34–35). The descent of the Holy Spirit at Jesus' baptism is to empower Jesus as he 'began his ministry' (3:22–23). By the Spirit Jesus faces temptation as the new Adam

---

32. These are contrasted with simply speaking 'a word against the Son of Man', which will be forgiven (12:10a). The distinction between 'speaking a word against' and 'blaspheming' is either momentary versus permanent rejection, or acting in ignorance versus hardened opposition (cf. Stein, *Luke*, p. 348). The passive voice in 'will be denied' (v. 9) and 'not be forgiven' refers to God's action.

33. We see the humanity of the Son also when he, understandably (revealing the awfulness of the judgment ahead), asks if it is possible for the cup of wrath to be removed, yet willingly agrees with the Father's will (22:42). Similarly, it is to the Father that he entrusts his spirit on the cross (23:46), having just promised that the criminal on the cross will be with him that day in paradise (23:43).

34. Though, as we have seen above, everything Jesus does he does as the one person of the divine-human Son. Cf. Wellum, 'Deity', p. 76, n. 42. Cf. also John Owen, *The Works of John Owen*, ed. W. Goold, 16 vols. (Edinburgh: Banner of Truth, 1965–8), vol. 3, p. 162: 'Whatever the Son of God wrought in, by, or upon the human nature, he did it by the Holy Ghost, who is his Spirit, as he is the Spirit of the Father.'

(4:1), proclaims the good news as the Isaianic Servant/prophet (4:14, 18) and speaks words of joyful praise as Son to the Father (10:21).

Luke's Gospel also points forward to Jesus' activity in sending the Spirit beyond his earthly ministry. Before Jesus even begins his public ministry, John announces that one 'mightier' than him will baptize 'with the Holy Spirit' (3:16). Interestingly, whereas in 12:12 Jesus reassures his disciples that the Holy Spirit will help them to speak when they are brought before rulers, in 21:15 Jesus says that he himself will give them the words to say. Although not clarified at this point in Luke's narrative, this anticipates the book of Acts in which Jesus accomplishes his purposes through the Spirit who empowers his people. In the closing verses of Luke's Gospel we get a clearer anticipation of Luke's trinitarian emphasis to come in Acts. Just prior to the ascension Jesus tells the disciples that he is the one who will send the Holy Spirit, even though, as Jesus says, the Spirit is 'the promise of my Father' (Luke 24:49). The sending of this promised Holy Spirit will mean that Jesus' disciples will be 'clothed with power from on high' in order to proclaim the name of Jesus. And so it is to the book of Acts we turn to see the unfolding of the saving plan of the triune God.

The Trinity in Acts

The God who keeps his promises

In the book of Acts Luke continues to outline evidence that God has indeed accomplished his saving purposes as promised.[35] Thus Luke continues to refer to God (*theos*) as the God of Israel and the nations, the God who keeps his promises and saves his people. The first and last references to God in the narrative of Acts refer to the 'kingdom' or saving rule of God (1:3; 28:31). Throughout the narrative of Acts continuity with the God of Israel is constantly assumed. God is 'the God of Abraham, the God of Isaac, and the God of Jacob, the God of our fathers' (3:13; cf. 5:30; 7:32; 22:14; 24:14), he is the 'living God' and the sovereign creator of everything (14:15; 17:24). Idolatry (7:41–42; 14:15; 15:19–20; 17:29–30), sorcery (8:9; 13:6; 19:19) and false worship of a human being (8:10; 10:25–26; 12:22–23; 14:11–15) or anything else in creation (7:42) rather than God alone are therefore ruled out. The God of Israel sovereignly guided Israel's history, graciously providing land, tabernacle, temple,

---

35. For expanded discussion of this see Alan J. Thompson, *The Acts of the Risen Lord Jesus: Luke's Account of God's Unfolding Plan*, NSBT 27 (Apollos: Inter-Varsity Press; Downers Grove: InterVarsity Press, 2011).

judges and kings (7:1–50; 13:16–22). God's gracious provision culminates in bringing to Israel the 'Saviour, Jesus, as he promised' (13:23). God accomplished his saving purposes through the life (2:22; 10:37–38), death (2:23; 4:27–28), resurrection and exaltation (2:24, 32–33; 3:15; 5:30–31; etc.) of Jesus. God is the one responsible for the inclusion of Gentiles together with Jews among the people of God (10:1 – 11:18; 13:26, 48; 15:7–8, 14; 21:19) by grace through faith (10:43; 13:39; 14:1; 15:9).

Jesus as Lord

As with Luke's Gospel, so also in Acts, God's saving purposes for Israel and the nations come through Jesus Christ and the forgiveness of sins that is offered through his life, death and resurrection. Continuity with the Christology of Luke's Gospel is explicitly stated in the opening verse of Acts. Luke's Gospel is about all that Jesus *'began* to do and teach' (Acts 1:1). The implication, therefore, is that Acts is about all that Jesus *continues* to do and teach. Thus Luke's multi-faceted Christology continues: Jesus is the promised royal descendant of David (2:30–31; 13:23), the prophet Moses spoke of (3:22–23), the Servant of the Lord (3:13, 26), a man accredited by God (2:22) and anointed with the Holy Spirit (10:38). Once again, however, does this mean that Jesus is merely a human agent of God's saving purposes? Having already established that Jesus is the incarnate Lord who is to be worshipped, it is no surprise that Luke continues to use 'Lord' (*kyrios*) for both Jesus and God the Father.

This wider narrative context of Luke-Acts helps us understand the statement of Peter that God 'has made him both Lord and Christ' (2:36). It is obvious from Luke's Gospel (e.g. Luke 2:11), and already from the opening chapters of Acts (e.g. 1:6; 2:31), that this does not mean Jesus was not Lord or Christ before his resurrection and enthronement. Rather, Jesus has entered 'his glory' after suffering (Luke 24:26) and, upon enthronement, is now the reigning 'Spirit-giving Lord of glory'.[36] Furthermore, because it is Jesus who now grants forgiveness of sins and the gift of the Spirit (2:33, 38), the name of the Lord (Yahweh in Joel), who must be called upon in order to be saved from judgment on the 'day of the Lord', is the Lord Jesus, David's Lord who sits at the right hand of the Lord (2:34).[37]

---

36. Gathercole, 'Trinity', p. 62. Rowe argues that this is 'God's reversal of the human rejection of Jesus' (*Early Narrative Christology*, p. 195). Thus Jesus' identity as Lord continues, though this is something all Israel should now 'know for certain' (Acts 2:36).

37. Cf. 'calls upon the name' in 2:21 (see also 9:14, 21; 22:16). See below on 7:59.

So Acts emphasizes that it is the risen and reigning Lord *Jesus* who continues to accomplish *God's* saving rule. There are regular statements that show that the Lord Jesus is continuing to rule as he directs the spread of the word by adding to the church (2:47; 11:21; 16:14), healing people (3:16; 9:34) and directing the whole of Paul's movements and ministry (9:15; 18:10; 23:11). Indeed, Jesus is 'Lord *of all*' (10:36)! Although there is much more that could be said, the following examples show that Luke views the Lord Jesus not only as continuing to be involved in the world, but as the divine Lord and Saviour of his people (4:12). In Acts 11:21, for instance, we are told that the reason why a 'great number who believed turned to the Lord' in Antioch is because 'the hand of the Lord' was with those who were telling people about the Lord Jesus. The phrase 'the hand of the Lord' is an idiomatic expression found throughout the Old Testament to refer to the power and presence of Yahweh, whether in judgment or in salvation and help for his people.[38] In this context the Lord whose 'hand' is referred to must be the Lord Jesus, because immediately prior to this is the reference to the spread of the good news about 'the Lord Jesus' (11:20), and immediately following this is the reference to 'a great number' of people believing and turning to 'the Lord' (11:21). Therefore the reason given for why people are responding in faith and repentance here is because the Lord Jesus is empowering his people in their proclamation such that he effects faith and repentance in 'a great number' of people.

Another instance of the Lord Jesus' acting with divine prerogatives is found in the story of Lydia's conversion. The reason why Lydia responded to Paul's message about Jesus is because 'the Lord opened her heart' (16:14). Once again Lydia's description of herself in the following verse as a 'believer in the Lord' (NIV) indicates that the Lord who opened her heart here is the Lord Jesus. As in Luke's Gospel, the Lord Jesus is the one who knows and, in this example, changes human hearts.[39] In the Old Testament Yahweh is the one who knows human hearts and directs them according to his sovereign will.[40]

Jesus is also prayed to as the sovereign Lord who has divine power. After choosing two men who fitted the qualifications for being an apostle (Joseph-Barsabbas and Matthias), the disciples prayed, 'You, Lord, who know the hearts

---

38. Cf. the phrase *cheir kyriou* in e.g. Num. 11:23; Isa. 41:20; 59:1; 66:14. In the NT the phrase is used only by Luke (Luke 1:66 [Yahweh]; Acts 11:21; 13:11 [probably the Lord Jesus in view of 13:12]).

39. See above on Luke 5:22; 7:39–40; 9:47; 11:17. See also below on Acts 1:24; 15:8.

40. In addition to 2 Chr. 6:30 see also Prov. 15:11; 21:1–2.

of all, show which one of these two you have chosen' (Acts 1:23–24). Two explicit links to the opening verses of this chapter and the use of 'Lord' in the immediately preceding verses confirm that this is a prayer to the Lord Jesus. First, the phrase 'the day when he was taken up from us' in 1:22 recalls the same phrase in 1:2, and the phrase 'you have chosen' in their prayer (1:24) recalls those same opening verses where the apostles are described as those 'whom he [Jesus] had chosen' (1:2; cf. Luke 6:13; 10:22). These two explicit links indicate that Jesus' 'choosing' activity in 1:2 is in the background here. Second, in the verses immediately preceding this prayer, the 'Lord' is explicitly 'the Lord Jesus'. The potentially qualified replacement apostle must have been with the disciples 'all the time that *the Lord Jesus*' was among them (1:21–22).[41] Their prayer to the 'Lord', therefore, shows that they expect the Lord Jesus to choose from heaven this twelfth apostle as he chose the apostles during his earthly ministry. Praying to Jesus as the 'Lord' who chooses his apostles, describing Jesus as someone who knows 'the hearts of all',[42] and then casting lots (cf. Prov. 16:33), an action that in this context acknowledges sovereignty over seemingly random events, all attribute divine prerogatives to the Lord Jesus, who continues to rule over his church.

A further example of prayer to Jesus as Lord is found in the description of Stephen's dying moments in Acts 7:59–60. At the conclusion of his sermon Stephen directs his angry attackers to look to Jesus, the Danielic Son of Man in heaven, in the glorious presence of God, and in a position of power and authority 'at the right hand of God' (7:55–56). This final declaration concerning Jesus and the location of God's presence, in contrast to the temple, is the final straw for this angry mob; they cover their ears, yell at the top of their voices, and stone him to death (7:57–58). In the face of death, however, Stephen utters two prayers – to the Lord Jesus! This in itself is remarkable. We have just been informed that Stephen has seen 'the glory of God, and Jesus standing at the right hand of God'. Yet when Stephen prays, he prays to the Lord Jesus!

Furthermore, Stephen's prayers attribute divine prerogatives to Jesus. First, he calls upon the Lord Jesus to receive his spirit (7:59) – Jesus is the Lord to call upon to grant access to heaven.[43] Then he asks that the Lord Jesus not hold this sin against his attackers (7:60) – Jesus has the power to forgive murderers.

41. The only other use of 'Lord' in Acts 1, apart from 1:21, 24, also refers to Jesus (cf. 1:6).

42. God is described as a 'heart knower' in 15:8.

43. The same term, *epikaleō* (call upon), is used regarding 'the Lord', Yahweh, in 2:21.

At one level Stephen clearly reflects the character of the Lord Jesus here (cf. Luke 23:34, 46). Stephen is going further, however, than merely following Jesus' example. In the context of his speech Stephen's concluding words and dying prayers declare Jesus to be the fulfilment of the temple. Jesus, in the presence of God, is the one who is prayed to, grants access to heaven and provides forgiveness of sin.

Jesus is the Lord, Yahweh, who must be called upon to be saved, the Lord who enables the growth of God's people and who knows and opens hearts, the Lord who answers prayer, grants access to heaven, and forgives murderers! He is the divine Saviour! Let us turn now to treat briefly some of the evidence in Acts for the unity of God the Father, Son and Holy Spirit as well as the distinctions also evident.

The triunity of God, Jesus and Holy Spirit
Jesus and God

As with Luke's Gospel, in Acts 'God' (*theos*) refers to God the Father in distinction from Jesus, the Lord. However, Acts also continues the pattern in Luke's Gospel of closely associating Jesus and 'God'. For instance, Peter begins his sermon on the day of Pentecost with a quotation from Joel 2 in which '*God* says "*I* will pour out my Spirit"' (Acts 2:17–18). Yet in Acts 2:33 Peter says *Jesus* has 'poured out what you now see and hear' (NIV).[44] Likewise, in Acts 11:15–17 Peter explains the 'pouring out' (cf. 10:45) of the Holy Spirit on the Gentiles by recalling the 'word of the Lord' (11:16).[45] In this context the 'word of the Lord' is the teaching of *Jesus*, who contrasted John's water baptism with the promise that his disciples would be baptized with the Holy Spirit (cf. 1:5).[46] Then Peter declares that *God* has given these Gentiles 'the same gift he gave us, who believed in the Lord Jesus Christ' (11:17 NIV; cf. also 5:32). Thus Acts 2 and 11 show interchangeable references to what 'God' did and what 'the Lord Jesus' did in sending the Holy Spirit.

Luke's correlation of Jesus' activity with God's activity is also seen in the accounts of Paul's conversion and call. In Acts 9:15 the Lord Jesus tells Ananias that Paul is '*my* chosen instrument' (NIV) and, in an outline of the rest of Paul's life, declares that he will bear Jesus' name before the Gentiles, their kings and

---

44. The verb *ekcheō* (poured out) in 2:33 deliberately recalls the reference to Joel 2:28 in Acts 2:17–18.

45. The 'word of the LORD' is a common expression in the OT for God's word (e.g. Gen. 15:1; Isa. 40:8).

46. Cf. Luke 3:16; 24:49; Jesus will 'baptize with' or 'send' the Holy Spirit.

the people of Israel. Interestingly, in the additional details given in Acts 22 Paul recounts Ananias's message that '*the God of our fathers* appointed you to know his will' (22:14). Then in Acts 26 Paul recounts the words of the Lord Jesus that *he* has appeared to Paul 'to appoint you as a servant and witness' (26:16). *Jesus'* initiative and purpose in Acts 9 and 26 is described in terms of *God's* initiative and purpose in Acts 22. In fact, the same term, 'chosen/appointed', is used for God's activity (in 22:14) and Jesus' activity (in 26:16).[47]

Similar associations are sometimes found in Luke's descriptions of people who respond to the gospel. For instance, Paul's response to the Philippian jailer's question about how to be saved is that he must 'believe in the *Lord Jesus*' (16:31). A few verses later, however, Luke says that the reason for the jailor's joy is because he has 'believed in *God*' (16:34).[48] Elsewhere in Acts Paul describes the required response to the gospel as both 'repentance towards God' and 'faith in our Lord Jesus Christ' (20:21). Similarly, repentance can be described as 'turning' to God (14:15; 15:19; 26:18, 20) or 'turning' to the Lord Jesus (9:35 [cf. 9:42]; 11:21). Repentance can be described as a gift from God (11:18) or the Lord Jesus (5:31). Faith can also be described as granted by God (14:27) or the Lord Jesus (3:16).

The Spirit and God

Whereas the previous references have identified Jesus with God in the action of pouring out the Spirit, the conversion and calling of Paul, and responses to the gospel, on other occasions the Spirit is also clearly identified with God. Thus, on the one hand, Peter can declare that Ananias has told a 'lie to the Holy Spirit' (5:3), but in the next verse (in keeping with the distinction made between 'man' and 'God' found through Luke-Acts) Peter declares that Ananias has 'not lied to men but to God' (5:4). Peter also says that Ananias and Sapphira agreed to test the 'Spirit of the Lord' (5:9), which is a common phrase in the Old Testament for the presence of Yahweh by his Spirit (e.g. Judg. 3:10; 2 Sam. 23:2–3). Elsewhere in Acts we are told that the Spirit is living, active and communicates his will: he speaks God's authoritative word (1:16; 13:2, 26–27; 21:11; 28:25; cf. also 8:29; 10:19), bears witness (5:32), has purposes (13:2; 15:28), sends (13:4; cf. 8:39), prevents (16:6), encourages (9:31) and warns (20:23).

---

47. I.e. 'chosen/appointed' (*procheirizomai*) is used for God in 22:14 and Jesus in 26:16. A different phrase (*skeuos eklogēs*, 'chosen instrument') is used in 9:15.

48. In Acts the object of faith is most often the Lord Jesus (9:42; 10:43; 11:17; 14:23; 19:4; 22:19; 24:24; 26:18). God is the object of faith in 16:34 and 27:25.

In Acts the unity of God, Jesus and the Holy Spirit is seen in the decision
of Paul and his companions to travel over to Macedonia (Acts 16:6–10). First,
'the Holy Spirit' prevented them from preaching the word in Asia (16:6).
Then 'the Spirit of Jesus' would not allow them to enter Bithynia (16:7). This
second reference is still to the Holy Spirit, though the designation 'Spirit of
Jesus' recalls the day of Pentecost when Jesus, in fulfilment of his promise in
Luke 24:49, is the one who pours out the Holy Spirit (Acts 2:33). In this way
the more common phrase of the Old Testament, 'the Spirit of the Lord', is now
applied to Jesus and draws attention to the ongoing reign of the Lord Jesus over
the spread of the word by the Holy Spirit. After describing the directing activity
of 'the Holy Spirit', or 'the Spirit of Jesus', and a vision of a Macedonian man
calling for help, Luke then notes that the decision to travel to Macedonia is made
because they concluded that '*God* had called us to preach the gospel to them'
(16:10). These descriptions of the directing activity of 'the Holy Spirit', 'the
Spirit of Jesus' and 'God' in the space of four verses indicate that Luke is able
to move seamlessly between references to all three in describing how the spread
of the gospel is directed. Luke regularly refers to the Trinity in ways that would
suggest a common identity: sometimes Luke can speak of what Jesus does
as what God does, a response to Jesus as a response to God, a response to
the Spirit as a response to God, or the activity of the Spirit as the activity of the
Spirit of Jesus and the activity of God. It is also clear, however, that the three
are distinguishable; it is to these distinctions that we now turn.

Father, Son and Spirit

In many of the same passages where all three, Father, Son and Spirit, are
mentioned together, clear distinctions are also made. The Lord Jesus pours out
the Spirit from 'the right hand of God' (2:33). Here we have the divine authority
and co-regency of the Lord Jesus (2:30) with the Father, in a position of power
and authority ('at the right hand'). A distinction is clearly made, however, as the
Lord is at the 'right hand' of the Father, who is also Lord (2:34). A similar distinction is seen in Stephen's concluding words: Stephen, full of the Spirit, is
enabled to see both 'the glory of God' and 'Jesus standing at the right hand of
God' (7:55). Likewise, in Peter's association of the events in Cornelius' house
with the events of Pentecost, the three are mentioned together: the gift of the
Spirit is given by God to those who believed in the Lord Jesus – just as Jesus,
the Lord, had said (11:15–17)! The Spirit, though God (5:4), is also the 'gift of
God' (8:20; cf. 2:38; 11:17). The three are also mentioned together in Paul's
exhortation to the Ephesian elders to watch out for the church (20:28): the elders
have been appointed (or equipped) as overseers of the flock by the Holy Spirit;
the flock is the church of God; the church has been purchased by God at the

costly price of 'the blood of his own Son' (NET).[49] Thus all three are included
in one verse. Clear distinctions, however, are made: the Spirit equips the elders,
God owns the church, and the Son was the means by which God acquired the
church.

There are only three references to God as 'Father' in Acts, all in the first two
chapters. In keeping with the pattern we have seen in Luke's Gospel, the first
two references are found in Jesus' words (1:4, 7). Although Jesus is the Lord
who will restore the kingdom to Israel (1:6), and the disciples will be *his* witnesses
(1:8), the timing of this restoration is ultimately set by the Father's authority
(1:6–8).[50] The only reference to the Father in Luke-Acts that is not spoken by
Jesus is Peter's statement (which reflects Jesus' own teaching, Luke 24:49; Acts
1:4) that Jesus received 'from the Father the promised Holy Spirit' (2:33 NIV).
Thus all three are mentioned together; yet they are distinguishable. Ultimately
then, although it is as true to say that God sent the Spirit as it is to say that Jesus
sent the Spirit (as noted above); more precisely, it is the Father who initiates,
promises and grants to the Son, and the Son who sends. The divine authority
to judge 'the living and the dead' belongs to Jesus, but this is a position to which
he has been 'appointed' by God the Father (10:42; 17:31; cf. Luke 10:22a). The
Father–Son distinction and order that characterized Jesus' earthly ministry is
continued in his post-exaltation position of power at the right hand of the
Father.

Conclusion

The overarching emphasis in Luke and Acts is that believers in the Lord Jesus,
such as Theophilus, may most certainly be assured that the triune God is the
sovereign Saviour; his kingdom, or saving rule, has come! The saving actions
and promises of God in the history of Israel culminate in the life, death and
resurrection of the incarnate Lord, who accomplishes the saving purposes of
his Father by the power of the Spirit. This incarnate Lord Jesus has ascended

---

49. The genitive *tou idiou* (one's own) is understood here as a term of endearment
    referring to the Son. On the options see Steve Walton, *Leadership and Lifestyle:
    The Portrait of Paul in the Miletus Speech and 1 Thessalonians*, SNTSMS 108 (Cambridge:
    Cambridge University Press, 2000), pp. 91–98.

50. On the significance of these verses for the kingdom in Acts see Thompson, *Acts*,
    pp. 103–108. The language of 'you will be my witnesses' (v. 8) reflects the wording
    of Isa. 43:12; 44:8 (that Yahweh, the Lord, is the only Saviour).

and now reigns at the right hand of the Father, so that God's saving rule continues to be accomplished among the nations by the Lord Jesus through the Spirit who was promised by the Father and sent by the Son. The Father directs his saving plan under his authority, according to his timing. The Lord Jesus reigns, answers prayer and opens hearts. The Spirit empowers God's people – those who believe in the Son – to bear witness to the Son and his salvation. God is one, yet three, and all three act inseparably yet distinctly. The promised salvation of Israel and the nations is the united work of the three-in-one – all glory and praise belong to the triune God . . . alone!

© Alan J. Thompson, 2016

4. THE TRINITY AND THE GOSPEL OF JOHN

Richard Bauckham

The Gospel of John has played a hugely important role in the formation of classical Christian trinitarian doctrine and in continued reflection on the Trinity, including critical discussion. Sometimes (especially in the case of the trinitarian relationships within the immanent Trinity) it has been pressed to yield more than it can reasonably give, but in many ways the broad shape of trinitarian doctrine in Christian tradition corresponds well to what this Gospel has to say about the Father, the Son and the Holy Spirit. It is important, however, for Christian theology not merely to acknowledge its Johannine roots but also continually to return to them. Important as the classical statements of trinitarian doctrine are, they are no more than summaries of the rich reflections offered by the Gospel itself. Fresh readings of these – for example, in the light of the shape of Jewish monotheism in the Gospel's original context, or with close attention to their pervasive soteriological significance – have much to offer. They can contribute to a revitalization of what may otherwise become merely the lifeless repetition of orthodox formulae. Like the God of the whole Bible, the God of the Gospel of John is above all the living God and the loving God, who gives life and love to creation from the infinite resources of his own being. In what the Gospel says about the Father, the Son and the Spirit, we are invited to contemplate the irreducibly relational nature of the life and the love that God is, both in himself and with us. We can do no better than start where John starts – with the relationality of God as it was already 'in the beginning': 'the Word was with God, and the Word was God' (1:1)[1].

The prologue: from the Word to the only Son

Before beginning to tell the story of Jesus from its traditional starting point, the ministry of John the Baptist, the evangelist John provides a prologue that tells his readers who Jesus is and what he came to do. Essentially it fulfils the same function as Mark's very short prologue (Mark 1:1), which may have given John the idea for his much more elaborate prologue. In both cases readers are equipped from the start with the knowledge of Jesus' identity that it takes characters in the story the whole length of the story fully to realize.[2] Thus in John's case it is not until after the resurrection that Thomas recognizes that Jesus is 'God' (20:28), but the prologue already calls Jesus 'God' emphatically and with necessary explanation (1:1–2, 18). By comparison with Mark's very brief prologue John's is a quasi-poetic piece of highly concentrated theology, and whereas Mark signals merely 'the beginning' of the gospel, John's begins at 'the beginning' of everything, the beginning at which Genesis and the whole biblical story began. To let his readers into the secret of who Jesus really is, John thinks it necessary to begin at the earliest possible beginning, when God the Creator was on the brink of bringing the whole cosmos into being. For anyone who knew Genesis, the identity between the opening words of Genesis and those of John's Gospel ('In the beginning') would be obvious and would provide the key to the meaning of the way the prologue continues.[3]

The first part of the prologue (1:1–5) is set in what we might call primordial time, the time of Genesis 1, while the second part (1:6–18), which begins in the style of Old Testament historical narrative (1:6), is set in historical time and, by featuring John the Baptist (1:6–8, 15), connects with the opening section of the gospel story (1:19–34). The first part of the prologue takes the form of a

---

1. Unless stated otherwise, Scripture quotations in this chapter are from the NRSV.

2. See Morna D. Hooker, 'The Johannine Prologue and the Messianic Secret', *NTS* 21 (1974–5), pp. 40–58.

3. Note that Jewish allusions to creation frequently use the words 'in the beginning' or 'the beginning' in allusion to Gen. 1:1 (Masanobu Endo, *Creation and Christology: A Study on the Johannine Prologue in the Light of Early Jewish Creation Accounts*, WUNT 2.149 [Tübingen: Mohr Siebeck, 2002], pp. 206–207).

retelling of Genesis 1:1–5,[4] comparable in some ways with other Jewish retellings of the Genesis creation narrative in Second Temple period literature.[5] The allusions to Genesis are clear and must determine what John means by 'the Word' (*ho logos*). In Genesis 1 God creates by speaking words. The noun 'word' does not occur there, but it does in the short summary of the story of creation in Psalm 33:6–9,[6] and Jewish retellings of the Genesis account frequently state that God created by his word.[7] Sometimes they refer to this creative word of God simply as 'the word', as John does.[8]

The Greek word *logos* has other meanings besides 'word', including 'reason', but the allusion to Genesis requires that in John's prologue the primary meaning must be 'word' and there is no strong reason for positing any further meaning, such as a philosophical (Stoic or Platonic) notion of a cosmic reason,[9] appealing though such a meaning was to later readers. Most recent commentators on John have thought that the figure of divine Wisdom, which features in some Jewish literature in connection with creation, has influenced the prologue. It is possible that John identified God's Word with God's Wisdom, especially in view of the connection between Genesis 1:1 and Proverbs 8:22 (both refer to 'the beginning'), but Jewish narratives of creation refer to the word of God considerably more often than they do to the wisdom of God,[10] while the two are sometimes distinguished and given different roles (God's wisdom devised the plan and his word executed it).[11] What John says of the Word in 1:1–4 is quite sufficiently explained

---

4. See esp. Peder Borgen, 'Observations on the Targumic Character of the Prologue of John' and 'Logos was the True Light: Contributions to the Interpretation of the Prologue of John', both in idem, *Logos Was the True Light and Other Essays on the Gospel of John* (Trondheim: Tapir, 1983), pp. 13–20, 95–110.

5. These are studied and compared with the prologue to John in Endo, *Creation and Christology*.

6. Ps. 33:6a, 'By the word of the LORD the heavens were made.'

7. Endo, *Creation and Christology*, pp. 163, 210.

8. *2 Bar.* 14.17; 48.8; 54.3.

9. Philo's ideas about the Logos were strongly influenced by Stoic and especially Middle Platonic notions. Thomas H. Tobin, 'The Prologue of John and Hellenistic Jewish Speculation', *CBQ* 52 (1990), pp. 252–269, argues that the prologue to John belongs within the same sphere of Hellenistic Jewish speculation, such that John's Logos is comparable with Philo's. I do not think the parallels are sufficiently distinctive to establish the case.

10. See the table in Endo, *Creation and Christology*, p. 163.

11. *2 En.* 33.4; Wis. 9.1–2.

on the basis of Jewish references to the role of God's word in creation,[12] while other alleged similarities to Wisdom ideas in the rest of the prologue are possible but not compelling.[13] We should certainly not make interpretation of the prologue depend upon detecting Wisdom somewhere behind it.

The first three verses of the prologue are an expression of Jewish creational monotheism. The simplest and clearest way in which Jewish writers maintained the uniqueness of their God was to assert that the one and only God was the creator of all things.[14] Everything except God was created by God. Sometimes it was emphasized that no one assisted God in creation; it was all his own work.[15] But this uniqueness of God did not prevent certain distinctions being made between God and aspects or attributes of his: God and his Wisdom, God and his Word, God and his Spirit. Such distinctions were no threat to the uniqueness of the one God because such aspects or attributes belonged to his own identity. They were not some divine entity in addition to God himself, but precisely *his* Wisdom, *his* Word, *his* Spirit.[16]

The prologue therefore begins by stating, in a way that is not only poetic but also very precise, the relationship between God and his Word before creation, when the Word through which God would express himself in creating the world already belonged to God's identity:

In the beginning was the Word,
    and the Word was with God [*ho logos ēn pros ton theon*],[17]
    and the Word was God [*theos ēn ho logos*].
He[18] was in the beginning with God [*pros ton theon*].

---

12. That the Word was 'with God' in the beginning (John 1:2) could reflect Prov. 8:30 (cf. also Wis. 9.9), but it could be John's own attempt to elucidate the relationship between God and his Word.

13. See e.g. John Painter, *The Quest for the Messiah: The History, Literature and Theology of the Johannine Community*, 2nd ed. (Edinburgh: T&T Clark, 1993), pp. 145–147.

14. Richard Bauckham, *Jesus and the God of Israel: God Crucified and Other Studies on the New Testament's Christology of Divine Identity* (Milton Keynes: Paternoster; Grand Rapids: Eerdmans, 2008), pp. 9–10.

15. E.g. Sir. 42.21; *2 En.* 47.3–5; *4 Ezra* 3.4; 6.6.

16. Bauckham, *Jesus*, pp. 16–17.

17. This use of *pros* is unusual but not unparalleled (Matt. 13:56; Mark 6:3; 9:19; 14:49; Luke 9:41).

18. The personal pronoun ('he' rather than 'it') is unavoidable in English, even though in the Greek it is not unequivocally clear at this stage that the Word is personified or personal.

The effect of the repetition is to highlight the two different relationships in which the Word stands to God: he was 'with God' and he 'was God', and both were simultaneously true. He is distinguishable from God and yet shares the same divine identity. In the repeated statement that the Word 'was with God', the word 'God' has the article ('the God'), but in the statement that the Word 'was God', the word 'God' is anarthrous (i.e. it lacks the article). This may be a grammatical necessity (to distinguish the subject of the sentence [*ho logos*] from the predicate [*theos*]).[19] It certainly does not mean that the Word 'was a god' or 'was divine' in some lesser sense than the full deity of God himself, for the function of the statement is precisely to negate the possibility that the preceding statement ('the Word was with God') refers to some independent entity alongside or subordinate to God. Here, in the beginning, before creation, there is no room for any beings other than the one God.

The meaning of 'the Word was God' is often discussed without reference to the rest of the prologue. But the word 'God' (*theos*) occurs eight times in the prologue (including the disputed reading *theos* in 1:18b), and with the exception of the two occurrences in the phrase 'the Word was with God' (1:1a, 2), all other occurrences are anarthrous (1:1, 6, 12, 13, 18a, 18b). Of these six occurrences, the first and last refer to the Word, but the intervening four all refer to God as such, not the Word. This high percentage of the anarthrous *theos* in the prologue is out of line with usage in the rest of the Gospel and would seem therefore to be intentional and significant.[20] When John in the prologue wishes to distinguish between God and the Word, he uses *ho theos* for God, but otherwise uses the anarthrous *theos* equally for God and the Word, indicating that he means the identity of the Word with God as seriously as he means the distinction between them.

That John is thinking in terms of Jewish creational monotheism becomes especially clear in verse 3:

> All things came into being through him,
> and without him not one thing has come into being
> that has come into being.[21]

---

19. Colwell's rule (named after E. C. Colwell) states that predicate nouns that precede the verb usually lack the article.

20. D. A. Fennema, 'John 1.18: "God the Only Son"', *NTS* 31 (1983), pp. 124–135, here 128–129.

21. My tr. I prefer this punctuation to the alternative reading that takes *ho gegonen* with the following verse, 'what has come into being in him was life'. But the difference is not of great significance for the present argument.

We should recall that the often repeated affirmation of the uniqueness of the one God was that he alone 'created all things'. The prologue's words reflect another common statement about creation: that God created 'by his word'. This, as we have seen, is quite consistent with the claim that God alone created. The apparently laboured repetition in verse 3 of the prologue, where the positive statement is reinforced by the equivalent negative statement, is explicable as a monotheistic insistence that the creative role of the Word is included in the creative act of God. In the distinction between Creator and creation there should be no doubt that the Word belongs to God's side of the distinction. The Word himself is not among the things that have 'come into being'. This is not to say that the prologue refers to the Word's role in creation solely to make this monotheistic point. As verse 10 makes clear, it is also important that the one who came into the world to make eternal life available to creatures was the one who had created all things in the beginning. But the emphatic repetition in verse 3 functions to underline that the Word belongs to the identity of the unique creator of all.

The Gospel of John depicts two principal aspects of the saving work of Jesus: he reveals the Father and he gives eternal life. The prologue introduces both these soteriological themes, rooting them both in its reading of the Genesis creation narrative (light and life). What the Word was in primordial time he is also when he comes into the world in historical time: the Light who gives light to the world (vv. 8–9) and the Creator who gives life to the world (vv. 10–13). But in the climactic section of the prologue (vv. 13–18), which begins with the first use of the term 'the Word' since verse 1, a use that turns out also to be the last use of this term (in this sense) in the whole Gospel, the theme of revelation is dominant, along with the terms 'only Son' (*monogenēs*) and 'Father'. These two terms occur for the first time in verse 14 and occur again at the end of the prologue (v. 18), forming an inclusio around this discrete part of the prologue.

For our present purposes we must confine our attention to the two references to Jesus Christ as 'only Son' (*monogenēs*). Outside the prologue the term occurs again only at 3:16, 18, where, unlike in the prologue, it is combined with the word 'son' (*huios*). There is now a consensus that the word *monogenēs* does not mean 'only-begotten' but 'one of a kind', 'one and only', 'unique'.[22] However, it was frequently used for an only child, and, especially in these verses of the prologue where reference is also made to a 'father', it stands adequately on its own as meaning 'only son'. (The addition of *huios* in 3:16, 18 is understandable since

---

22. See esp. Gerard Pendrick, '*Monogenēs*', *NTS* 41 (1995), pp. 587–600.

God is not there called 'Father'.) This is one reason why the reading *monogenēs theos* in verse 18 should probably be preferred to the alternative reading *ho monogenēs huios*, and why it should be translated as 'God the only Son'.[23]

When the Word became flesh, the eyewitnesses (those who saw with both eyes and insight)[24] saw 'his glory, glory as of an only son from a father'[25] (v. 14). The terminology of 'only son' and 'father' is introduced here by way of a simile, but is applied directly when it recurs in verse 18: 'No one has ever seen God; God the only Son, who is on the breast of the Father, he has made him known' (my tr.). The references to the only Son and the Father here form an inclusio with verse 14. But furthermore the whole phrase 'God the only Son, who is on the breast of the Father' forms an inclusio with the beginning of the prologue, where the Word was with God and was God. The statement that 'the Word was with God' is now unpacked in the more vividly personal language 'the only Son, who is on the breast of the Father'. Additionally (if we accept the reading *monogenēs theos* in v. 18), the word *theos* is applied in both cases to the Word or only Son, anticipating at both ends of the prologue the climax of the Gospel story in Thomas's confession at 20:28.

In this final section of the prologue (vv. 13–18) it has become clear that 'the Word' was only a preliminary designation of the one who is revealed in the

---

23. For detailed discussion see Fennema, 'John 1.18'; Elizabeth Harris, *Prologue and Gospel: The Theology of the Fourth Evangelist*, JSNTSup 107 (Sheffield: Sheffield Academic Press, 1994), pp. 101–109. For the view that *theos* is not original see James F. McGrath, *The Only True God: Early Christian Monotheism in Its Jewish Context* (Urbana: University of Illinois Press, 2009), pp. 65–66.

24. In my view this is the meaning of the first person plural in v. 14, contrasted with 'we all' (all Christian believers) in v. 16.

25. This phrase is not likely to mean 'a father's only son' (NRSV), for which one would expect *ek*, not *para*. If *para theou* is taken with *doxan*, the meaning is 'glory such as an only son receives from his father'; if with *monogenous*, the meaning is 'glory as of an only son coming from his father'. For the former meaning, cf. 5:44; for the latter meaning, cf. 6:46; 7:29; 16:27–28; 17:8. See John Henry Bernard, *A Critical and Exegetical Commentary on the Gospel According to St. John*, ICC, vol. 1 (Edinburgh: T&T Clark, 1928), p. 23. The use of *hōs* with the anarthrous nouns suggests the indefinite sense 'glory like that of an only son from a father'. But it is possible to understand *hōs* as specifying the glory, 'glory of the kind that the only Son receives from the Father' or 'the glory that is unique to the only Son from the Father'. See Edwyn Clement Hoskyns, *The Fourth Gospel*, ed. Francis Noel Davey (London: Faber & Faber, 1947), p. 149.

incarnation to be the only Son.[26] This is why 'the Word' never appears in the Gospel (in this sense) after 1:14, which makes a transition from 'the Word' to 'the only Son' of the Father.[27] The implication of this transition is that not only is the Word now revealed to be the only Son, but also God is now revealed to be the Father. The Hebrew Bible and later Jewish literature speak of God as the Father of his people Israel, but in John's Gospel the term Father always refers to God as the Father of Jesus his Son (with the single significant exception of 20:17).[28] By being in his humanity the divine Son, Jesus reveals both the Father as his Father and his relationship with the Father as an eternal relationship within the divine identity.

Eternal Son?

I have said that in incarnation the Word was *revealed to be* the only Son of the Father. This would mean that the Word had always been the only Son of the Father, eternally 'on the breast of the Father', but that only in incarnation was this revealed. John will have used the term 'Word' in verses 1–14 because this was the usage of the Hebrew Bible, switching to 'only Son' in verses 14–18 because this is who the Word has been revealed to be in incarnation. But a few scholars argue that, according to the prologue, the Word *became* the Son at the incarnation. John A. T. Robinson argued that the Word, that is, God's self-expression and self-revelation, came, in Jesus, to be 'embodied totally in and as a human being, became a person'.[29] Making use of patristic terminology, Robinson follows Piet Schoonenberg's suggestion that, rather than thinking of the anhypostatic human nature of Jesus becoming hypostatic ('a person or hypostasis') when assumed by the Logos, as the Fathers and the tradition did, we should think of the Logos as anhypostatic 'until the Word of God finally came to self-expression not merely in nature

---

26. This is not to deny that throughout the Gospel narrative Jesus is the 'Word' in the sense that he reveals God.

27. Cf. Mark Stibbe, 'Telling the Father's Story: The Gospel of John as Narrative Theology', in John Lierman (ed.), *Challenging Perspectives on the Gospel of John*, WUNT 2.219 (Tübingen: Mohr Siebeck, 2006), pp. 170–193, here 175: 'the God/Logos distinction is redefined as a Father/Son distinction'.

28. Marianne Meye Thompson, *The God of the Gospel of John* (Grand Rapids: Eerdmans, 2001), pp. 50–51, 70–71.

29. John A. T. Robinson, *The Priority of John* (London: SCM, 1985), p. 380.

and in a people, but in an individual historical person, and thus *became* hypostatic'.[30]

Robinson understands Jesus' 'sonship' to be the ideal human form of relationship to God, which Jesus instantiates perfectly, thereby revealing God his Father. He admits that John represents Jesus as speaking in the first person of his own pre-existence and post-existence as 'a heavenly person', but understands this to be 'the language of myth . . . pushing the truth of the sonship that Jesus embodied back to the very beginning of God's purpose'.[31] Jesus, according to John, 'is not a divine being who came to earth . . . in the form of a man, but the uniquely normal human being in whom the Logos or self-expressive activity of God was totally embodied'.[32]

More recently, Keith Ward, arguing for a 'reformulation' of the doctrine of the Trinity, takes 'the Word' in John's prologue to be 'the self-expressive thought of God', 'the eternally expressed thought of God. It is the Thought which is *monogenēs theos* (John I, 18), the uniquely generated aspect of God. Then God's Thought is made real and particular in material form in Jesus.' There is only one personal 'subject' in Jesus, the human subject, 'but that subject perfectly expresses the divine Ideal or self-communicative expression of God'.[33] Ward does not explicitly discuss what John means by calling Jesus 'the Son', but it seems clear that, like Robinson, he thinks the term can properly apply only to Jesus the human being.[34] As a constructive theologian, Ward is concerned, like Robinson, to maintain the integrity of the humanity of Jesus, which requires a fully human subject, but also to oppose the notion of a 'social trinity' that posits intersubjective relationships in God's eternal trinitarian being.

I will limit my argument here to the contention that John's Gospel does not present the 'sonship' of Jesus as appertaining only to his human relationship with God. One might still argue, theologically, that the idea of Jesus' personal pre-existence, whether the New Testament writers *meant* it metaphysically or only figuratively, is a 'mythological' way of saying that he was the climax of

---

30. Ibid., pp. 380–381; cf. Piet Schoonenberg, *The Christ*, tr. Della Couling (London: Sheed & Ward, 1972), pp. 80–91, emphasis original.

31. Robinson, *Priority*, p. 389.

32. Ibid., pp. 393–394.

33. Keith Ward, *Christ and the Cosmos: A Reformulation of Trinitarian Doctrine* (Cambridge: Cambridge University Press, 2015), pp. 56–57.

34. Ward is careful to say he is offering 'an interpretation of John from within my own very different historical context' (ibid., p. 63) and 'not, of course, suggesting that this is the one correct interpretation' (p. 64).

God's eternal purpose for humanity.[35] But it will still be important to establish just how the Gospel presents it.

The most decisive evidence that the Son, as Son, pre-existed the incarnation is to be found in the prayer of Jesus in chapter 17, which in some respects is a counterpart to the prologue.[36] Only in chapter 17 does the perspective of the Gospel turn back to 'the beginning' with which it began (17:5, 24). Here, on the brink of completing the work the Father has given him to do (17:4), Jesus looks back to the glory he had with the Father 'before the world existed' (17:5). He looks back in order to look forward to the imminent moment when he will return to the Father and receive once again that primordial glory from the Father. His prayer is, 'So now, Father, glorify me in your presence [*para seautō*] with the glory I had in your presence [*para soi*] before the world existed' (17:5, my tr.). Here 'in your presence' (more literally, 'close to you')[37] is equivalent to 'with God', said of the Word in 1:1–2, and even more to 'on the breast of the Father', said of 'God the only Son' in 1:18. Moreover, the reference to 'glory' picks up the phrase in 1:14, 'we have seen his glory, glory as of an only son from a father'. The glory the eyewitnesses saw (1:14) must therefore be the earthly manifestation of the glory the Son had with the Father before the world existed (17:5). If it could be called, in its incarnate form, 'glory as of an only son from a father', then it must have been 'glory as of a father's only son' already in eternity.

Jesus returns to this theme towards the end of the prayer, when he prays that those who believe in him may in the future 'be with me where I am, to see my glory, which you have given me because you loved me before the foundation of the world' (17:24). This is the last occurrence in the Gospel of the key word 'glory' and it matches the first occurrence: 'we have seen his glory' (1:14). Those who have seen his glory in its earthly form will in the future see his glory in its heavenly form. Here the glory is linked to the Father's eternal love for the Son. It is the glory the Father gave him because he loved him 'before the foundation of the world'. It cannot be doubted that the Gospel here speaks of an

---

35. This is the argument of Karl-Josef Kuschel, *Born Before All Time? The Dispute over Christ's Origin*, tr. John Bowden (London: SCM, 1992).

36. Note that only in these two passages is Jesus called 'Jesus Christ' (1:17; 17:3). In my view Thomas L. Brodie, *The Gospel According to John: A Literary and Theological Commentary* (New York: Oxford University Press, 1993), pp. 508–511, pushes correspondences between the prologue and ch. 17 too far, but certainly establishes a relationship.

37. Cf. 8:38.

intersubjective relationship of love between the Father and the Son in eternity.[38] Just as, at the end of the prologue, the relationship of the Word to God is restated as the only Son's (implicitly loving) intimacy with his Father, so Jesus himself, communing with his Father at the conclusion of his work, sees it as the enjoyment of his Father's love in his intimate presence. Moreover, here in chapter 17 there is no question that the reference is to the same pre-mundane eternity of which the beginning of the prologue speaks. What the prologue said of God and the Word at the beginning was no more than a preliminary indication of the relationship that chapter 17 more adequately depicts as that between the Father and his Son.

The binitarian shape of Johannine monotheism

In using the term 'binitarian' here I am not intending to exclude the Spirit from John's understanding of monotheism, but simply to focus for the time being on the relationship between Jesus and God. We need to give full weight to two aspects of the way John speaks of this:

1. Jesus as *uniquely associated with God*. In such cases John adds Jesus to 'God' (i.e. the God of Israel), distinguished from but closely associated with God.
2. Jesus as *identified with God*. In such cases John includes Jesus in the unique identity of the God of Israel.

These two aspects are already stressed in the opening verses of the prologue (the Word was 'with God'[39] and 'was God'), which should warn us against collapsing either into the other. A signal example of aspect 1 is in Jesus' words to the Father 'that they may know you, the only true God, and Jesus Christ whom you have sent' (17:3). Here the terminology of Jewish monotheism ('the only true God') is applied to the Father, from whom Jesus the Son is distinguished

---

38. In Wis. 8.3 it is said of Wisdom that 'the Lord of all loves her', following reference in 8.2 to Solomon's love for Wisdom, personified as a beautiful woman he wishes to marry. But in John 17:24, in the context of Jesus' personal address to the Father, one can scarcely reduce the meaning of 'loved me' to 'God loved [i.e. set high value on] the Word.' It is not that sort of love that Jesus wishes to be in his disciples (17:26).

39. During Jesus' earthly life this relationship seems to be expressed by the reverse formulation: God is 'with' Jesus (8:29; 16:32).

(cf. also 5:44). But, on the other hand, in an equally signal facet of aspect 2, Jesus claims that 'the Father and I are one' (10:30). 'The Jews' perceive this claim as blasphemous, as 'making yourself God' (10:31, 33), probably because it echoes the terminology of the Shema ('the Lord, the Lord your God is one'),[40] and so includes Jesus in the unique identity of the God of Israel, as Paul's version of the Shema in 1 Corinthians 8:6 also does.[41] (Contrast 'the Jews'' own version of the Shema: 'We have one Father, God' [8:41].)

The divine prerogatives

In the Jewish definition of the one God's exclusive divinity, as well as being sole creator of all things (as in the prologue to John), God was also understood as the sole sovereign ruler of all things. A key aspect of this was his sovereignty over life and death (Deut. 32:39). God is the only living one, that is, the only one to whom life belongs eternally and intrinsically. All other life derives from him, is given by him and taken back by him. Another key aspect was his prerogative of judgment, the implementation of justice. Such divine prerogatives have to be understood, not as mere functions that God may delegate to others, but as intrinsic to the divine identity. Ruling over all, giving life to all, exercising judgment on all – these belong integrally to the Jewish understanding of *who God is*.

These divine prerogatives, intrinsic to divinity as such, are the focus of the first major passage in the Gospel in which Jesus speaks about his own identity in discussion with the Jewish leaders: chapter 5. Here Jesus defends his act of healing on the Sabbath by claiming God's unique prerogative of working on the Sabbath: 'My Father is still working [i.e. his work did not cease with his creation of all things but continues in his sovereign rule over all things], and I also am working' (5:17). (Since people are born and die on Sabbaths, it is clear that God exercises his sovereignty over life and death and his prerogative of judgment on the Sabbath as on other days. Jesus claims to do the same.) The Jewish leaders take this to mean that Jesus 'was making himself equal to God' (5:18), and the discourse of Jesus that follows implies that in one sense they are

---

40. See Richard Bauckham, *The Testimony of the Beloved Disciple: Narrative, History, and Theology in the Gospel of John* (Grand Rapids: Baker Academic, 2007), pp. 250–251; *Gospel of Glory: Major Themes in Johannine Theology* (Grand Rapids: Baker Academic, 2015), pp. 32–34.

41. See the full study in Erik Waaler, *The* Shema *and the First Commandment in First Corinthians*, WUNT 2.253 (Tübingen: Mohr Siebeck, 2008).

right but in another, wrong. In all that he does Jesus is wholly dependent on his Father and in no way sets himself up as a rival to him. He is not equal to God in the sense the Jewish leaders intend, but is equal to God in the sense that what the Father gives him to do are the uniquely divine prerogatives. He does not simply act as God's agent in implementing some aspects of God's sovereignty. He exercises the full divine sovereignty (*'whatever* the Father does, the Son does likewise' [5:19])[42] as given him by his Father but as also fully his own: 'just as the Father raises the dead and gives them life, so also the Son gives life to *whomever he wishes*' (5:21); 'the Father judges no one, but has given *all judgment* to the Son' (5:22); 'just as the Father has life in himself, so he has granted the Son to have *life in himself*' (5:26). Jesus thus shares in the divine identity as the only living one, the only giver of life, the only judge of all.

In sayings such as these we see how the two aspects of the binitarian shape of monotheism are closely related. As the plenipotentiary agent of his Father, Jesus is distinguished from God but *uniquely associated with him*. At the same time, as plenipotentiary agent he alone exercises uniquely divine prerogatives, which belong to the unique identity of the one God. This must mean that the unique divine identity *includes* the specific relationship of dependence and divine authority that Jesus the Son has with God his Father. In that sense he is *identified with God*. That this is a correct understanding of the Johannine passage is confirmed by the words 'The Father . . . has given all judgment to the Son, so that all may honor the Son just as they honor the Father' (5:22–23). In the Jewish tradition worship was intimately connected with monotheism. The only true God must be worshipped and he is the only one who may be worshipped. This is because worship is precisely the recognition of the unique divine identity. In Jewish religious practice it was worship that distinguished the one God from all other beings who, however exalted, are his creatures and subject to his sovereign rule.

The absolute 'I am' sayings

The Gospel contains two series of sayings of Jesus including the words 'I am' (Greek *egō eimi*, where the pronoun *egō*, which is not always necessary in Greek, is used for emphasis along with the verb). There are seven sayings in each series. One series is easily recognized by readers of the Gospel in English translation.[43]

---

42. See also 3:35; 13:3; 17:2.

43. (1) 6:35, 41, 48; (2) 8:12; cf. 9:5; (3) 10:7, 9; (4) 10:11, 14; (5) 11:25; (6) 14:6; (7) 15:1.

These are the 'I am' sayings with predicates, in which the 'I am' is followed by a noun. They are metaphorical sayings in which Jesus describes himself in some way as the one who gives salvation (e.g. the bread of life, the light of the world, the true vine). Our present concern is with the other series, known as the absolute 'I am' sayings, in which the words 'I am' (Greek *egō eimi*) stand by themselves without a predicate.[44] These are less easy to identify in English translations, because the translators adopt a variety of translation strategies in order to make intelligible English of them in context.[45] Sometimes the phrase is rendered 'I am he', sometimes 'It is I' and at least once 'I am' (8:58).

In three cases the phrase appears at first sight to have a quite ordinary meaning, for example 4:26 ('I . . . am he'; i.e. Jesus identifies himself as the Messiah just mentioned); 6:20 ('It is I'; i.e. Jesus identifies himself to the disciples); 18:5, 6, 8 (when the soldiers say they are looking for Jesus, he replies, 'I am he'). But in four cases no such ordinary meaning is available and the phrase 'I am' is as strangely incomplete in the Greek as it is in literal English translation. Three of these appear in close succession in the second half of chapter 8: 'You will die in your sins unless you believe that I am' (8:28 NRSV margin); 'When you have lifted up the Son of Man, then you will realise that I am' (8:38 NRSV margin); 'Before Abraham was, I am' (8:58). In 8:24 and 8:28 Jesus is evidently making some kind of remarkable claim that is obscure to his hearers. In the case of 8:58 the reaction of the Jewish leaders is to try to stone Jesus for blasphemy (8:59). The reaction shows that Jesus is understood to be claiming not merely to have pre-existed Abraham, but some kind of divine identity. The fourth case in which 'I am' cannot be given an ordinary meaning is in 13:19: 'I tell you this now, before it occurs, so that when it does occur you may believe that I am.'

In view of these four cases where a special meaning is indicated it is best to take all seven sayings as a set, while understanding those in which an ordinary

---

44. (1) 4:26; (2) 6:20; (3) 8:24; (4) 8:28; (5) 8:58; (6) 13:19; (7) 18:5–6, 8. For a fuller discussion of these sayings see Bauckham, *Testimony*, pp. 243–249. The definitive study is Catrin H. Williams, *I Am He: The Interpretation of 'Anî Hû in Jewish and Early Christian Literature*, WUNT 2.113 (Tübingen: Mohr Siebeck, 2000). See also David M. Ball, *'I Am' in John's Gospel: Literary Function, Background and Theological Implications*, JSNTSup 124 (Sheffield: Sheffield Academic Press, 1996). The two series of 'I am' sayings, with and without predicates, are connected in that Jesus' identification with God (the absolute sayings) is the basis for his role as Saviour (the sayings with predicates).

45. In every case the NRSV helps English readers to recognize the resemblance between all these sayings by giving the literal translation 'I am' in a footnote.

meaning is possible as instances of *double entendre* (a frequent literary device in John). In these cases the more obvious meaning is not wrong, but a more profound meaning is hidden beneath it. This can be seen most clearly in the seventh of these absolute 'I am' sayings, which forms an emphatic climax to the set by means of threefold repetition (18:5, 6, 8). Here the ordinary meaning, a reply to the soldiers' question, fails to account for the soldiers' reaction. They fall prostrate on the ground, suggesting, as in 8:58–59, that Jesus has made some kind of divine claim.

But how do the words 'I am' express such a claim? One suggestion, often made specifically with reference to 8:58, is that 'I am' is a form of the divine Name, the Tetragrammaton (YHWH).[46] In Exodus 3:14, when God reveals his Name to Moses, he interprets it as meaning 'I am who I am' (this is one of several possible translations of the Hebrew), and then uses a short version of this as a form of the Name: 'Thus shall you say to the Israelites, "I AM has sent me to you."' One difficulty with this suggestion is that no Greek version of Exodus 3:14 uses the translation *egō eimi*, the Greek phrase in John. A more serious obstacle is that nowhere in Jewish literature outside Exodus 3:14 is the phrase 'I am' used as a version of the divine Name.

A more adequate explanation of these sayings in John is that they reflect the divine self-declaration 'I am he.'[47] The LXX Greek uses the phrase *egō eimi* in Deuteronomy 32:39 and on several occasions in Isaiah 40 – 55 (41:4; 43:10; 46:4) to translate the Hebrew phrase *'ănî hû'*, which is usually translated in English as 'I am he.' In the two cases (43:25; 51:2) where the Hebrew has the more emphatic form of the same phrase, *'ānōkî 'ānōkî hû'*, the LXX has the double expression *egō eimi egō eimi*. This phrase 'I am he' is an extraordinarily significant one. It is a divine self-declaration, encapsulating YHWH's claim to unique and exclusive divinity. In the Hebrew Bible it occurs first in what are almost the last words God himself speaks in the Torah, where it is an emphatically monotheistic assertion: 'Behold, I, even I am he; there is no god besides me' (Deut. 32:39, my tr.). In the prophecies of Isaiah 40 – 55 this form of divine self-declaration (in Hebrew: Isa. 41:4; 43:10, 13, 25; 46:4; 48:12; 51:12; 52:6) expresses emphatically the absolute uniqueness of the God of Israel, who in these chapters constantly asserts his unique deity in contrast with the idols of the nations, and defines his uniqueness as that of the eternal creator of all things and the unique sovereign ruler of all history. His great act of eschatological salvation will

----

46. E.g. Jerome H. Neyrey, *An Ideology of Revolt: John's Christology in Social-Science Perspective* (Philadelphia: Fortress, 1988), pp. 213–224.

47. This is argued by Ball, *'I Am'*; Williams, *I Am He*.

demonstrate him to be the one and only God in the sight of all the nations, revealing his glory so that all the ends of earth will acknowledge him as God and turn to him for salvation.

The 'I am he' declarations are among the most emphatically monotheistic assertions of the Hebrew Bible, and if Jesus in John's Gospel repeats them he is unambiguously identifying himself with the one and only God, YHWH, the God of Israel. It does not do justice to these sayings to see them, as some scholars do, merely as an expression of an 'agent' Christology, according to which Jesus is the plenipotentiary agent of God.[48] This undoubtedly is an important aspect of the understanding of Jesus in John (where Jesus is frequently said to have been 'sent' by the Father). But in the total context of the Gospel, including the absolute 'I am' sayings, it is clear that God does not send *someone else* to act as his agent in salvation. As we saw in the last section, what this agent does is not something God can delegate to someone other than God, since it belongs to the uniquely divine prerogatives of the one God. Only one who truly shares the unique divine identity can give eternal life and reveal God's glory in the world. Jesus' absolute 'I am' sayings express his unique and exclusive participation in God's unique and exclusive deity. Just as 'I am he' in the Hebrew Bible sums up what it is to be truly God, so in John it identifies Jesus as truly God in the fullest sense.

The Father and the Son

The relationship of God the Father to Jesus the Son is at the centre of the theology of this Gospel. It is the climax of the prologue (1:18), the subject of much of Jesus' discourse about himself and his mission, the wellspring of the narrative that takes Jesus to the cross in obedience to the Father (10:17–18; 18:11), and disclosed in Jesus' prayers, especially chapter 17. More than any other New Testament writer, John emphasizes the uniqueness of Jesus' sonship. Not content to characterize him as the 'only Son' (*monogenēs*; 1:14, 18; 3:16, 18), John even confines the term 'son' (*huios*) to Jesus. Those whom he enables to be 'born from God' are not 'sons' but 'children' (*tekna*) (1:12; 11:52; cf. 13:33). Unlike them, the Son is never said to have been born, which could imply temporal origin. Uniquely, the Son was with God eternally (17:5). He alone has seen God

---

48. E.g. James F. McGrath, *John's Apologetic Christology: Legitimation and Development in Johannine Christology*, SNTSMS 111 (Cambridge: Cambridge University Press, 2001), chs. 4–5.

(6:46) and thereby can reveal him (1:18; 12:45; 14:9). They enjoy mutual knowledge (10:15) and everything in common (17:10). Thus Jesus' sonship is more than just the perfect instantiation of human being, though his earthly life does model what it means to be truly human in unimpeded relationship with God.

What I have said about Jesus as plenipotentiary agency of God exercising the uniquely divine prerogatives belongs within this larger category of Father–Son relationship.[49] He exercises all these prerogatives not as a mere agent of an absent sender but as the Son to whom his Father is always present.[50] Yet he does not exercise them in the way the Father does, but in his own filial manner. On the one hand, the Father *gives* him the exercise of these prerogatives, but, on the other hand, the Father gives them for him to have '*in himself*' (5:26).[51] Thompson comments:

> Precisely in holding together the affirmations [*sic*] that the Son has 'life in himself' [5:26] with the affirmation that he has 'been *given*' such life by the Father [6:57], we find the uniquely Johannine characterization of the relationship of the Father and the Son.[52]

We could say that this combination of dependence and possession – or possession as intrinsically given – constitutes the Son's own way of being God.[53] Within the unique divine identity that the Son shares with the Father there is a differentiated relationship of Father and Son.

Again and again the Gospel stresses the absolute and continuous dependence of the Son on the Father for everything he says and does (5:19, 30; 7:16, 28; 11:41–42; 12:49–50; 17:7–8; 18:11), for the divine Name (17:11–12), for glory (8:54; 17:22) and for all who believe in him (6:37; 10:29; 17:6, 9, 24). He is given

---

49. Sjef van Tilborg, *Imaginative Love in John*, BibInt 2 (Leiden: Brill, 1993), pp. 25–28.

50. William R. G. Loader, 'John 5,19–47: A Deviation from Envoy Christology', in Joseph Verheyden, Geert van Oyen, Michael Labahn and Reimund Bieringer (eds.), *Studies in the Gospel of John and Its Christology: Festschrift Gilbert van Belle*, BETL 265 (Leuven: Peeters, 2014), pp. 149–164.

51. Cf. 1:4, 'In him was life'.

52. Thompson, *God*, p. 79, emphasis original. In my view Thompson's emphasis on the dependence of the Son on the Father for *life* is one-sided. The Son is dependent on the Father for *everything*.

53. Note esp. 8:28, where Jesus' identification with God ('I am he') is accompanied by his dependence on the Father ('I do nothing on my own').

literally *everything* (3:35; 13:3; 17:2) and everything he has is *given*. The Father is the unique source of everything, the Son the one who uniquely receives everything from the Father, so that he can give to others. But in doing the work his Father has given him to do, in sharing with others what the Father has given him, the Son also gives to the Father: love (14:31), honour and glory (7:18; 8:49; 17:1, 4).

One aspect of Jesus' absolute dependence on the Father is his obedience to the Father's command (10:18; 12:49; 14:31), expressed also as, 'I always do what is pleasing to him' (8:29). This, of course, is what was expected of a son. However, this relationship of authority and obedience should not be over-stressed, given that the Father also gives the Son authority over everything (3:35; 13:3; 17:2). In the Father–Son relationship the asymmetrical relationship of giving (the Father gives the Son everything) is greater than and encompasses that of command and obedience. In the much-debated statement 'the Father is greater than I' (14:28) the reference is probably to the Son's dependence on the Father's giving, not to the Son's obedience to the Father, which is not relevant to the context. The use of the term 'subordination', which implies a hierarchy of rank, may therefore not be very helpful.[54] The Johannine account implies not that the Son ranks below the Father, but that the Son owes everything to the Father. Since *everything* is *given*, there is both asymmetry (14:28) and complete commonality (16:15; 17:10). The Son has an equality with the Father that the Father has given him (5:17–29).[55]

---

54. This issue requires much fuller discussion; see e.g. Charles Kingsley Barrett, '"The Father is Greater Than I" John 14.28: Subordinationist Christology in the New Testament', in idem, *Essays on John* (London: SPCK, 1982), pp. 19–36; Craig S. Keener, 'Is Subordination Within the Trinity Really Heresy? A Study of John 5:18 in Context', *TrinJ* 20 (1999), pp. 39–51; Thompson, *God*, pp. 92–98; Christopher Cowan, 'The Father and Son in the Fourth Gospel: Johannine Subordination Revisited', *JETS* 49 (2006), pp. 115–135; Andreas J. Köstenberger and Scott R. Swain, *Father, Son and Spirit: The Trinity and John's Gospel*, NSBT 24 (Downers Grove: InterVarsity Press, 2008), pp. 114–127.

55. We should be careful to follow the outlines of the way the Gospel actually depicts the Father–Son relationship, which does not conform in every respect to the relationship of human fathers and sons in the ancient world. A key difference is the fact that both Father and Son are eternal. In a restricted sense the Son's position resembles that of a son who has inherited his father's status and estate at the latter's death. In the Gospel the Father gives everything to the Son while remaining the living source.

It is important to realize that John's account of the relationship of the Father and the Son always has in view their 'work', the work that the Father has given the Son to accomplish on earth. In terms of classical trinitarian doctrine this is the 'economic' Trinity. What I have called 'the Son's way of being God' is actually the *incarnate* Son's way of being God, his way of being God *as the man Jesus*. We should therefore be cautious about attributing to the Son in the 'immanent' Trinity every aspect of his relationship to the Father that the Gospel attributes to the incarnate Son (such as obedience).[56] But we may surely suppose that the Son's eternal relationship to the Father was such that a genuinely human version of it was possible. If the eternal Son's way of being God was in absolute dependence on the Father, then it was a way of being God that could be lived out in the human form of the life, death and exaltation of Jesus. This is how this Gospel's version of the story of Jesus is able to stress the unreserved involvement of God in it, yet without Docetism, without compromising the genuine humanity of Jesus.

Personal coinherence[57]

There is one respect in which the Gospel is quite clear about (to use the classical theological conceptuality) the correspondence between the economic and the immanent Trinity. This concerns the Father's love for the Son. As the prologue already declares, what is revealed by the incarnation is the intimate relationship between the Father and the Son (1:18). It is surely no accident that the Gospel's series of references to the Father's love for the Son (3:35; 5:20; 15:9–10; 10:17; 17:23, 24, 26)[58] climax in an emphatic cluster of three at the end of Jesus' prayer

---

56. The Gospel's very frequent assertion that the Father sent the Son is often taken as requiring a notion of the Son's obedience within the immanent Trinity, but this sending occurs on the very boundary between the immanent and the economic Trinity.

57. On this theme see Bauckham, *Gospel of Glory*, pp. 9–13, 36–41; David Crump, 'Re-examining the Johannine Trinity: Perichoresis or Deification?', *SJT* 59 (2006), pp. 395–412. The term *perichoresis* was used by the Greek Fathers to refer to the 'in-one-anotherness' of all three trinitarian persons and has been taken up by modern trinitarian theologians such as Jürgen Moltmann. The neglect of this theme by both Thompson, *God*, and Köstenberger and Swain, *Father, Son and Spirit*, seems to me a serious omission.

58. For the Father's love for the Son, *agapaō* is used six times, *agapē* once (15:10) and *phileō* (which in John is synonymous with *agapaō*) once (5:20). Only once is Jesus said to love the Father (14:31), but this reference shows that his whole life of obedience to the Father is grounded in his love for the Father.

to the Father in chapter 17, which, as we have noticed, to some extent corresponds to the prologue by reprising and extending its themes. The Son's participation in the uniquely divine prerogatives is grounded in the Father's love for him (3:35; 5:20), as is his heavenly glory (17:24). It is the most profound reality, not only of his earthly life, but also of his pre-existence in eternity (17:24). Moreover, looking back from the vantage point of the conclusion of Jesus' prayer, we could say that the whole story of salvation that the Gospel tells stems from the love between the Father and the Son and has as its goal the inclusion of humans within this loving relationship ('that the love with which you have loved me may be in them, and I in them', 17:26). The love between the Father and the Son is the deepest dimension not only of the Gospel's understanding of God, but also of the Gospel's soteriology.

Another way in which the Gospel portrays the intimacy of Father and Son is by means of the formula 'the Father is in the Son and the Son is in the Father' (10:38; 14:10–11; 17:21; cf. 14:20). It is significant that this uniquely Johannine formulation occurs first in 10:38, following the remarkable version of the Shema in 10:30 ('I and the Father are one'). Jesus' self-defence against the charge of blasphemy that this provokes culminates in the equally audacious claim, also perceived as blasphemy, 'the Father is in me and I am in the Father' (10:38). This seems to function as equivalent to or a further explication of the first claim. The inner reality of the unity of the Father and the Son, the way in which together they comprise the one God of Jewish faith, is their intimate personal communion. This shows that their oneness, according to 10:30, is not simply their common purpose, as commentators sometimes suppose. There is, within the identity of the one God, a personal relationship that is the ground and source of the unity of purpose and action between the Father and the Son.

This distinctive 'in one another' language seems to have been coined by John to express the personal coinherence that mutual love involves.[59] Coinherence, a kind of overlapping of identity, is a feature of human mutual love to an extent,[60] but only to a limited extent. The love of the Father and the Son, given by the Father (17:24) and reciprocated by the Son (14:31), is a relationship of complete self-giving to each other, such that, while remaining distinct in the way of being God that is proper to each, they also comprise one God. It is true

---

59. The reciprocity distinguishes it from Pauline language such as 'in Christ'. That John's 'in one another' language refers to mutual love is clear especially from 15:4–10 and 17:26. In 14:23 a different, though parallel, image is used.

60. Cf. Daniel B. Stevick, *Jesus and His Own: A Commentary on John 13–17* (Grand Rapids: Eerdmans, 2011), p. 157: 'What we love never stands altogether outside us.'

that the Gospel uses the 'in one another' language not only of the relationship of the Father and the Son, but also of the relationship between the individual believer and Jesus (6:56; cf. 15:5) and the relationship between believers as a group and Jesus (14:20; cf. 15:4, 7). In his prayer to the Father Jesus mixes these relationships: 'As you, Father, are in me and I in you, may they also be in us' (17:21); 'that they may be one, as we are one, I in them and you in me' (17:22–23; cf. 11); 'so that the love with which you loved me may be in them, and I in them' (17:26). The comparison between the unity of the Father and the Son and the unity of believers (17:22–23) does not mean that they are alike in every respect, but that there is an analogy.[61] It is notable that believers are not said to be one through being 'in one another', but through the presence in them of Jesus, and the Father's presence in him. The highly compressed language of this climactic passage of the prayer surely means that the love of the Father for the Son, which makes them one, overflows, through the Son,[62] to unite believers with both the Son and the Father.

The Spirit of life and truth

Important though the Spirit is in the Gospel of John, there is much less to be said about the place of the Spirit in the Johannine understanding of God than there is about the Son. We should begin by recognizing that the Spirit appears in this Gospel in two different roles. Outside the farewell discourse (chapters 13–16) the Spirit is associated largely with life and probably to some extent with power.[63] (The only passage that does not obviously fit these categories is 4:23–24, which is perhaps closer to the Paraclete passages.) In the farewell discourses, on the other hand, the Spirit appears in the special role of the Paraclete or 'the Spirit of truth'. The use of the term 'Holy Spirit' (which seems to have become popular in Second Temple period Judaism and the New Testament as a way of distinguishing the Spirit *of God* from other uses of the term, e.g. for

---

61. Bauckham, *Gospel of Glory*, pp. 34–36; Francis Watson, 'Trinity and Community: A Reading of John 17', *IJST* 1 (1999), pp. 168–184, here 171.

62. Note the love of the Father for the world (3:16) and the love of Jesus for his disciples (13:1, 34; 15:9–10; etc.).

63. John 1:32–33; 3:5–8, 34; 6:63; 7:37–39; 20:22. In addition, in the light of 7:38–39, we should probably take 'the living water' of 4:10–14 to symbolize the Spirit, while the 'water' of 19:34 is probably also a symbol of the life-giving Spirit, just as the blood in that passage identifies Jesus' death as a sacrifice.

angels or human spirits) in 14:26, as well as 1:33 and 20:22, makes it clear that it is the same divine Spirit who appears in these different roles. The roles correlate roughly with the two main strands of Johannine soteriology: the gift of eternal life from God and the revelation of God.

The association of the divine Spirit with life and power derives originally from the usage of the Hebrew Bible,[64] as does the imagery of breath (20:22), wind (3:8) and water (1:33; 7:38),[65] but in the Gospel the reference is to eternal life, the divine life that Jesus came to share with humans, the life that makes them 'children of God'.[66] Jesus receives the Spirit 'without measure' in order to bestow him onto others (1:32–33; 3:34; 20:22; cf. 7:37–39). He gives him from within himself (symbolized as water and breath coming from within him: 7:37–39; 19:34; 20:22),[67] in accordance with his claim that the Father 'has granted the Son also to have life in himself' (5:26).[68] Since giving life is the prerogative of the Father, in which the Son also shares (1:4; 5:26–29; 1:25–26), there can be no doubt that the Spirit is integral to the divine identity. But really this is something John can take for granted, simply because in the tradition of the Hebrew Bible the Spirit is God's Spirit, just as the Word is God's Word. The unity of God and his Spirit does not have to be extensively explicated in the way the unity of the Father and the Son does.

In most of these passages the language used does not attribute to the Spirit 'his' own agency, and in the two cases where the Spirit is the subject of an active verb (1:33; 3:8) the language can hardly be pressed to show that the Spirit actually is an agent distinguishable from the Father and the Son. However, the passages about the Paraclete or Spirit of truth in the farewell discourse make a very different impression. Whatever the precise meaning of *paraklētos*,[69] it is undoubtedly a human personal image. Evidently Jesus himself is a *paraklētos*, and the Spirit, in this role, another such (14:16). The Paraclete teaches, reminds, testifies,

---

64. E.g. 1 Sam. 11:6; Job 33:4; Ps. 104:39.

65. Isa. 40:7; 44:3; Ezek. 37:1–10; 39:29.

66. Had John wished to make explicit reference to the Spirit in the prologue, he could have done so in 1:12–13.

67. John 20:22 echoes Gen. 2:7.

68. This point is made by Thompson, *God*, pp. 175–177.

69. See e.g. Kenneth Grayston, 'The Meaning of PARAKLĒTOS', *JSNT* 13 (1981), pp. 67–82; Gary M. Burge, *The Anointed Community: The Holy Spirit in the Johannine Tradition* (Grand Rapids: Eerdmans, 1987), pp. 6–31; Andrew T. Lincoln, *Truth on Trial: The Lawsuit Motif in the Fourth Gospel* (Peabody, Mass.: Hendrickson, 2000), pp. 113–114.

convicts, guides, speaks, declares (14:26; 15:26; 16:8, 13–15). (Merely listing these activities illustrates well why he is called 'the Spirit of truth'; 14:17; 15:26; 16:13.)[70]

While these activities put the Paraclete in the role of a successor to Jesus in relation to the disciples and the world, taking over from Jesus when Jesus goes to be with the Father (16:7), sent by the Father at Jesus' request (14:16, 26) or, in an alternative formulation, sent by Jesus from the Father (15:26; 16:7), there is one suggestion of a closer and less easily conceptualized relationship between the Paraclete, on the one hand, and the Father and the Son, on the other. This is implied by the statement that the Paraclete 'abides [*menei*] with you [the disciples], and he will be in you' (14:17), which resembles Jesus' promise that he will abide in the disciples and they in him (15:4–5). However, the parallel is not exact, since 14:17 notably lacks the reciprocal language of personal coinherence that characterizes relationships between the Father, the Son and the disciples. Perhaps more significantly, 14:17 is followed in 14:23 by the distinctive promise that Jesus and the Father 'will come to them and make our home [*monēn*] with them' (14:23). It is hard to be sure of the connections of thought in this passage,[71] but many commentators have concluded that here the 'Spirit is the mediator of the presence of Jesus and God to believers'.[72]

Some of the ways in which the Gospel relates the Paraclete to the Father and the Son parallel relationships between the Father and the Son. The Paraclete is sent by the Father, just as the Son is (and as the disciples are by Jesus), and comes from the Father (15:26), as Jesus does. He 'will not speak on his own, but will speak whatever he hears' Jesus say (16:13), just as Jesus spoke only what he heard from the Father. He will glorify the Son (16:14), as the Son glorified the Father and the Father the Son. (But it is surely reading too much into 16:14–15 to say that 'the Spirit holds all things in common with the Father and the Son' and

---

70. The term is paralleled at Qumran, but is also an instance of a standard formation ('Spirit of' + an abstract term) used to specify a particular form of the Spirit's activity (e.g. Deut. 34:9; Isa. 11:2; Zech. 12:10; Rom. 8:2; 2 Tim. 1:7; Heb. 10:29).

71. Thi Tuong Oanh Nguyen, 'The Allusion to the Trinity in Jesus' Understanding of His Mission: A Theological Interpretation of ΠΕΜΠΩ and ΑΠΟΣΤΕΛΛΩ in the Fourth Gospel', in G. Van Belle, M. Labahn and P. Maritz (eds.), *Repetitions and Variations in the Fourth Gospel: Style, Text, Interpretation*, BETL 223 (Leuven: Peeters, 2009), pp. 257–294, here 292–293, argues that the references to the Paraclete in 14:15–17 and 14:26 form an inclusio linking the Paraclete with the passage about the coming of Jesus and the Father.

72. Andrew T. Lincoln, *The Gospel According to Saint John*, BNTC (London: Continuum, 2005), p. 396.

thus 'shares . . . the unique divine identity' with them.)[73] These parallels between the Son–Paraclete relationship and the Father–Son relationship go some way to integrate the Paraclete into a pattern of trinitarian relationship, but they are limited. Centrally important aspects of the Father–Son relationship – notably love, personal coinherence and 'oneness' – have no parallel involving the Paraclete. To put the same point differently, there is no mutuality between the Paraclete and either the Father or the Son.[74] Whereas in the love between the Father and the Son we see something of their eternal relationship, the Spirit, as portrayed both in the Paraclete passages and elsewhere in the Gospel, functions solely to relate God to the world (especially believers). As David Crump puts it, 'While the Father and the Son embrace each other in perichoretic communion, the Spirit engages the world head-on and does not look back.'[75]

It may be that, in the Johannine understanding of God's relation to the world in Jesus Christ, a glimpse of the eternal relationship of the Father and the Son is required, since it is this relationship that took human form in incarnation, but that there is no such need to reflect on the Spirit in God's eternity. The Gospel therefore presents us with the two different roles of the Spirit in the world: as the divine life that flows from the Father and the Son to be the abundant life of creation united with God, and as the divine agent who makes the revelation of the Father in Jesus known after Jesus' exaltation. It also leaves us with impersonal and personal representations of the Spirit, each appropriate to one of these two roles. Thus the Spirit is God in ways different from the Father's way of being God and the Son's way of being God, but belongs no less integrally to the identity of the one God.

© Richard Bauckham, 2016

---

73. Köstenberger and Swain, *Father, Son and Spirit*, p. 135.

74. Thus he gives glory, but he does not receive it.

75. Crump, 'Re-examining', p. 409. The point is well taken, but neglects the fact that the Son too 'engages the world head-on' out of the love for the world he shares with the Father.

5. PAUL AND THE TRINITY

Brian S. Rosner

Paul and the Trinity

Paul's letters rank alongside the Gospel of John as containing the richest vein of trinitarian theology in the New Testament. While the doctrine of the Trinity is not assembled in any one place, and the key terminology for the classical expression of the Trinity (person, substance, etc.) is obviously not present, there are at least three places in his letters that can be described as explicitly trinitarian:[1]

> There are different kinds of gifts, but *the same Spirit* distributes them. There are different kinds of service, but *the same Lord*. There are different kinds of working, but in all of them and in everyone it is *the same God* at work. (1 Cor. 12:4–6)[2]

> May the grace of the Lord Jesus Christ, and the love of God, and the fellowship of the Holy Spirit be with you all. (2 Cor. 13:14)

---

1. Cf. Gordon D. Fee, *Paul, the Spirit, and the People of God* (Peabody, Mass.: Hendrickson, 1996), p. 39.
2. Unless otherwise indicated, translations are taken from the NIV. Italics normally indicate emphasis added.

There is one body and *one Spirit*, just as you were called to one hope when you
were called; *one Lord*, one faith, one baptism; *one God and Father of all*, who is over
all and through all and in all.

But to each one of us grace has been given as *Christ* apportioned it.
(Eph. 4:4–7)

These three passages offer profound and searching observations about God.
They reflect three divine identities, along with a sense of the oneness of
God. However, these verses are striking not only for their profound reflections
on the doctrine of God, but also because they appear in so-called practical
sections of Paul's epistles. You might have expected Paul's deepest thinking
about Theology Proper to be found in those sections of his letters focused on
matters of doctrine and belief. Instead, we find Paul's descriptions of one
loving God the Father, one gracious Lord Jesus Christ, and one generous Holy
Spirit, three working together as one for our good in perfect balance and
harmony in a discussion of the misuse of the spiritual gifts (1 Cor. 12), in a
mundane letter-closing (2 Cor. 13) and in an appeal for unity (Eph. 4) respect-
ively. While there may be many ways into the subject of the Trinity in Paul's
letters, the relationship between his trinitarian thinking and his practical
teaching is among the most fascinating, edifying and, at the same time, un-
explored angles.

How should we read Paul's letters in the light of the Trinity? There are two
extremes to avoid. First, we must beware of anachronistic interpretation of
Paul whereby we read later patristic formulations of the Trinity into his letters.
The doctrine of the Trinity is a synthetic judgment about the teaching of all of
Scripture rather than a statement found anywhere within it. But equally, we must
not adopt a minimalist and non-theological reading of Paul on these matters.
E. P. Sanders was right in one sense when he wrote that 'Paul did not spend his
time reflecting on the nature of the deity.' But Sanders was certainly wrong
when he asserted that 'from Paul we learn nothing new or remarkable about
God'.[3] Paul did not write about God in abstraction. But that does not mean
that a weighty doctrine of God does not emerge from his highly occasional
letters.

When noticing and appreciating the doctrine of God in Paul's letters it is
important not to limit Paul's trinitarian thinking to those passages that explicitly
mention the Father, the Son and the Spirit; more subtle textual features such as

---

3. E. P. Sanders, *Paul and Palestinian Judaism: A Comparison of Patterns of Religion*
(Philadelphia: Fortress, 1977), p. 509.

other names for the three persons of the Godhead,[4] the use of terms such as 'Lord', the use of pronouns and divine passives[5] should not escape our notice. And when reading Paul's letters, along with observing three distinct divine identities, it is vital to notice the ways in which he affirms their unity and the oneness of God.

We should also not neglect the trinitarian dimensions of Paul's doctrines of Christ and the Spirit. According to Joseph Fitzmyer, being seized by Christ on the road to Damascus changed Paul's Christology rather than his Theology Proper.[6] However, many of Paul's discussions of Christology and pneumatology also reflect his understanding of God. In 1 Corinthians 8:6, for example, Paul affirms his belief that Jesus Christ has the status of unique Lord: 'yet for us there is but one God, the Father, from whom all things came and for whom we live; and there is but one Lord, Jesus Christ, through whom all things came and through whom we live'.

The key words of this verse, namely 'Lord', 'God' and 'one', are taken from Israel's great Shema, Deuteronomy 6:4 ('the LORD our God, the LORD is one'), in which *Lord* and *God* both refer to the same (*one*) God. As N. T. Wright observes, in 1 Corinthians 8:6 Paul

> has glossed 'God' with 'the Father', and 'Lord' with 'Jesus Christ', adding in each case an explanatory phrase: 'God' is the Father, 'from whom are all things and we to him', and the 'Lord' is Jesus the Messiah, 'through whom are all things and we through him.'[7]

---

4. 'God', *theos* in Gk., almost always refers to God the Father in Paul's letters. See the references to 'God' in the three texts that open this chapter: 1 Cor. 12:6; 2 Cor. 13:14; and esp. Eph. 4:5 ('one God and Father of all'). Cf. Eph. 1:17: 'the God of our Lord Jesus Christ, the glorious Father', and Eph. 5:20, 'God the Father'. Two possible exceptions appear in Rom. 9:5 and Titus 2:13, where *theos* may refer to Christ.

5. A divine passive is where God is the implied agent performing the action with a verb in the passive voice.

6. Joseph A. Fitzmyer, *Paul and His Theology: A Brief Sketch* (Englewood, N.J.: Prentice-Hall, 1989), p. 30.

7. N. T. Wright, 'Monotheism, Christology, and Ethics: 1 Corinthians 8', in idem, *The Climax of the Covenant: Christ and the Law in Pauline Theology* (Minneapolis: Fortress, 1992), p. 129. It is indeed remarkable how often Paul's trinitarian reflections have a basis in the OT.

In 1 Corinthians 8:6 Paul simultaneously reaffirms strict Jewish monotheism and asserts the highest possible Christology imaginable, finding the identity of Christ within the very definition of that one God/Lord of Israel. Many of Paul's discussions of Christology and the Spirit also have relevance to the Trinity.

Often New Testament scholars, even evangelicals, will only go as far as admitting that Paul engages in 'unselfconscious trinitarianism' at best. The problem is that in such a climate we run the risk of not allowing such elements in Paul's letters to reach anyone's consciousness.

What, then, are the trinitarian dimensions of Paul's practical teaching? In the following sections of this chapter we consider his treatments of four practical matters in relation to the Trinity: assurance of salvation, confidence in prayer, intimate fellowship and moral renewal.

Salvation and the Trinity

Assurance of salvation is a theological problem with keen pastoral dimensions. Even the most committed believers with a good understanding of justification by grace sometimes doubt their own election and salvation. What do we talk about at such times? Does the Trinity come up in such conversations? It is striking how often Paul's efforts to reassure believers of God's love are set within a trinitarian framework.

In 1 Corinthians 6 Paul deals with two egregious faults in the church of God in Corinth, namely civil litigation and going to prostitutes. In 1 Corinthians 6:9–10, in the midst of such serious moral failure, Paul warns them that people whose lives are characterized by greed and sexual immorality, and the like, 'will not inherit the kingdom of God'. Such warnings should not be seen as undermining the eternal security of believers; indeed, they are one means by which God enables believers to persevere. Nonetheless, an unintended effect of strong words of judgment can be to destabilize the confidence of God's people. Hence in 1 Corinthians 6:11 Paul writes to remind the Corinthian believers of the genuineness of their conversion: 'And that is what some of you were. But you were washed, you were sanctified, you were justified in the name of the Lord Jesus Christ and by the Spirit of our God.'

To reassure believers in Corinth Paul refers to their washing and forgiveness, positional sanctification and forensic justification. However, we must also notice that the cooperative work of all three persons of the Godhead, to use the language of Chalcedon, is foundational to Paul's understanding of eternal salvation.[8] The terms Paul uses in 1 Corinthians 6:11 also reinforce the eschatological nature of the transformation the Corinthians (along with all other believers in Christ) have experienced. God's establishment of the Messiah (Christ) as Lord over all and his transformation of his people by the cleansing and renewing power and presence of the Holy Spirit were both part of the Old Testament picture of the wonderful changes that would be introduced with the in-breaking of the age to come and its overcoming of this present evil age.[9]

As it turns out, when Paul discusses justification by grace through faith as the basis for our assurance, he regularly underscores the roles of the Father, Christ and the Spirit. In Romans 5:1–11 Paul describes the life of those who have been justified and the fruit of that status: 'Therefore, since we have been justified through faith' (5:1a). In the face of suffering Paul assures us that 'God's love has been poured out into our hearts through the Holy Spirit' (5:5), a love that is demonstrated beyond any doubt, for 'Christ died for us' (5:8; cf. 5:6). In telling the full story of the love of God Paul cannot help but mention the work of Christ and the Spirit. Salvation is the narrative of the saving Trinity's acting on behalf of human beings.

Likewise, in Titus 3:4–7 the basis of our future hope is having been 'justified by his grace' (3:7). Paul states that two facts assure us of the 'love of God' (3:4): first, that 'he saved us, not because of righteous things we had done, but because of his mercy' (3:5); and second, of 'the washing of rebirth and renewal by the Holy Spirit, whom he [i.e. God] poured out on us generously through Jesus Christ our Saviour' (3:5–6). If the collaborative work of God, Jesus Christ and the Holy Spirit in Titus 3:5–6 underscores three distinct divine identities, the unity of God and Christ can be seen in that in Titus 3:4, 6 Paul describes them both as 'our Saviour'.

In Ephesians 3 Paul is concerned that believers not lose heart over his imprisonment: 'I ask you, therefore, not to be discouraged because of my sufferings

---

8. See 1 Cor. 1:4–7, 2:4–5, 12 and 6:19–20 (cf. also 2 Cor. 1:21–22), where salvation is predicated either explicitly or implicitly on the threefold work of the triune God. Gordon D. Fee, 'Christology and Pneumatology in Romans 8:9–11 – and Elsewhere: Some Reflections on Paul as a Trinitarian', in J. B. Green and M. Turner (eds.), *Jesus of Nazareth: Lord and Christ* (Grand Rapids: Eerdmans, 1994), pp. 312–331.

9. E.g. note God's establishment of his Son over all other powers in Ps. 2, and in Ezek. 36:23–27 his sanctification of his name by the cleansing and sanctification of his people by the Spirit so that they no longer profane his name among the nations but, rather, obey him from the heart. See Roy E. Ciampa and Brian S. Rosner, *The First Letter to the Corinthians*, PNTC (Grand Rapids: Eerdmans, 2010), p. 245, n. 96.

for you' (3:13). When faced with the discouragement of the experience of suffering, it is natural to doubt God's love. In this light Paul prays for them in Ephesians 3:14–19:

> For this reason I kneel before the Father, from whom every family in heaven and on earth derives its name. I pray that out of his glorious riches he may strengthen you with power through his Spirit in your inner being, so that Christ may dwell in your hearts through faith. And I pray that you, being rooted and established in love, may have power, together with all the Lord's holy people, to grasp how wide and long and high and deep is the love of Christ and to know this love that surpasses knowledge – that you may be filled to the measure of all the fullness of God.

As in the texts from 1 Corinthians, Romans and Titus (see above), Paul's encouragement in Ephesians 3:14–19 is set in the context of the joint work of the Father, Christ and the Spirit.[10] The prayer is directed to *the Father* and his petitions include a strengthening in the inner being *by the Spirit* and in the heart, *where Christ dwells*. In spite of the reality of suffering, believers can know that they belong to the Lord as his holy people, a status in which strength and power can be found. The final petition is that God's people would appreciate *the love of Christ* and be filled with *the fullness of God*. Both the Spirit and Christ play a role in the heart; and both the Father and Christ are needed for a full experience of God's love.

Similarly, Romans 8 deals with the 'present sufferings' of believers (8:18) and Paul goes to great lengths to reassure them of God's love in the face of hardship. Romans 8:38–39 concludes that nothing 'in all creation, will be able to separate us from *the love of God* that is *in Christ Jesus our Lord*'. Once again a clearly trinitarian foundation is laid in support of such reassurance. If '*the Spirit* himself testifies with our spirit that we are God's children' (8:16), Paul insists that both God and Christ are also on our side:

> If God is for us, who can be against us? He who did not spare his own Son, but gave him up for us all – how will he not also, along with him, graciously give us all things? Who will bring any charge against those whom God has chosen? It is God who justifies. Who then is the one who condemns? No one. Christ Jesus who died – more than that, who was raised to life – is at the right hand of God and is also interceding for us. (8:31–34)

---

10. Cf. also the trinitarian structure of the prayer in Eph. 1:17: 'I keep asking that the God of our Lord Jesus Christ, the glorious Father, may give you the Spirit of wisdom and revelation, so that you may know him better.'

Another example of Paul's conception of the unity and oneness of the Father and the Son can be seen in his description of God's favourable stance towards us both as 'the love of Christ' (8:35) and 'the love of God' (8:39). For God to be 'for us' (8:31) means that we can be sure of the love of God and Christ; 'we are more than conquerors through him [Christ] who loved us' (8:37).

Two more passages may be mentioned as revealing Paul's consistent pattern of appealing to the harmonious and united work of God, Christ and the Spirit when he points to the security of Christians. First, in 2 Thessalonians 2:13b–14 Paul highlights the past electing work of God, the present sanctifying work of the Spirit and the prospect of sharing the future glory of Jesus Christ: 'God chose you as firstfruits to be saved through the sanctifying work of the Spirit and through belief in the truth. He called you to this through our gospel, that you might share in the glory of our Lord Jesus Christ.'

And second, in 2 Corinthians 1:21–22 notions of standing firm, being anointed, belonging to God and having a guaranteed future are again predicated on the united threefold work of God, Christ and God's Spirit: 'Now it is God who makes both us and you stand firm in Christ. He anointed us, set his seal of ownership on us, and put his Spirit in our hearts as a deposit, guaranteeing what is to come.'

Nothing magnifies grace like appreciating the triune God's work in salvation. And nothing gives believers more confidence that they are known and loved by God than pointing out the collaborative activity of God, the Lord Jesus Christ and God's Spirit.

Prayer and the Trinity

The privilege of prayer is one of the clearest expressions of trinitarian thought in Paul's letters.[11] Yet despite this, many monographs and articles addressing the nature of the Trinity in relation to Paul focus on the question of to whom prayers are directed, rather than the Trinity's enabling of the act (or fact) of prayer itself. However, within the Pauline corpus several passages detail the impact of the Trinity on prayer. Within the very life of God there is communication. Two

---

11. Cf. Paul Fiddes, 'Participating in the Trinity', *PRSt* 33 (2006), p. 382: 'Foremost among practical experiences of participation in which talk of God as triune comes alive is that of prayer. The New Testament portrays prayer as being "to" the Father, "through" the Son and "in" the Spirit.'

aspects of this communication are intercession for the saints and the enabling of their own prayerfulness.

Two of the most concise examples of texts that reflect on prayer and the Trinity appear in Ephesians 2 and Galatians 4. In Ephesians 2 Paul lays out the achievements of Christ in making peace, both peace between us and God, and also peace with each other in bringing Jews and Gentiles together as one body of Christ (Eph. 3:6): 'For through him [i.e. Christ] we both have access to the Father by one Spirit' (Eph. 2:18). Possibly Paul's most liturgical and formulaic utterance about prayer, this verse indicates that we pray to the Father, through the Son, by the Spirit.

The goal of prayer, which the work of the Son and the Spirit enable, is 'access' to the Father. The word in question, *prosagōgē* in Greek, is used just twice more by Paul and appears nowhere else in the New Testament. On both occasions it refers to a secure 'way of approach' to God:[12]

> in whom [Christ] we have *access* to God in boldness and confidence through faith in him [Christ]. (Eph. 3:12 NRSV)

> through whom [Christ] we have gained *access* [to God] by faith into this grace in which we now stand. (Rom. 5:2a)

For Paul prayer is not a 'hit-and-miss' affair, like shooting arrows at the moon. We do not pray timidly and uncertainly, blindly hoping that God may hear us. We either have access to God or we do not. And since Christ guarantees our access to God, we come boldly and confidently with the help of the Spirit. Despite being rarely heard as an encouragement to pray, this specifically trinitarian account of the basis for prayer is the most effective inducement to prayer in the Bible.

A similar shape to prayer is evident in Galatians 4:6, 'Because you are his sons, God sent the Spirit of his Son into our hearts, the Spirit who calls out, "*Abba*, Father."' Climaxing a passage celebrating our adoption into God's family as his sons and heirs, Paul describes the privilege of addressing God as Father in prayer in trinitarian terms: we pray to our Father through the Spirit of his Son. As in Ephesians 2:18, prayer here is no 'fingers-crossed' exercise in uncertain desperation, but a participation in the life of God. The basis for prayer is that 'God sent the Spirit of his Son into our hearts'. And that Spirit actually prays on our behalf. The same note of grace is struck in the following verses where Paul describes the Galatian Christians as those who now know God,

---

12. BDAG, p. 876.

before swiftly correcting himself by saying that a better way of putting it is that God knows us (Gal. 4:8–9; cf. 1 Cor. 8:2).[13] This puts the whole business of prayer in a different light, one that is expanded in similar terms in Romans 8.

In Romans 8 Paul is realistic about the difficulty of praying and spells out why praying is so difficult. In response he offers the Trinity as the solution:

> In the same way, *the Spirit* helps us in our weakness. We do not know what we ought to pray for, but *the Spirit* himself intercedes for us through wordless groans. And *he* [God] who searches our hearts knows the mind of *the Spirit*, because *the Spirit* intercedes for God's people in accordance with *the will of God*. (Rom. 8:26–27)

We find it hard to pray because of our weakness and uncertainty as to what to pray (8:26), and because we know neither our own hearts nor the will of God (8:27). Paul's encouragement to pray is that the Spirit helps us[14] in our weakness and makes requests to God on our behalf. The reason the Spirit knows what we need is because God knows both our hearts and the mind of the Spirit. The Spirit then makes our requests in accordance with the will of God, which guarantees that God will grant those requests. If that were not enough, Christ Jesus is also involved in that, along with the Spirit, he also intercedes for us, and from the right hand of God no less (Rom. 8:34).

One could hardly conceive of a more theocentric account of prayer than Romans 8. Being weak, we find it hard to know how to pray. Paul responds that our intercessions are brought to God by (1) the Spirit and (2) Christ Jesus. These intercessions are based on (1) God's knowing our hearts, (2) God's knowing the mind of the Spirit and (3) the Spirit's knowing the will of God. If some parts of Romans 8:26–27 are unclear (e.g. the nature of 'wordless groans'), one thing is clear: the triune God facilitates our prayers from start to finish.

Fellowship and the Trinity

The life of God as the Trinity and his work within Christians brings about a particular way of life for believers. Paul uses a variety of terms for the life of

---

13. Cf. Brian S. Rosner, 'Known by God: The Meaning and Value of a Neglected Biblical Concept', *TynB* 59 (2008), pp. 207–230.

14. Gk. *synantilambanomai*. Cf. BDAG, 'συναντιλαμβάνομαι', p. 965, 'come to the aid of, be of assistance to'. The role of the Spirit here is comparable to the Advocate/ Comforter (Gk. *paraklētos*) in John 14:16, 26; 15:26; 16:7.

believers as those who have been reconciled to God and to each other. Indeed, the intimacy of restored relationships, both vertical and horizontal, is a constant refrain in Paul's letters. And this two-directional fellowship is not some esoteric indulgence, but rather has practical implications for our life together in the service of God.

The famous benediction at the end of 2 Corinthians reveals the trinitarian basis for Paul's vision of the Christian life: 'May the grace of the Lord Jesus Christ, and the love of God, and the fellowship of the Holy Spirit be with you all' (2 Cor. 13:14). Undergirding all of Paul's instructions to the Corinthians is the work of the triune God. Gordon Fee points out that not only does 2 Corinthians 13:14 contain a solid triadic reference to God, but it also models the intimate fellowship extended from God to the Corinthians. He writes:

> The *participation in the Holy Spirit* continually actualizes that love and grace in the life of the believer and the believing community. The *koinonia* ('fellowship/participation in') *of the Holy Spirit* is how the living God not only brings people into an intimate and abiding relationship with himself, as the God of all grace, but also causes them to participate in all the benefits of that grace and salvation.[15]

This fellowship, or participation, extends both to our relationship to God and to each other in the church. There is no autonomous life for the Christian, either horizontally or vertically without reference to the God known in Christ.[16]

Philippians 2:1–2 likewise grounds our life together in divine blessings:

> If then there is any encouragement in Christ, any consolation from [Christ's] love, any sharing in the Spirit, any compassion and sympathy, make my joy complete: be of the same mind, having the same love, being in full accord and of one mind. (NRSV)

At first blush this passage seems to offer a 'binitarian' basis for Christian fellowship: union with Christ and the love of Christ supplemented by 'sharing in the Spirit' (*koinōnia pneumatos*). Here too *koinōnia* in the Spirit flows out from the

---

15. Gordon D. Fee, 'Paul and the Trinity: The Experience of Christ and the Spirit for Paul's Understanding of God', in Stephen T. Davis, Daniel Kendall and Gerald O'Collins (eds.), *The Trinity: An Interdisciplinary Symposium on the Trinity* (Oxford: Oxford University Press, 2000), pp. 53, emphases original.

16. Cf. C. Kavin Rowe, 'The Trinity in the Letters of St. Paul and Hebrews', in Gilles Emery, O. P., and Matthew Levering (eds.), *The Oxford Handbook of the Trinity* (Oxford: Oxford University Press, 2012), pp. 49–51.

vertical aspect of being united with Christ to the horizontal aspect of relationship with others in the body.[17]

However, a trinitarian basis for Paul's encouragement to unity and love in Philippians 2:1–2 may also be present. The four 'if' clauses contain an implied passive verb, the agency for which is almost certainly God: 'If there is any encouragement [from God] in Christ, any consolation [from God] from Christ's love', and so on. For Paul the most personal and subjective benefits of faith in Christ (encouragement, consolation, sharing, compassion and sympathy), which form the basis for harmonious church life, derive from the work of God, Christ and the Spirit. Elsewhere in Philippians Paul describes believers as those 'who serve God by his Spirit, who boast in Christ Jesus' (Phil. 3:3).

In Ephesians 1:17–20 Paul prays that believers may know God, the sure hope and rich inheritance he has given them, as well as God's great power exemplified in raising Christ from the dead. In order to grasp more fully these spiritual blessings, Paul appeals to the united work of Father, Christ and Spirit: 'I keep asking that the God of our Lord Jesus Christ, the glorious Father, may give you the Spirit of wisdom and revelation, so that you may know him better' (Eph. 1:17).

Finally, the qualities of the corporate life of believers that Paul recommends, expressed in joyful praise and thanksgiving and teaching one another, are encapsulated in two well-known passages from the Prison Epistles. In Ephesians 5:18 this life springs from being filled with the Spirit; in Colossians 3:16 it comes from being filled with the word of Christ. In both passages a trinitarian pattern is clearly evident in the descriptions of Christian fellowship. In particular, note in both cases the call to give thanks to God the Father in the name of the Lord Jesus Christ and the heart-felt singing springing from the Spirit:

> Do not get drunk on wine, which leads to debauchery. Instead, be filled with the Spirit, speaking to one another with psalms, hymns, and songs from the Spirit. Sing and make music from your heart to the Lord, always giving thanks to God the Father for everything, in the name of our Lord Jesus Christ. (Eph. 5:18–20)

> Let the word of Christ dwell among you richly as you teach and admonish one another with all wisdom through psalms, hymns, and songs from the Spirit, singing to God with gratitude in your hearts. And whatever you do, whether in word or deed, do it all in the name of the Lord Jesus, giving thanks to God the Father through him. (Col. 3:16–17 NIV modified)

---

17. A. Katherine Grieb, 'People of God, Body of Christ, Koinonia of Spirit: The Role of Ethical Ecclesiology in Paul's "Trinitarian" Language', *AThR* 87 (2005), pp. 225–252.

In Romans 14:17–18 Paul responds to the dispute among the Roman Christians concerning kosher food by pointing out there is something far more important than what our stomachs consume:

> For the kingdom of God is not a matter of eating and drinking, but of righteousness, peace and joy in the Holy Spirit, because anyone who serves Christ in this way is pleasing to God and receives human approval.

Whereas Paul can speak of the kingdom of God as a future inheritance (as in 1 Cor. 6:9–10; 15:50; Gal. 5:21), here it is a present reality in the life of Christians (as in 1 Cor. 4:20). And the character of this life under God's rule is described in terms of 'righteousness, peace and joy' springing from the Holy Spirit.[18] What Paul stresses as vitally important in Romans 14:17 is simply the outworking of our justification and reconciliation to God for our corporate life in the kingdom of God: being declared righteous with God must lead to righteousness in human relationships; finding peace with God must lead to living at peace with others. In other words, the joy of being right with God and Christian hope should spill over into the joy of Christian fellowship. This will lead to living a life that is 'pleasing to God', which can also be described in terms of 'serving Christ'. According to Paul, the corporate life of believers is supported not just by God, but also by Christ and the Holy Spirit.

Doing good and the Trinity

A fourth aspect of Paul's practical teaching that has trinitarian dimensions concerns the simple matter of doing good.[19] Two texts stand out with respect to the specific language of 'doing good' to others, including those outside the church.

First, Galatians 2:19–20 speaks of 'living for God' in terms of sharing in the life of Christ:

---

18. It is no accident that two of these three qualities appear in the fruit of the Spirit in Gal. 5:22 ('joy' and 'peace').

19. Cf. Rowan Williams, 'Interiority and Epiphany: A Reading in New Testament Ethics', *Modern Theology* 13.1 (1997), p. 42: 'Generosity, mercy and welcome are imperatives for the Christian because they are a participation in the divine activity; but they are also imperative because they show God's glory and invite or attract human beings to "give glory" to God – that is, to reflect back to God what God is.'

For through the law I died to the law so that I might live for God. I have been
crucified with Christ and I no longer live, but Christ lives in me. The life I now live
in the body, I live by faith in the Son of God, who loved me and gave himself for me.

As Miroslav Volf contends, 'A soteriology based on the indwelling of the
Crucified by the Spirit (Galatians 2:19–20) grounds a social practice modeled
on God's passion for the salvation of the world.'[20] Paul elaborates on the details
of such a life in Galatians 5 in terms of walking by the Spirit (5:16) and exhibiting
the fruit of the Spirit (5:22–23). Then in Galatians 6:9–10 he uses the language
of 'doing good' to reinforce his point: 'Let us not become weary in *doing good*,
for at the proper time we will reap a harvest if we do not give up. Therefore, as
we have opportunity, let us *do good* to all people . . .'

Along with the role of the Spirit in shaping Christian behaviour we should
notice a Christological dimension. Paul's language of 'Christ lives in me' (Gal.
2:20) recalls his frequent description of believers in Christ as those who are 'in
Christ'. Pregnant with meaning, not surprisingly, this phrase has been variously
interpreted. If some interpreters have stressed the mystical and experiential
sense of the phrase, a religious energy in the soul of the believer, others underscore the eschatological status of being-in-Christ as the mode of existence of
God's new creation (cf. 2 Cor. 5:17: 'if anyone is in Christ, there is a new creation'
[NRSV]). Charting a middle course, it is best to argue that the emphases on state
and status both have some validity, for Christian experience derives from the
objective standing of being in Christ. But this happy position is not to be
construed privately or individually. In one sense Paul expounds being 'in Christ'
in 1 Corinthians 12:12–27 with the metaphor of the body of Christ in which
all believers are members. To be in Christ is to enjoy both a secure and an
objective status before God and a new mode of eschatological existence in
solidarity with other believers. The point to note in the context of Paul's reflections on the shape of the Christian life and the Trinity is that 'doing good' is
about being conformed to Christlikeness by the power of the Holy Spirit, which
is the proper goal of every human life.

In Romans 8:29–30 Paul gives an indication of the goal to which the Christian
is heading and the process involved:

For those whom he foreknew he also predestined to be conformed to the image of
his Son, in order that he might be the firstborn within a large family. And those whom

---

20. Miroslav Volf, '"The Trinity Is Our Social Program": The Doctrine of the Trinity
and the Shape of Social Engagement', *Modern Theology* 14 (1998), p. 417.

he predestined he also called; and those whom he called he also justified; and those whom he justified he also glorified. (NRSV)

God's goal for his children is tied up with Jesus: so that he may have the place of honour among many brothers and sisters; he is also the template to which believers are conformed. Christians can look forward to sharing in his glorification as the end of the process. As Romans 8:17 promises, 'if children, then heirs, heirs of God and joint heirs with Christ – if, in fact, we suffer with him so that we may also be glorified with him' (NRSV).

Paul's practical instructions in Romans 12 – 13 are also driven by this goal of conformity to Christ. Impressive verbal parallels suggest that the transformation insisted upon in 12:1–2 represents a reversal of 'the downward spiral' of 1:18–32.[21] According to Thompson, 'underpinning 12.1–2 is Jesus' foundational and exemplary sacrifice. For Paul, Christ's image is the goal of the transforming process.'[22] This emerges at a number of points. The call for Christians to offer themselves as 'living sacrifices' recalls the application of cultic language to Jesus' atoning death (3:24–25; 5:8–9; 8:3–4) repeatedly in the letter. Where his was necessarily a bloody sacrifice to effect atonement, believers offer a living sacrifice. The language of 'being transformed' echoes the goal of conformity to Jesus. The closing verse of the section, Romans 13:14, also suggests that Jesus is in mind as Paul shares his vision of humanity: 'Instead, put on the Lord Jesus Christ, and make no provision for the flesh, to gratify its desires.'

A second example of Paul's setting good works in a trinitarian framework can be found in Titus 3:4–8a:

> But when *the kindness and love of God our Saviour* appeared, he saved us, not because of righteous things we had done, but because of his mercy. *He* [God] *saved us* through the washing of rebirth and renewal *by the Holy Spirit*, whom he poured out on us generously *through Jesus Christ our Saviour*, so that, having been justified by his [God's] grace, we might become heirs having the hope of eternal life. This is a trustworthy saying. And I want you to stress these things, so that those who have trusted *in God* may be careful to devote themselves to doing what is good.

The basis for Paul's appeal that believers be devoted to 'doing what is good' is salvation by God's kindness, love and mercy and justification by God's grace.

---

21. Michael Thompson, *Clothed with Christ: The Example and Teaching of Jesus in Romans 12.1–15.13*, JSNTSup 59 (Sheffield: JSOT Press, 1991), pp. 78–82.

22. Ibid., p. 85.

Interestingly, both God and Jesus Christ are given the title of 'Saviour' (cf. Titus 3:4, 6 above). If the passage affirms that God is the agent of our salvation, we are saved through the washing and rebirth given by the Spirit, who is poured out on us through Jesus Christ. Even in the most mundane and practical of matters, 'doing good', Paul offers a thoroughly trinitarian rationale and motivation.

Conclusion

What are the practical implications of the doctrine of the Trinity for Paul in his letters? While this is a good question to ask, it is more in keeping with the nature of Paul and his letters to think about things the other way around: *What are the trinitarian dimensions of Paul's practical teaching?* It is not that Paul inherits or arrives at a doctrine of the Trinity in a vacuum, which he then applies in his practical theology. Rather, in following his vocation as a servant and apostle of Jesus Christ to preach the gospel and to instruct believers as to how to conduct their life together in a manner worthy of the gospel he inevitably plumbs the depths of the doctrine of the triune God. While it is possible to talk about assurance of salvation, the act of praying, Christian fellowship and the shape of the Christian life without mentioning the Trinity, this is not the way Paul goes about it. Repeatedly, and to great effect, when Paul deals with matters of pastoral concern, he cannot help but mention the united and collaborative work of God, Christ and the Spirit, three divine identities, who together constitute one God.[23]

© Brian S. Rosner, 2016

---

23. I would like to thank Chris Porter for help in research for this chapter and Scott Harrower for helpful suggestions on an earlier draft.

6. HEBREWS AND THE TRINITY

Jonathan I. Griffiths

The character and work of the trinitarian God is expounded on every page of Hebrews. The writer calls for allegiance to the One God of Israel and makes him known as Father, Son and Holy Spirit.[1] Hebrews is not, of course, a doctrinal tract on the Trinity. It is first and foremost a sermon urging faltering believers to continue with Christ.[2] However, as the writer expounds Scripture and exhorts the addressees to respond with faith and obedience, he says a great deal that illumines the trinitarian character of God. To examine adequately all the relevant material in Hebrews would require a monograph of its own, and so the aim of this present study is more modest: to consider the ways in which the writer presents the three divine persons in relation to two central themes of his discourse, the themes of revelation and

---

1. For a recent defence of the view that Hebrews is a trinitarian work see Nathan D. Holsteen, 'The Trinity in the Book of Hebrews', *BibSac* 169 (2011), pp. 334–346; see also C. Kavin Rowe, 'The Trinity in the Letters of St Paul and Hebrews', in Gilles Emery, O. P., and Matthew Levering (eds.), *The Oxford Handbook of the Trinity* (Oxford: Oxford University Press, 2011), pp. 41–54.

2. On the sermonic genre of Hebrews see Jonathan I. Griffiths, *Hebrews and Divine Speech*, LNTS 507 (London: Bloomsbury T&T Clark, 2014), pp. 16–24.

redemption.[3] To what extent are the divine projects of revelation and redemption undertaken explicitly by the Father, Son and Holy Spirit? What is shown concerning the identity and role of each person, and concerning the ways in which they interrelate?

Revelation

A personal Word

Hebrews opens with the affirmation that God, having spoken 'in [*en*] the prophets' in former times, has spoken in these last days 'in' (*en*) his Son (1:1–2). The following verses express with eloquence and economy the manner and substance of God's speech in the Son (note that 1:1–4 is all a single Greek sentence). God has made himself known through all that the Son is and does. The Son is himself 'the radiance of the glory of God and the exact imprint of his nature' (1:3).[4] His activity in making and upholding the universe, providing purification for sins and taking his seat on high all constitutes God's self-revelation. Thus his speech 'in' the Son is personal – even ontological – in its character. Although the terms in which Hebrews expresses this theology of personal revelation through the Son differ from the terms of John's prologue, there is here in Hebrews a similar idea: the Son is himself God's revelatory Word, his speech in personal form.[5]

Greater than the angels

Having introduced the idea that the Son is the personal revelation of God in 1:1–4, the writer then turns in 1:5–14 to consider the nature and implications of his sonship through citing a number of Old Testament passages, primarily from the Psalms. On one level the writer's purpose here is clear enough: he wishes to demonstrate that the Son is superior to angels. But why is it important that the Son should be seen to be superior to the angels? Some insight is given in 2:1–4, where the writer moves from making his biblical

---

3. Holsteen's more broad-ranging study of the Trinity in Hebrews likewise draws attention to these two important themes and develops them briefly ('Trinity', pp. 342–344).

4. English Scripture quotations are taken from the ESV, except in cases where alternative renderings of individual words or phrases are required in order to elucidate points of exegesis.

5. For further exploration of this point see Griffiths, *Divine Speech*, pp. 42–48.

case to exhorting his addressees to respond to the truth he has declared to them:[6]

> Therefore we must pay much closer attention to what we have heard, lest we drift away from it. For since the message declared by angels proved to be reliable, and every transgression or disobedience received a just retribution, how shall we escape if we neglect such a great salvation? (2:1–3a)

Traditionally, Jewish interpretation viewed angels as the agents by whom God delivered the Law at Sinai;[7] hence the writer's reference to 'the message declared by angels' (cf. Acts 7:38, 53; Gal. 3:19). The writer's agenda here is to prove that Jesus is superior to the angels in order that the addressees may pay closer attention to the salvation message they heard through him.

But how does the writer think that this series of Old Testament citations will prove his point? He begins in 1:5 by quoting Psalm 2:7 and 2 Samuel 7:14 as words spoken by the Father to the Son. These, of course, are key verses speaking of the promised messianic king in the line of David. He then proceeds (after a brief citation of Psalm 104 at verse 7)[8] to quote two more psalms that address the Davidic king (Pss 45 and 110), applying them to Jesus.[9] However, the writer's primary agenda in this section is not to demonstrate that Jesus is a

---

6. Hebrews is made up of a series of expositions of biblical texts and themes, each of which ends with an exhortation ('Therefore, let us . . .'). Observing the exhortation that concludes a given section of exposition helps the reader to identify the central concern(s) of the writer in that section of exposition. See ibid., pp. 28–35.

7. See Deut. 33:2 LXX, *Jub.* 1.27, 29; 2.1; 6.22; 30.12, 21; 50.1–2; Josephus, *Ant.* 15.136.

8. Here the focus is on the angels' status as 'ministers' in God's service and under his authority.

9. D. A. Carson has recently drawn attention to the fact that (in the light of 2 Sam. 7:14 esp.) the appellation 'son' could be applied to the Davidic king in the OT without carrying the necessary implication of ontological sonship. Similarly, the Davidic king could be referred to in a 'hyperbolic' way as a 'god' (see 1:8) without actually implying his divinity (D. A. Carson, *Jesus the Son of God: A Christological Title Often Overlooked, Sometimes Misunderstood, and Currently Disputed* [Nottingham: Inter-Varsity Press; Wheaton: Crossway, 2012], pp. 13–62). This is a necessary reminder that the kingly OT texts of Heb. 1 had significant levels of application to historical Davidic kings within their original context (a fact often largely overlooked in Christian exegesis of them).

Davidic king. Indeed, Jesus' status as a Davidic king (even as *the* Davidic king) would not necessarily imply his superiority to angels.

It is important to bear in mind the intended audience of Hebrews: Jewish converts who have put their trust in Jesus as the Messiah, but who are questioning whether they are secure in him and are tempted to revert to old covenant religion.[10] The writer's argument takes it for granted that if Jesus is the promised Davidic king, then the various unquestionably kingly/messianic texts cited in chapter 1 do apply legitimately to him. The writer does not offer an argument for their applicability to Jesus, but rather draws out the striking implications of his messianic identity through the writer's selection of extracts: the messianic king is called 'Son' and even 'God'.

G. B. Caird rightly observed that Hebrews treats the Old Testament as being *self-consciously* and 'avowedly' incomplete.[11] Hebrews takes it for granted that without the incarnation, death and resurrection of Jesus there were very significant aspects of the Old Testament that ultimately did not make sense. In his programme of reconvincing these tottering Jewish believers to trust in Jesus the writer takes them precisely to those Old Testament texts that most clearly cry out for fulfilment in the Messiah.[12] Here in chapter 1 the writer invites his addressees to consider afresh some familiar kingly/messianic texts (as well as one or two less obviously kingly texts) and notice that they identify the Davidic king as both 'Son' and 'God'. Yes, there was a limited and 'hyperbolic' sense in which Davidic kings could have been called both 'son' and 'god' within the context of Old Testament history. But none of these kings was truly and ontologically God or the Son of God. And so, the writer reasons, texts that ascribe such titles to the Davidic king present an obvious difficulty for any reader of the Old Testament who will not accept that Jesus is the person of whom they speak. Without Jesus those texts lead ultimately to positions of logical incoherence or theological impossibility.

---

10. This summary represents a fairly broad scholarly consensus concerning the intended audience of the discourse. The introductions to most major commentaries on Hebrews outline and engage with this basic position.

11. George B. Caird, 'The Exegetical Method of the Epistle to the Hebrews', *CJT* 5 (1959), pp. 44–51, here 49.

12. See Motyer's analysis of the OT hermeneutic operating in Heb. 1. Building upon Caird's observations, he highlights the writer's interest in the tensions between OT texts within their original historical context 'which allow him . . . to assert that Jesus is the fulfilment, the answer to the puzzle' (Stephen Motyer, 'The Psalm Quotations of Hebrews 1: A Hermeneutic-Free Zone?', *TynB* 50 [1999], pp. 3–22, here 21).

The writer has already introduced a Christology of pre-existence ('through whom also he created the world', 1:2) and ontological sonship ('He is the radiance of the glory of God and the exact imprint of his nature', 1:3). He judges that the addressees recognize the authority of the Old Testament and should be receptive to a persuasive argument from it (they are, after all, tempted to return to old covenant religion). And so he seeks to demonstrate that the Old Testament itself points to a Davidic king who is both truly Son and truly God. Here, then, is the force of the argument: this promised king, *whom Scripture attests to be both Son of God and God himself*, is inestimably greater than the angels, and so merits urgent and careful attention (2:1).

A divine conversation

For the writer, the words of the Old Testament citations in Hebrews 1 are (and always were) words fundamentally about Christ and, in a number of cases, addressed to Christ.[13] In affirming that God 'says' these words to or of the Son, the writer is not carrying out an exegetical sleight of hand for a dramatic purpose. The words of the Old Testament citations might have been scripted centuries before, and have been spoken many times in the life and worship of God's people, but they had an appointed time of ultimate and full expression in the life and work of the Son. In the case of the Old Testament citations in Hebrews 1 the divine conversation they record takes place at the time of the enthronement of the Son on high.[14] The same principles undergird Hebrews 2:12–13,

---

13. The writer's treatment of other OT figures and institutions parallels this approach to the Davidic monarchy to some extent. Melchizedek is important as a historical anticipation and prefiguration of the Son, not because Jesus will reflect him, but rather because Melchizedek 'resembles' the Son of God (7:3). The Son is the prior and fundamental reality to whom Melchizedek is a partial witness. The tabernacle in the wilderness preceded the new covenant in historical terms, but is only a 'copy and shadow' (8:5) of the heavenly sanctuary where Jesus, the high priest of the new covenant, now serves as priest. Thus the OT structure was a reflection of, and witness to, the more fundamental heavenly reality, which is connected to Christ's ministry in the new covenant.

14. Heb. 1:3b–4 has made reference to the ascension/enthronement of the Son, and the OT quotation in 1:6 is prefaced by the words 'when he brings the firstborn into the word [*oikoumenē*], he says'. In 2:5 the term *oikoumenē* will refer explicitly to the 'world to come' that has been subjected to the Son. This is the world into which he came when he was 'crowned with glory and honour' (2:9). The writer's mention of this 'world to come' as being that 'of which we are speaking' (2:5) 'explicitly takes up 1:6 and suggests that

where the Son responds to the Father by using words from Psalm 22 and Isaiah 8. These words were spoken in an anticipatory way by the psalmist and the prophet, but are ultimately the Son's words. Thus the writer presents the Old Testament citations in Hebrews 1 and 2 as offering a window into a conversation that takes place between two divine persons within the Godhead. The significance of the fact that God converses with the Son through these citations should not be overlooked. It powerfully affirms the Father and the Son are not interchangeably the same, but rather true persons who relate – even converse – one with another.

Extending the conversation – the role of the Spirit

The quotations in Hebrews 1 constitute the most concentrated catena of separate Old Testament citations in the book, but there is a steady stream of other Old Testament citations throughout the letter, and many of these are similarly introduced as words spoken by a divine person. On a few occasions the Holy Spirit is named as the speaker. The quotation of Psalm 95:7–11 in Hebrews 3:7–11 is introduced by the words 'as the Holy Spirit says'. The words of warning of the psalm recall the rebellion in the wilderness but are not tied to a single moment of historical fulfilment or relevance. Rather, the warning is for the people of God to heed God's voice whenever they hear it:

> Today, if you hear his voice,
> do not harden your hearts as in the rebellion . . .

The Holy Spirit is the named speaker again in Hebrews 10:15, where the words of the Old Testament citation are directed to 'us', that is, to the addressees of the letter. In both these instances where the Holy Spirit is named as the speaker of Scripture words, the direction of speech is from the Godhead to the people of God.[15]

---

they both speak of Christ's return to the divine realm after his death and resurrection' (Peter T. O'Brien, *The Letter to the Hebrews*, PNTC [Grand Rapids: Eerdmans; Nottingham: Apollos, 2010], p. 69); see also Ardel B. Caneday, 'The Eschatological World Already Subjected to the Son: The Οἰκουμένη of Hebrews 1.6 and the Son's Enthronement', in Richard Bauckham et al. (eds.), *A Cloud of Witnesses: The Theology of Hebrews in Its Ancient Contexts*, LNTS 387 (London: T&T Clark, 2008), pp. 28–39.

15. As Ken Schenck has already observed in 'God Has Spoken: Hebrews' Theology of the Scriptures', in Richard Bauckham et al. (eds.), *The Epistle to the Hebrews and Christian Theology* (Grand Rapids: Eerdmans, 2009), pp. 321–336, esp. 334–335.

On two other occasions in Hebrews the Holy Spirit is shown to have a revelatory role, and in both these cases the intended recipients of this revelation
are again the people of God. Speaking of the revelation of the message of
'salvation' at 2:3–4, the writer notes:

> It was declared at first by the Lord, and it was attested to us by those who heard, while
> God also bore witness by signs and wonders and various miracles and by gifts of the
> Holy Spirit distributed according to his will.

These gifts of the Spirit form a key part of God's 'bearing witness' to the authenticity of the salvation message declared 'at first by the Lord' (i.e. Jesus) and then
'attested' by eyewitnesses (quite possibly the apostles). Beyond noting that the
Spirit's role in this context is to facilitate and reinforce the divine work of revelation
to the people of God, two further observations are relevant. First, this important
summary statement of the means by which the salvation message was revealed
and disseminated presents that complex of events as a collaborative work of the
three persons of the Godhead: the Lord Jesus declares the message, God
the Father bears witness to it and he does so in part 'by gifts of the Holy Spirit'.
Second, the Spirit acts specifically as the agent for the Father in this collaborative
project of revelation. God (the Father, as distinguished from 'the Lord', who is
the Son here) is the one bearing witness; the distributions of the Spirit form part
of his bearing witness and are given in accordance 'to his will' (2:4b).

At 9:8 there is one further instance where the Holy Spirit reveals truth to
contemporary readers of Scripture. Speaking of the biblical pattern given for
the tabernacle in the wilderness with its two parts (the 'holy place' and the 'most
holy place'),[16] the author says, 'By this the Holy Spirit indicates that the way
into the holy places is not yet opened as long as the first section is still standing
(which is symbolic for the present age)' (9:8–9a). The writer contends that the
arrangement of the tabernacle as given to Moses (see 8:5) and recorded
in Exodus was a 'parable' or 'symbol' that had a revelatory purpose tied to
'the present age' (9:9a).[17] The work that the Holy Spirit performs in this regard

---

16. There is not scope here to consider the exegetical questions surrounding the
    description of the 'first' and 'second' tabernacle. For a detailed treatment of these
    descriptors see David Gooding, 'The Tabernacle: No Museum Piece', in Jonathan
    Griffiths (ed.), *The Perfect Saviour: Key Themes in Hebrews* (Nottingham: Inter-Varsity
    Press, 2012), pp. 69–88.
17. The 'present age' is best understood to be the same as the 'time of reformation'
    (9:10) and as referring to the present era of fulfilment, which was ushered in 'when

is that of 'indicating' (*dēlountos*) the relevance of the arrangement of the tabernacle.

Commentators differ in their assessment of the nature of the Spirit's activity, some locating the work of 'indication' in the original inspiration of the covenant documents,[18] and some locating the activity in a work of the Spirit in giving the writer of Hebrews (and perhaps his addressees) fresh insight into the ancient text.[19] The range of meaning of the participle *dēlountos* would allow for both.[20] These options should not necessarily be seen as mutually exclusive, especially given Hebrews's clear insistence that God continues to speak the scriptural words he once spoke. But the writer's broader patterns of Old Testament hermeneutics indicate that the balance falls on the Spirit's inspiring the Scripture (and then continuing to say what he originally said), rather than affording new insight. The writer's point in 9:8–9a is that, *in its original design* as laid out in the covenant documents, the Holy Spirit intended the tabernacle to indicate that 'the way into the holy places is not yet opened'. The Spirit thus pointed to 'the present age', when there is no division and direct access to the heavenly sanctuary is available through Christ. That was what the Spirit meant to 'indicate' from the moment of inspiration of the covenant Scriptures, and that is what he continues to 'indicate' through those same Scriptures.

Here once again is an instance of the Spirit's speaking the words and message of Scripture to the people of God – both ancient and contemporary.

Christ appeared as a high priest of the good things that have come' (9:11). So Harold W. Attridge, *The Epistle to the Hebrews*, Hermeneia (Philadelphia: Fortress, 1989), p. 241; see further the discussion there.

18. So e.g. Cockerill: '"the Holy Spirit" as the inspirer of Scripture is even now "revealing" the inadequacy of the old order through the biblical description of its limitations. The pastor claims no esoteric divine disclosure. What he has to say is drawn from the plain biblical description of the old order understood in light of its fulfilment' (Gareth Lee Cockerill, *The Epistle to the Hebrews*, NICNT [Grand Rapids: Eerdmans, 2012], pp. 380–381).

19. So e.g. O'Brien (*Hebrews*, p. 312, emphases original): 'The phrase, the *Holy Spirit was showing by this*, signifies more than a recognition of the Spirit's role in the inspiration of the scriptural text, although this may be presupposed . . . Rather, the author is claiming special insight from the *Holy Spirit* into the meaning and purpose of these OT provisions in light of their fulfilment in Christ.'

20. The verb *dēloō* can mean either to 'reveal' something that was not previously known or to 'explain' or 'clarify' something (BDAG, 'δηλόω', p. 222).

Redemption

As already noted, in the single Greek sentence in 1:1–4 the writer presents the person and work of the Son as the means by which God the Father has spoken in 'these last days'. Because the Son perfectly represents and reveals the Father (1:3a), the work that he achieves in 'making purification for sins' is part of the Father's self-revelation 'in' the Son. But the Father's role in the drama of redemption is not passive: he is the one who bequeaths to the Son the name he inherits in the ascension and enthronement on high (4:4–5). The opening verses of the letter thus give us a summary picture of the whole sweep of redemption as a joint work of Father and Son.

The perfection of the Son

Having established Jesus' exalted status as the divine Son in chapter 1, the writer goes on to consider his descent in the incarnation in chapter 2. Here the reader encounters one of the most (initially, at least) perplexing aspects of the theology of Hebrews – its teaching concerning the 'perfecting of the Son'. The writer addresses the theme first in Hebrews 2:10, and returns to it in 5:7–10:

> For it was fitting that he, for whom and by whom all things exist, in bringing many sons to glory, should make the founder of their salvation perfect through suffering. (2:10)

> In the days of his flesh, Jesus offered up prayers and supplications, with loud cries and tears, to him who was able to save him from death, and he was heard because of his reverence. Although he was a son, he learned obedience through what he suffered. And being made perfect, he became the source of eternal salvation to all who obey him, being designated by God a high priest after the order of Melchizedek. (5:7–10)

Both references to the 'perfecting' of Christ are made in the context of a discussion of his preparation for, and appointment to, the office of high priest. Although the language of 'perfection' may sound like a process by which some 'imperfection' is removed or overcome, the context indicates that the Father's 'perfecting' of the Son through suffering refers positively to his vocational shaping, preparation and training for his work as high priest.[21] This role is, of

---

21. For a thorough treatment of the theme of perfection and the case that it is to be understood vocationally see David G. Peterson, 'Perfection: Achieved and Experienced', in Jonathan Griffiths (ed.), *The Perfect Saviour: Key Themes in Hebrews*

course, a role he takes on *as the incarnate Son* (see esp. 2:9 and 5:7), and for which he is prepared in his incarnate life on earth. Thus his shaping and development for this role may be compared to other human processes of development he experiences in the incarnation.[22]

Of central interest here is the interaction between the Father and the incarnate Son in the process of 'perfection'. The Father is shown to be the primary actor, while the incarnate Son experiences and willingly endures the suffering involved in the process. In his suffering he cries out to the Father and is heard because of the 'reverence' with which he responds to the Father in this process. As the incarnate Son, faced with trials he had never before faced (and here the writer must be recalling the Garden of Gethsemane and the lead-up to the cross), his obedience to the Father was tested and tried in new ways, and he 'learned obedience through what he suffered' (5:8). It is not the case that he was previously disobedient; rather, he had never before been called to obey in the context of human suffering of this kind.

This interaction between the Father and the Son in the process of the Son's 'perfection' is fundamental to the accomplishment of redemption. More than that, this relational dynamic shapes the nature of the redemption the Son achieves for his people.

A family of 'brothers' and 'sons'

At this point in our discussion it will be useful to trace the broader flow of the logic of 2:5–11. The writer continues his case for the superiority of the Son over the angels by noting that the 'world to come' has not been subjected to them and demonstrates, centrally through an exposition of Psalm 8, that it *has been subjected to the Son* as representative leader of a new humanity:

> Now it was not to angels that God subjected the world to come, of which we are speaking. It has been testified somewhere,

> 'What is man, that you are mindful of him,
>   or the son of man, that you care for him?
> You made him for a little while lower than the angels;
>   you have crowned him with glory and honour,
>   putting everything in subjection under his feet.'

(Nottingham: Inter-Varsity Press, 2012), pp. 125–145; *Hebrews and Perfection*, SNTSMS 47 (Cambridge: Cambridge University Press, 1982).
22. Cf. e.g. Jesus' growth in wisdom in his youth (Luke 2:40, 52).

Now in putting everything in subjection to him, he left nothing outside his control. At present, we do not yet see everything in subjection to him. But we see him who for a little while was made lower than the angels, namely Jesus, crowned with glory and honour because of the suffering of death, so that by the grace of God he might taste death for everyone. (2:5–9)

Psalm 8 looks back to the creation pattern of Genesis 1:26–28 and the special dignity given to humanity in its call to exercise dominion over the rest of the natural world. But the writer notes that in the present fallen world humanity does not exercise this dominion according to the original design (2:8). Adam as representative leader of humanity ('man', 'son of man') was given a high calling, but through sin failed to exercise his role rightly. There is, however, one great exception to the pattern of fallen humanity: Jesus, who was for a time made lower than the angels in his incarnation, suffering and death, is now enthroned on high (2:9a). In order to address Adam's failure and restore humanity to the 'glory and honour' of its original position Jesus stepped into Adam's shoes and became 'son of man' in the incarnation 'so that by the grace of God he might taste death for everyone' (2:9b; see 2:17). He became a human being in order that he might die as a fitting substitute for other humans.

Now the writer further draws out the significance of the humanity of the Son for the salvation he achieves:

For it was fitting that he, for whom and by whom all things exist, in bringing many sons to glory, should make the founder of their salvation perfect through suffering. For he who sanctifies and those who are sanctified all have one source. That is why he is not ashamed to call them brothers, saying,

'I will tell of your name to my brothers;
in the midst of the congregation I will sing your praise.'
(2:10–12, citing Ps. 22:22)

Through his incarnation, suffering, death, resurrection and ascension, Jesus 'brings many sons to glory' – now not simply restoring the original creation pattern in Adam, but exalting humanity to something even higher. In the incarnation the Son of God became a son of man and so became able to call other human beings 'brothers'. But more than that, he became the 'founder' or 'pioneer' (the representative leader) of their salvation, leading them up to the glory he himself entered in the ascension.

Those 'sons' whom the Son redeems become his 'brothers' and share in the glory of his resurrected and ascended life in the presence of the Father. The 'congregation' or 'assembly' (*ekklēsia*) in which the Son sings the praise of the Father (2:12) is at once the heavenly 'assembly' pictured in 12:22–24 and the earthly gatherings of God's people that mirror and anticipate it.[23] Significantly, the writer refers to this heavenly gathering as 'the assembly of the firstborn' (*ekklēsia prōtotokōn*, 12:23). Hebrews has already identified Jesus as 'the first-born' Son of the Father (1:6a). But now all his redeemed people – gathered in the divine presence (12:22–23) through his shed blood and priestly mediation (12:24) – are identified as an assembly of 'firstborn' children.[24]

It would be clearly too much to say that the unique trinitarian category of sonship is extended to redeemed humanity, but Hebrews nonetheless affirms that Jesus' saved people join the divine 'family' as brothers of the Son and sons of the Father.[25]

The shared experience of sonship

This extension of the 'family' relationship from the Son to other sons undoubt-edly shapes many aspects of the way in which new covenant believers are called to relate to the Father in Hebrews. It certainly accounts (at least in part) for their ability to approach his presence through Christ. The Son has been welcomed into the Father's presence (1:3b); believers, already part of the heavenly 'assembly of the firstborn' (12:23), are invited to approach the divine presence with boldness themselves (4:16; 10:22). At least in some cases this new relational dynamic explicitly underpins the extension of divine discourse to the people of God (Jesus addresses his 'brothers' in the 'congregation', 2:12; the Father addresses his people as 'sons' by using words of Scripture, 12:5–6).[26]

---

23. O'Brien, *Hebrews*, pp. 111–112.

24. Ibid., pp. 485–486; Peterson, *Hebrews and Perfection*, p. 162.

25. In 2:13b–14 Christian people are described as 'children' given by God to the Son. Cockerill's comment here is judicious: 'There is no contradiction between God's people being Christ's "children" and God's "sons and daughters." The Greek word for "children" [*paidia*] is often used as a general term for younger people with a close relationship to and respect for the one addressing them as "children." Thus Christ's calling them his "children" preserves the uniqueness of the Son, affirms his solidarity with the "sons and daughters," and suggests that they are in need of his assistance' (*Hebrews*, p. 145).

26. Mackie argues that the 'Son's conferral of family membership' on his people provides the basis for the call for them as siblings to 'vocalize their commitment to and identification with the Son (4:14; 10:23)' through the 'sacral act of confession' as they draw near to the divine presence (Scott D. Mackie, *Eschatology and Exhortation in*

Most strikingly and clearly, this shared experience of sonship emerges as the underlying assumption in the discussion of fatherly 'discipline' in Hebrews 12:3–11. The writer has just called the addressees to 'run with endurance the race that is set before us' (12:1), drawing their attention to Jesus, 'the founder [or 'leader' or 'pioneer', *archēgos*, see 2:10] and perfecter of our faith, who for the joy that was set before him endured the cross, despising the shame' (2:2). The endurance of Jesus is then given as a model for responding to the hostility believers face from a sinful world:

> Consider him who endured from sinners such hostility against himself, so that you may not grow weary or faint-hearted. In your struggle against sin [i.e. against sinful opposition in the world, in parallel to the opposition Jesus faced from sinners] you have not yet resisted to the point of shedding your blood. (12:3–4)

Like in chapter 2, Jesus as *archēgos* is representative leader of his people in 12:2, enduring suffering on the way to the joy of the final destination. As the discussion proceeds, the category of sonship returns explicitly to view once more, now as a category applied specifically to believers as the Father addresses the listeners explicitly as 'sons' in the words of Scripture:

> And have you forgotten the exhortation that addresses you as sons?

> 'My son, do not regard lightly the discipline of the Lord,
>   nor be weary when reproved by him.
> For the Lord disciplines the one he loves,
>   and chastises every son whom he receives.'
>   (12:5–6, quoting Prov. 3:11–12)

Although God has been referred to as Father of the Son in 1:5, he has never before in Hebrews been referred to as Father of his people. But now, as the

---

(*Footnote 26 cont.*) *the Epistle to the Hebrews*, WUNT 2.223 [Tübingen: Mohr Siebeck, 2007], p. 217); see also his 'Confession of the Son of God in Hebrews', *NTS* 53 (2007), pp. 114–129. According to this view, the shared experience of sonship would not only provide the basis for the addressees to hear God speak to them, but also for them to respond to God and thus participate in a two-way conversation. Mackie's suggestion certainly coheres with the exegetical findings of this present study, although it must be accepted somewhat tentatively because the response of 'confession' is nowhere in the text linked explicitly to a status of shared sonship for the addressees.

people of God follow in the footsteps of Jesus their *archēgos* in enduring suffering, they share in an experience that is basic for all true sons as they relate to their father – they receive discipline from his hand. Indeed, this experience is a mark of their legitimacy as true sons (12:7–8), demonstrating that God is rightly called their 'Father' (12:9).[27]

The Spirit and the self-offering of Christ

Although the Spirit is only infrequently mentioned in connection with the work of redemption, Hebrews indicates that his role is integral. Most striking in this regard is Hebrews 9:14, where the writer affirms that Christ 'through the eternal Spirit offered himself without blemish to God'. Previous references to the Holy Spirit in the discourse (2:4; 3:7; 6:4; 9:8; 10:15) prepared the reader to understand the mention of 'Spirit' here as referring to the Holy Spirit, rather than to a separate aspect of Christ's own being.[28] The nature of the Spirit's work in Christ's self-offering is neither limited to a specific function nor clearly tied to a specific conceptual background here.[29] Rather, the whole process by which Christ ultimately came to offer himself to God the Father as a sacrifice is to be understood as a Spirit-enabled process.

Three specific observations should be noted. First, the writer records in this context that Christ offered himself 'without blemish'. This lack of blemish most

---

27. The designation 'Father of spirits' distinguishes God from his people's human 'fleshly fathers' (12:9a).

28. Cockerill, *Hebrews*, p. 398; Peterson, *Hebrews and Perfection*, p. 138; O'Brien, *Hebrews*, p. 324. Attridge, who finds that '[t]he precise import of this phrase is difficult to determine', is nonetheless quick to dismiss any trinitarian understanding here: 'Trinitarian speculation . . . is not involved. Hebrews' references to the Spirit are too diffuse and ill-focused to support a Trinitarian theology in this context' (*Hebrews*, p. 250). However, the fact that references to the Spirit are scattered through the discourse (without the Spirit's receiving sustained attention at any one point) could indicate equally that the writer had a coherent theology of the Spirit that he assumed his addressees would share and that he did not need to defend or develop.

29. The numerous attempts to identify a precise biblical or traditional background that the writer intended to evoke here generally fail to convince. For an overview of such proposals see Martin Emmrich, '"*Amtscharisma*": Through the Eternal Spirit (Hebrews 9:14)', *BBR* 12 (2002), pp. 17–32. Emmrich's own proposal that the writer here reflects a traditional association (esp. in rabbinic literature) between an anointing by the Spirit and the priestly office is intriguing, but again lacks sufficient evidence from within Hebrews to establish it conclusively.

naturally refers to his moral rather than physical perfection.[30] Implicit, then, is a work of the Spirit that enabled the incarnate Christ to endure trial – including the final trial of his sufferings leading up to his death – without sin (see 4:15), and thus reach the point of his self-offering as morally unblemished.

Second, the designation of the Spirit as the 'eternal Spirit' (*pneumatos aiōniou*) is unique in the New Testament. The writer has already affirmed that Christ secured 'an eternal redemption' for his people upon his entry to the 'holy places' (9:12; cf. 5:9). Verse 15 will again echo the term 'eternal' in speaking of the 'eternal inheritance' that Christ secures for his people through his self-offering. Certainly, an implication here is that the Holy Spirit enables Christ by his self-offering to achieve temporally enduring benefits. But the context suggests that beyond this temporal connotation to the designation 'eternal' there is also a spatial connotation.[31] Christ's self-offering to God culminates in his 'appearance' and 'entry' into God's very presence in the heavenly sanctuary, distinguished from the sanctuary on earth that is made by hands and is part of this creation (9:11–12, 24).

2 Corinthians 4:18 provides an interesting point of comparison. Here Paul indicates that he understands the 'eternal' realm to be not simply the temporally abiding realm, but also the unseen realm: 'For the things that are seen are transient, but the things that are unseen are eternal.'[32] If it is right to see a spatial implication to the use of the term 'eternal' in Hebrews 9:14, then work of the 'eternal Spirit' gains added significance. Although the divine Son had taken on

---

30. O'Brien, *Hebrews*, p. 325.

31. Ellingworth emphasizes this, suggesting that although the term 'eternal' 'usually has temporal overtones in Hebrews . . . what is probably more important in this context is that it denotes the Godward side of reality, that which is "not of this creation"' (Paul Ellingworth, *The Epistle to the Hebrews: A Commentary on the Greek Text*, NIGTC [Grand Rapids: Eerdmans; Carlisle: Paternoster, 1993], p. 457). Cf. Attridge, *Hebrews*, p. 251.

32. Paul shows evidence of a similar understanding in 2 Cor. 4:17–18, where the eternal realm is not simply the abiding realm, but also the unseen realm: 'For this light and momentary affliction is preparing for us an eternal weight of glory beyond all comparison, as we look not to the things that are seen but to the things that are unseen. For the things that are seen are transient, but the things that are unseen are eternal.' On the conceptual overlap between the unseen and the eternal in Greek thought see Plato, *Phaedo* 79a; and Margaret E. Thrall, *A Critical and Exegetical Commentary on the Second Epistle to the Corinthians*, 2 vols., ICC (London: T&T Clark, 1994–2000), vol. 1, pp. 355–356.

the limitations of finite humanity in the incarnation, he was nonetheless enabled to secure redemption for his people in the heavenly places through the agency of the 'eternal Spirit'.[33] This redemption then provides the necessary internal cleansing of 'conscience' required for his people to 'serve [*latreuein*] the living God' (9:14b). The language of divine 'service' belongs to the priestly world of the temple (cf. 8:5) and points to the access to God's heavenly presence that believers enjoy even now through the high priestly work of Christ.[34] Thus there is a significant 'spatial' aspect to the 'eternal redemption' Christ achieves for his people by 'the eternal Spirit'.

Third, we have mention here in 9:14 of all three persons of the Trinity. By the agency of the eternal Spirit, Christ the Son offers himself to God the Father. Scholars generally agree that Hebrews 9:11–14 provides an important summary of key aspects of the theology of Hebrews.[35] It is striking that here, in this condensed statement of truths that are centrally important in the discourse, the writer so clearly mentions the role of each of the three persons of the Trinity and shows how they function together.

Summary and conclusions

Throughout Hebrews the God who reveals himself and redeems his people is unmistakably God the Trinity – Father, Son and Holy Spirit.

In the work of revelation the Father makes himself known in and through the person and work of the Son. The Father and the Son engage relationally with each other as they converse through pre-recorded words of Scripture. The

---

33. Presumably the work of the Spirit includes the action of raising Christ from the dead to the place of glory at the Father's right hand. It is often noted that the writer does not speak directly of the resurrection of Christ as a distinct event. He is very clear on the fact that Christ did indeed die (2:9; see 9:12, 17) but now remains alive for ever (7:16, 24), and so the resurrection is assumed. In his theology, resurrection and ascension are bound together, and it is probably a natural implication of 9:14 that the Spirit is the agent of the resurrection/ascension of Christ (cf. Rom. 1:4; 8:11; 1 Peter 3:18).

34. Cf. esp. 12:28. Believers 'have come' already to the divine presence in the heavenly Jerusalem (12:22–24) and so are able to 'serve' (*latreuein*, 12:28) before him, even while here on earth, through everyday acts of godly obedience (13:1–17).

35. See brief discussions and further references in Emmrich, '*Amtscharisma*', p. 17; William L. Lane, *Hebrews 9–13*, WBC 47B (Nashville: Nelson, 1991), pp. 234–235.

Spirit speaks words of Scripture as well, but words directed not to the Father and the Son but now to the people of God. Similarly, the Spirit acts as the Father's agent in confirming the revelation of the Son and his work through signs and wonders and the distribution of gifts.

One of the central exhortations of Hebrews is to listen – and to keep listening – to God's word. This word is fundamentally trinitarian in nature. It is spoken by the Father; its central theme is the person and work of the Son, in whom it is fully expressed; and it is brought to the people of God 'today' by the agency and power of the Spirit. Knowing that God the Trinity – Father, Son and Holy Spirit – is addressing his people through the scriptural word is a powerful prompt to listen.

In the great project of redemption the Son becomes man and learns obedience as a human Son of the Father. Through his death and resurrection, which he achieves by the agency of the eternal Spirit, he makes other sons of men his brothers and causes them to become sons of the Father. Having entered into the 'family' of God, these human sons share in the experience of the Father's disciplinary training – but do so knowing that it was first the experience of Christ the Son, their brother and forerunner.

A central pastoral concern of the writer is to urge the addressees to hold fast to the redemption they have received and to enjoy its benefits. This exhortation is repeatedly framed as a call to 'draw near' (4:16; 10:22). It is a call to approach God the Father through the mediation of the divine Son, who is high priest of his people. This exhortation prompts the believer to ask how possibly one on earth can approach God in heaven. From all that Hebrews has said and implied of the work of the 'eternal Spirit', it naturally follows that the Spirit – whose agency brings and confirms God's word to his people and who facilitated the offering of the Son before the Father – is the divine person who lifts the believer to the very presence of God in prayerful approach.

That the One God is Father, Son and Holy Spirit shapes not only the theological substance of the writer's message, but also the response he exhorts the addressees to make.[36]

---

36. I am grateful to my colleague Tim Ward for his kind help in providing feedback on a draft of this chapter.

7. THE TRINITY AND THE GENERAL EPISTLES

Brandon D. Crowe

The seven letters known as the General Epistles (James, 1–2 Peter, 1–3 John and Jude) are comparatively brief, but taken together reveal much about the trinitarian nature of God. These epistles move seamlessly between the persons of the Godhead and give us a peek into the trinitarian planning, accomplishment and application of salvation. I will address these letters in their canonical order.

James

The letter of James emphasizes the implications of the salvation wrought by Christ, but he does so in a robustly monotheistic way, even as he attributes a divine role to Jesus. James thus writes from the world view of a first-century Jewish believer in Christ. This means that the Old Testament Scriptures were viewed as the foundation for faith and life, yet as a believer in Jesus as the Messiah the teachings of Jesus were also of the utmost importance.

One God

The Jewish framework for James's teaching is evident in several ways. First, James addresses his letter to the twelve tribes of the Diaspora (1:1), which is the Jewish dispersion. Second, the world view of the Old Testament permeates James. Not only does he explicitly quote the Old Testament (e.g. Lev. 19:18 in Jas 2:8; Gen. 15:6 in Jas 2:23), but James's discussion throughout also reveals an author steeped in the language and imagery of the Old Testament (e.g. Abraham, Rahab, law, faith, wisdom). Third, building on the previous point, James identifies himself as a servant of God (1:1), which must also be the God of the Old Testament (so e.g. Prov. 3:34 in Jas 4:6). James therefore understands God to be the God of the Old Testament, even as he understands God in the light of the new revelation that has come through Jesus.

An important text that reveals that James shares the monotheistic outlook of the Old Testament is James 2:19a: 'You believe that God is one; you do well.'[1] Or, as the NIV captures the thrust, 'You believe that there is one God. Good!' Though James goes on to say that understanding the oneness of God is not enough to have genuine, saving faith (2:19b–26), he nevertheless confirms that it is vitally important to believe that God is one. James further identifies God as the source of wisdom (1:5), the giver of good gifts (1:17), the lawgiver and judge (4:12), the providential Lord (4:14–15), the Lord of hosts (5:4) and the compassionate and merciful Lord (5:11). Moreover, God is the one who is attributed with bringing us forth by his will (1:18), and the one who chose the poor to be rich in faith (2:5). These texts are consistent with the role of the Father in the economy of salvation elsewhere, as the one who plans salvation.

In addition, James's identification of God as Father reveals the New Testament emphasis that God is the Father of Jesus Christ. To be sure, God was already known as Father in the Old Testament (e.g. Deut. 32:4–6; Isa. 1:2; Hos. 11:1; etc.), yet the emphasis in the New Testament is more emphatically on the fatherhood of God in the light of the centrality of the sonship of Jesus Christ – Jesus is pre-eminently the Son of God. An important text in this regard is James 1:27, where God and Father both appear in the dative case in Greek, linked by *kai* (thus it reads, *tō theō kai patri*). Significantly, the Greek definite article is not repeated before 'Father' (cf. Matt. 28:19), which leads to the most natural reading that God is identical with the Father. This construction is an example of the Granville Sharp rule, which will also be relevant for our understanding of 2 Peter 1:1. In brief, the Granville Sharp rule states that when two singular, personal nouns are joined by *kai* and the article appears only before the first noun, then the two nouns refer to the same person.[2] James's emphasis

---

1. Unless otherwise noted, all translations in this chapter are from the ESV.

2. See Daniel B. Wallace, *Greek Grammar Beyond the Basics: An Exegetical Syntax of the New Testament* (Grand Rapids: Zondervan, 1996), pp. 270–272.

on God as Father also goes hand in hand with his emphasis on Jesus Christ, since fatherhood pre-eminently denotes God's fatherhood towards Jesus. God is our Father because God is the Father of Jesus Christ.[3]

Jesus, the Lord of glory

An additional key to the understanding of God in James is the identity of both the Father as Lord and the Son as Lord. Jesus is clearly identified as Lord in 1:1 ('the Lord Jesus Christ'), in 2:1 ('Jesus Christ, the Lord of glory') and 5:7 ('the coming of the Lord'). Additionally, the Father is clearly Lord in 1:27 ('God and Father'), in 3:9 ('our Lord and Father . . . people who are made in the likeness of God'),[4] and probably three times in 5:10–11 ('prophets who spoke in the name of the Lord'). Additionally, the Lord to whom prayer is made in 1:7 most likely refers to the Father, as does the Lord before whom we should humble ourselves in 4:10.

However, other occurrences of Lord appear to be more ambiguous, especially in James 5. Thus whereas James 5:4 seems to refer to the Father as Lord, closely thereafter in 5:7 James almost certainly refers to Jesus as Lord, since the return of Jesus as judge is in view (5:9). Yet, as noted above, in the next two verses Lord again seems to refer to the Father (5:10–11). Finally, James speaks of prayer in the name of the Lord for healing and the forgiveness of sins in 5:14–15. Given that most of the references to Lord in James refer to the Father, and since the most immediate antecedent for Lord is the Father, perhaps we should conclude that the name of the Lord in James 5:14–15 is the Father (cf. 4:10). However, we cannot be certain of this since it is also appropriate for healing and prayer to be done in the name of Jesus. In addition to the overlapping use of Lord for both Father and the Son, both the Father and Son in James are identified as *judge*. The Father is most likely in view as judge in James 4:12, in association with God the Father as lawgiver, whereas the returning judge in 5:9 is almost certainly to be understood as Jesus as Lord (cf. 5:7).

What are the implications of James's overlapping use of *judge* and *Lord* for the Father and the Son? First, we should note the ease with which James can use the same terms – divine terms – to speak of both the Father and the Son. We need not, however, conclude that James has a confused or modalistic

---

3. See Herman Bavinck, *Reformed Dogmatics*, ed. John Bolt, tr. John Vriend, 4 vols. (Grand Rapids: Baker Academic, 2003–8), vol. 2, pp. 269–273.

4. Jas 3:9 is probably another example of the Granville Sharp rule.

understanding of the persons of the Godhead since he clearly recognizes distinctions between the Father and the Son in some texts (e.g. 1:1).[5] Second, we must not miss the force of the appellation *Lord* for Jesus (1:1; 2:1; 5:7). In James 1:1 Jesus is identified as the *Lord* Jesus Christ. Given the familiarity many readers of the Bible have with the identification of Jesus as Lord, the impact of this phrase may not be felt as strongly as it should be. By identifying Jesus as Lord, James is claiming that Jesus is exalted in the highest heavens with God himself. This is further clarified in 2:1, where James identifies Jesus Christ as the Lord of glory.[6] Here James is making a most remarkable claim: that the man Jesus from Nazareth – who was probably James's half-brother! – was not only the Messiah, but could rightly be described as the glorious Lord of heaven! This is an astounding claim for a monotheist like James (2:19) to make about a person who lived on earth just a few years earlier. Yet James can describe both God the Father as (glorious) Lord and Jesus Christ as glorious Lord. A key implication of the uniqueness of God in the Old Testament is the truth that God does not give his glory to any other (e.g. Isa. 42:8; 48:9–11). Yet James, without undermining the one God of the Old Testament, teaches that the glory reserved for God belongs to both Father and Son.

Finally, though James does not explicitly mention the Holy Spirit, it is worth noting that Scripture speaks of the Holy Spirit in close association with the glory of the Lord.[7] Therefore, in James's reference to Jesus as Lord of glory (2:1) we may find an implicit allusion to the glory of the Holy Spirit, though admittedly James does not explore this possible relationship.

Conclusion: James

Though in some texts it may be difficult to determine whether James has in view the Father or the Son when he speaks of the judge or Lord, that James can use both terms to refer either to the Father or the Son reveals a Christology of the highest order. Jesus is the glorious Lord just as God is the all-glorious

---

5. The absence of the Greek article before *theou* makes it unlikely that Jas 1:1 has in view only one divine person.

6. For options on how to take the genitive construction 'Lord of glory' see Ralph P. Martin, *James*, WBC 48 (Waco, Tex.: Word, 1988), pp. 59–60.

7. 1 Peter 4:14; cf. Meredith M. Kline, 'The Holy Spirit as Covenant Witness' (ThM thesis, Westminster Theological Seminary, 1972), pp. 5–26; Meredith G. Kline, *Images of the Spirit* (Grand Rapids: Baker, 1980), p. 15.

One. James says less about the Holy Spirit, but thankfully we know more of the Holy Spirit's relationship to the Father and the Son through other portions of the New Testament, including 1 Peter, to which we now turn.

1 Peter

Trinitarian greeting

From the first verses of 1 Peter much is revealed about the trinitarian nature of God, where we read of 'the foreknowledge of God the Father, in the sanctification of the Spirit, for obedience to Jesus Christ and for sprinkling with his blood' (1:2). All three divine persons are included in Peter's greeting.[8] In 1 Peter 1:2 salvation is presented as a trinitarian blessing, with each person of the Godhead having a particular role in the outworking of salvation. God the Father is the one who foreknows his elect people (1:1). The sanctification of the Spirit in this context probably points to the Spirit's initial application of the work of Christ to God's elect people, setting them apart from the world. In other words, conversion ('obedience') is probably in view, which emphasizes that the Spirit's work is a divine act.[9] Conversion also comes through the covenantal blood of Jesus Christ, which points to forgiveness of sins through the shedding of Jesus' own blood.[10]

Much more could be said about the richness of 1 Peter's greeting, but for the present purposes it is significant that Peter views the work of salvation through a threefold lens. Salvation is a unified work of God the Father, God the Son and God the Holy Spirit. Significantly, Peter does not *argue for* the divine nature or actions of any of the persons of the Godhead, but *argues from* the presupposition of a salvation that has a unified, threefold dynamic.[11] Although Peter does not elaborate on the triune character of God, it is striking that his

---

8. I will refer to the author of 1 and 2 Peter as 'Peter', who is the purported author of both epistles. However, it makes little difference for the present argument whom one posits as the historical author(s) of these epistles. The trinitarian contours of both epistles remain.

9. So Thomas R. Schreiner, *1, 2 Peter, Jude*, NAC 37 (Nashville: B&H, 2003), p. 54; J. Ramsey Michaels, *1 Peter*, WBC 49 (Waco, Tex.: Word, 1988), p. 11.

10. On the OT background see Brandon D. Crowe, *The Message of the General Epistles in the History of Redemption: Wisdom from James, Peter, John, and Jude* (Phillipsburg, N.J.: P&R, 2015), pp. 12–13.

11. Cf. Bavinck, *Reformed Dogmatics*, vol. 2, pp. 269–270.

greeting stands very close to later trinitarian formulations that identify the Father as Creator, the Son as Redeemer and the Spirit as Sanctifier.[12] Peter's triadically shaped greeting is not anomalous, but fits well with the rest of 1 Peter, where we find Father, Son and Spirit woven throughout the letter.

God the Father and salvation

As we see throughout the New Testament, God is identified as the Father of the Lord Jesus Christ (1:3). At the same time, God is also the Father of his people (1:17) through Jesus Christ (1:21). God's power keeps his people for a salvation ready to be revealed in the last time (1:4). Just as Jesus trusted his Father through his earthly trials (2:21–24) and God raised him from the dead (1:21), so Peter instructs God's people in each succeeding generation as exiles to trust in God as Father in the face of difficulty (1:17; 2:19–20), since God has caused us to be born again through the resurrection of Jesus (1:3). As exiles we should honour all people, fearing God above all (2:13–17), knowing that if we humble ourselves under the hand of God, he will also lift us up in due time (5:6–7). Just as Jesus' suffering led to glory as he trusted his Father, so should Christians be encouraged in the sovereign control of God even in the face of suffering, since an eternal inheritance awaits (4:12–19).

The role of each person of the Godhead in salvation appears to be rather clearly defined in 1 Peter. In addition to what we have seen in the trinitarian greeting, Peter writes that God caused believers to be born again through the resurrection of Jesus Christ (1:3), we come to believe in God through Jesus Christ (1:21) and spiritual sacrifices are made to God through Jesus Christ (2:5). Similarly, Peter's hope is that the Gentiles will glorify God when Jesus returns (2:12; cf. 1:7, 13; 5:4), which accords with Peter's later doxological statements that God may be glorified through Jesus Christ (4:11), and his insight that God has called his people to his eternal glory in Christ (5:10). This brief overview indicates that 1 Peter has much to say about God the Father in relation to salvation, particularly in relationship to his Son. Of course, Peter has much more to say about Jesus, which is the topic of my next heading.

God the Son and salvation

The Son is identified in 1 Peter as the Lord Jesus Christ, which we have seen reveals an incredibly high Christology, since Jesus as Lord means he is Lord of the universe, having ascended to the Father's right hand. Jesus is also the returning Lord, who will be revealed at the last day (1:7, 13; 5:4). Since Jesus is

---

12. Ibid., pp. 319–320, 334; Schreiner, *1, 2 Peter, Jude*, p. 57.

Lord, Christians are to honour him appropriately (3:15). Along with his status as Lord, the Son is said to be foreknown before the foundation of the world (1:20). Although the Son and Father have always enjoyed perfect fellowship, the foreknowledge in view in 1:20 is most likely in relation to the Son's role as redeemer.[13]

In this light it is clear that Jesus Christ is the one who suffers for salvation in 1 Peter (2:21). Jesus is the spotless lamb whose blood takes away sin (1:2, 19). Jesus is the one who bore our sins in his body on the tree (2:24; 4:1, 13), having been put to death in the flesh (3:18). Peter was not a modalist. It was the Son who became incarnate (1:20) and suffered on the cross (2:24; 5:1), and the Son entrusted himself personally to his Father (2:23). Additionally, it is clear that Jesus Christ is the one who was raised from the dead (1:3, 11, 21; 3:18, 22; cf. 4:13; 5:1). As the Great Shepherd of the sheep (2:25; 5:4), Jesus is also the spotless lamb of God who shed his blood for the salvation of his people. And as Shepherd, Jesus is the glorious, returning Lord of all who tenderly cares for his flock, leaving an example for the elders to care for the flock until he returns, at which time they will receive an unfading crown of glory (5:1–4).

God the Holy Spirit and salvation

1 Peter also has much to say about the Holy Spirit. We have already seen that the Spirit is the one who sanctifies God's people (1:2), which is a divine act. Peter also speaks of the Holy Spirit's activity before the coming of Jesus Christ in at least one, and maybe two, passages. In 1 Peter 1:10–12 we read of the prophets who prophesied about the sufferings of Christ and his subsequent glories (1:11), though they themselves did not live in the age of fulfilment (1:20).[14] Significantly, Peter tells us that the prophets were inspired by the Spirit of Christ, who is also the Holy Spirit (1:12) and the sanctifying Spirit (1:2), which underscores the continuity of salvation through the ages. Indeed, this same Holy Spirit inspired the preaching of the gospel that led to the salvation of Peter's own audience (1:12). Additionally, by identifying the Holy Spirit as the Spirit of Christ, Peter is also alluding to the pre-existence of Jesus, as he does again in 1:20.[15]

More broadly, 1 Peter 1:3–21 offers additional glimpses into the trinitarian nature of God. Following closely after the trinitarian greeting (1:2), Peter speaks

---

13. See Edmund P. Clowney, *The Message of 1 Peter: The Way of the Cross*, BST (Downers Grove: InterVarsity Press, 1988), p. 72.

14. So Schreiner, *1, 2 Peter, Jude*, pp. 74–76.

15. Ibid., p. 73.

of all three divine persons in relation to salvation. God is the holy Father of the Lord Jesus Christ (1:3, 16–17, 21), it is Jesus Christ the Son who suffered, was raised and is returning (1:3, 7, 11, 13, 18–21), and it is the Holy Spirit who inspired the prophets to speak of the sufferings and glory of Christ before the incarnation (1:11), and who, moreover, continued to empower the preaching of the gospel of Jesus Christ unto salvation in Peter's own day (1:12). Peter speaks of one plan of salvation accomplished by one God in three persons. Something similar may be in view in 2:5, where Peter speaks of spiritual sacrifices, acceptable to God, through Jesus Christ. It is probably that the sacrifices are wrought by the Holy Spirit, especially in the light of his association with worship elsewhere in the New Testament (John 4:24; Rom. 12:1; 1 Cor. 11 – 14; Phil. 3:3), though here he may have in view all that Christians do by the power of the Holy Spirit.[16] If the sacrifices in 2:5 are indeed offered by means of the Holy Spirit, then we have another text in 1 Peter that reveals a triadic shape for God.

Another text that may speak of the Holy Spirit's role in the economy of salvation before the coming of Christ is 1 Peter 3:18–19. These verses constitute part of one of the most debated passages in the New Testament (3:18–22), and interpretive questions are legion. However, for the present argument we should observe the general movement in the text that speaks of Jesus' resurrection and glorification following his death (3:18, 22). However one takes *zōopoiētheis de pneumati* (3:18), it is quite likely that a reference to the Holy Spirit is in view, whether it is the agency or the sphere of the Spirit, since elsewhere in the New Testament the Holy Spirit is constitutive of the new life and new age inaugurated by Christ's resurrection (Rom. 1:3–4; 1 Cor. 15:42–49; cf. Rom. 8:11).[17] One's understanding of s/Spirit in 3:18 affects one's understanding of the proclamation to the spirits in 3:19. If one understands *pneumati* in 3:18 to refer to the Holy Spirit, then we may have in 3:19 a similar view to the role of the Spirit to what we saw in 1:11–12 – just as the Spirit of Christ spoke through the prophets, so the Spirit of Christ preached righteousness through Noah (cf. 2 Peter 2:5). However, this is by no means certain.

Finally, two passages in 1 Peter 4 further reveal aspects of the Holy Spirit. First, in 1 Peter 4:14 we read of 'the Spirit of glory and of God' (*to tēs doxēs kai to tou theou*), or possibly 'the Spirit of glory, namely the Spirit of God'. The Greek phrasing can be translated in various ways, but it seems eminently probable that Peter is somehow identifying the Holy Spirit (who rests on believers; cf. Isa.

---

16. Ibid., p. 107.
17. Cf. Michaels, *1 Peter*, p. 205.

11:2) with the divine glory. This is not the way one would speak of a *created* spirit. Peter's apparent mention of the divinity of the Spirit fits with the divine work of the Spirit mentioned earlier (1:2), and the emphasis on the glory of Christ through the Spirit elsewhere in 1 Peter (1:11, 21; 4:11, 13; 5:1, 4, 10). It is also instructive that we find Christ, the Spirit and God all mentioned in brief scope in 4:14: the same Spirit who was on Christ rests on believers in their identification with Jesus' suffering (4:13–14, 16), and is also known as the Spirit of God.[18]

A second text from 1 Peter that seems to speak of the Holy Spirit is 1 Peter 4:6, which speaks of living in or by the s/Spirit like God (*zōsi de kata theon pneumati*). It is usually a good exegetical instinct to understand *pneuma* language as a reference to the Holy Spirit when used in reference to God or Christ, and this seems to be the best option in 4:6. As we saw in 3:18, 1 Peter 4:6 sets up a contrast between flesh and s/Spirit. Since God is described as the one who lives according to the s/Spirit in 4:6, Peter is most likely referring again to the Holy Spirit, who is the same Spirit in view in relation to Jesus' resurrection life elsewhere in 1 Peter (3:18).[19]

Conclusion: 1 Peter

1 Peter has much to say about Father, Son and Spirit, but we must not miss the practical reasons for his letter. Peter was writing to encourage people who were facing difficulties because of their faith. Christ has not only redeemed his people, but set an example that we should follow in his steps, and this is ultimately for the glory of God (4:11; cf. 5:10–11).

2 Peter

2 Peter has much to say about the divinity of Jesus Christ. In fact, 2 Peter contains some of the most explicit language in the New Testament identifying Jesus as God. Therefore, we will look primarily at the divinity of Jesus in 2 Peter, before considering some triadic aspects as well.

Jesus as God

In 2 Peter 1:1 we find a reference to the righteousness of our God and Saviour Jesus Christ. The Greek phrasing (*tou theou hymōn kai sōtēros Iēsou Christou*) is

---

18. See ibid. pp. 264–265.

19. See also ibid. pp. 238–239; Schreiner, *1, 2 Peter, Jude*, pp. 208–210.

another example of the Granville Sharp rule we noted in James, which refers to one person.[20] In other words, Jesus is identified as our God and Saviour.[21] Further corroborating this view, in 1:3 we read that 'his' divine power has granted us 'all things that pertain to life and godliness'. The most natural antecedent to 1:3 is 'Jesus our Lord', which comes in the immediately preceding phrase (1:2). Moreover, 1:4 speaks of participating in the divine nature, which most likely has in view our growth in Christlikeness.[22] Therefore, to participate in the divine nature does not mean we become a part of God (the Creator–creature distinction is never abrogated), but that we become in practice more like Jesus Christ. To be like Jesus in holiness of character (1:4–10) is to participate in the divine nature.

Peter also states that Jesus will return (3:8–13; cf. 1:16), which is consistent with Jesus' identification as (resurrected and ascended) Lord throughout the letter (1:2, 8, 11, 14, 16; 2:20; 3:2, 10, 18). The certainty of Jesus' return is one of the key features of 2 Peter, which goes hand in hand with Jesus' identity as the glorious Lord. The glory of Jesus' exalted state, which will be revealed when he returns, was anticipated in the transfiguration during Jesus' earthly ministry, which points ahead to his power and coming (1:16–18).[23] 2 Peter ends in a similar way to how it opened, encouraging the audience to grow in the grace and knowledge of our (glorious) Lord and Saviour, Jesus Christ. Remarkably, 2 Peter ends with a doxology ascribing glory to Jesus Christ both now and for ever (3:18). Jesus is clearly divine in 2 Peter.

Father and Son
Although 2 Peter identifies Jesus as our God, he does not confuse the Father and the Son, though he does describe them in similar ways. 2 Peter speaks of the multiplication of grace and peace in the knowledge of God and of Jesus our Lord (*tou theou kai Iēsou tou kyriou hymōn*) in 1:2, which is most likely a reference to two divine persons: Father and Son.[24] Additionally, in 1:3 we clearly find a distinction between Father and Son, since God is identified as Father of the Lord Jesus Christ. Again we see that the Petrine epistles are not modalistic.

---

20. Wallace, *Greek Grammar*, pp. 270–277. Note similar constructions refer to one person in 2 Peter 1:11; 2:20; 3:18.

21. As noted earlier in this volume, *Saviour* is a divine title in the OT.

22. See Schreiner, *1, 2 Peter, Jude*, pp. 294–295; Gene L. Green, *Jude and 2 Peter*, BECNT (Grand Rapids: Baker Academic, 2008), p. 186.

23. Crowe, *Message of the General Epistles*, pp. 64–69.

24. See Richard J. Bauckham, *Jude, 2 Peter*, WBC 50 (Waco, Tex.: Word, 1983), p. 165.

At the same time, 2 Peter can also use interchangeable language (i.e. Lord or God) to refer to both the Father and the Son. Thus the Son is identified as God in 1:1, but elsewhere God seems most likely to refer to the Father (1:2–3, 17, 21; 2:4; 3:5). Likewise, the Father is sometimes identified as Lord (2:9, 11; 3:8–9), but this is a preferred title for Jesus in 2 Peter (1:2, 8, 11, 14, 16; 2:20; 3:2, 8–9, 15; 3:18) as in the context of early Christianity more broadly. One particularly noteworthy passage is 3:8–12, which seems to refer both to Jesus and the Father with the terminology of 'Lord' (cf. 3:8–9 with 3:10). Additionally, 3:12 refers to the coming of God. Is the Father or Jesus in view in 3:12? One's conclusion could go either way,[25] but it is clear that the Father and Son are distinct persons, and the return of Jesus can rightly be described as either the coming of the Lord (cf. 3:10) or the coming of God (cf. 1:1).

Father, Son and Spirit

We see the presence of all three divine persons together, albeit briefly, in the recounting of the transfiguration in 2 Peter 1:16–21. 2 Peter 1:17 speaks of the glory that the Son received from the Father, along with the voice from the majestic glory. Earlier, in the discussion of Matthew's Gospel, I suggested that in the biblical-theological context the glory cloud at the transfiguration (particularly in the light of the parallels with Jesus' baptism) may refer to the presence of the Holy Spirit. If so, the same may be true in the account of the transfiguration in 2 Peter 1:16–18. Even if one dismisses this possibility, however, a few verses later (1:21) we find explicit mention of the Holy Spirit, who inspired the prophets who spoke from God. What is striking is the continuity between God's speech, through the Holy Spirit, in Scripture in the light of the promise of Jesus' return. One could possibly construe the parallels as follows: just as God's word came from the majestic glory at the transfiguration (1:17–18, which may well be a reference to the Spirit's presence), providing a preview of the glory that will be manifested when Christ returns, so did the Spirit speak for God through the prophets of the return of Christ.[26] If this construal is correct, then the role of the Holy Spirit seems to point to the continuity of God's plan throughout the ages, as it did in 1 Peter. The word of God in Scripture, inspired by the Holy Spirit, is as sure as the voice Peter heard at the transfiguration. In sum, however one construes the details of 2 Peter 1:16–21, we clearly encounter all three divine

---

25. Cf. Schreiner, *1, 2 Peter, Jude*, p. 390; Bauckham, *Jude, 2 Peter*, p. 325.

26. Cf. Crowe, *Message of the General Epistles*, pp. 65–68; Kline, *Images*, p. 29. See also Vern S. Poythress, *The Manifestation of God: A Biblical Theology of God's Presence* (forthcoming), chs. 5, pp. 16–17, 43.

persons – Father, Son, and Spirit – in relation to the future salvation that will be consummated when Jesus returns.

1–3 John

Father and Son

The preface of 1 John (1:1–4) speaks of the pre-existence of the Son of God in a way that recalls the prologue of John's Gospel. 1 John speaks of the word of life that was from the beginning, which was with the Father. This life became manifest and was seen by John and his associates (1:1–2). Similarly, the Gospel of John speaks of the Word that was in the beginning with God (John 1:1–2; cf. Gen. 1:1), who was made flesh (John 1:14). In both texts the pre-existence of the Son of God is in view, who became incarnate and dwelt among us. Because of this our fellowship is with the Father and with his Son, Jesus Christ (1 John 1:3). Moreover, by identifying the Son as *eternal* life (1:2) John appears to speak of the timelessness of the Son's life – this is not just eternal life extending into the future, but eternal life that has always been true of the Son, in fellowship with his Father.[27] As the one who is defined by eternal life, Jesus has all life in himself, which is true only of God (cf. John 5:29). Creatures are limited by time; God is not.[28] Yet, remarkably, these verses also emphasize the fellowship we can have with the Son (1:3), who is eternal life.[29]

Throughout the Johannine epistles (especially 1 John) we see the unity of the Father and the Son. In addition to the preface of 1 John, we find that both Father and Son are sinless, in contrast to sinful humanity. God is light: in him there is no darkness of sin (1:5). If we say we do not sin, then the truth is not in us and we make God out to be a liar (1:8, 10). To walk in the light is to walk in fellowship with God, having our sins cleansed by the blood of Jesus Christ (1:7; cf. 1:9), our righteous Advocate with the Father (2:1). In addition, we read that the antichrist is the one who denies both Father and Son (2:22), whereas the one who confesses the Son also has the Father (2:23). Abiding in the message from the beginning ensures that we will continually abide with both Father and Son unto eternal life (2:24–25). Jesus is the life that became incarnate (1:2),

---

27. Cf. John R. W. Stott, *The Letters of John*, 2nd ed., TNTC 19 (Downer's Grove: InterVarsity Press, 1988), p. 63.

28. Cf. Bavinck, *Reformed Dogmatics*, vol. 2, pp. 160–164.

29. Cf. Stephen S. Smalley, *1, 2, 3, John*, WBC 51 (Waco, Tex.: Word, 1984), p. 10.

and Jesus is identified as (eternal) life throughout 1 John (5:11–13, 20). At the same time, life is constitutive of the Father (cf. John 5:21, 26), who grants eternal life (5:11, 16; cf. 2:25). In other words, one way we can perceive the unity of Father and Son is through the lens of life.

We also see the unity of Father and Son in the Father's sending of the Son (4:9–10, 14). Unfortunately, some have argued that the Father's sending of the Son to die amounts to an abusive, tyrannical act. However, this misguided view severely misunderstands the trinitarian works of God. We have seen that the outward works (*ad extra*) of the Trinity are indivisible. Therefore, both Father and Son (and Spirit) are united in the work of redemption; there is and can be absolutely no disharmony between Father, Son or Spirit.[30] Indeed, we read in 1 John 4:10 that the Father sent his Son to be a propitiation (*hilasmos*) for our sins because he loved us (cf. 4:19). This is the same love that characterizes the Son, who showed love by laying his life down for us (3:16; cf. 2 John 3). In addition, in 1 John to believe in the Son of God is tantamount to believing God (5:10). In the light of the profound unity we find between the Father and Son in 1 John it would not be out of character for the letter to end by identifying Jesus Christ, who is eternal life, as the true God (5:20).[31]

Though we clearly find the unity of the Father and Son in the Johannine epistles, we also do well to note distinctions between Father and Son. Thus it is the Father who sends the Son (4:9–10, 14), and it is the Son who becomes incarnate and serves as the propitiation for sins (1:2–3; 2:2, 22; 3:8, 16; 4:2, 10; 5:6–8). Though God cannot be seen (4:12, 20), we can see the Son of God who makes the Father known (1:1–3; 4:2, 14; 2 John 7). Additionally, our fellowship is with both the Father and his Son (1:3) at the same time, which bespeaks a distinction in persons.

Father, Son and Spirit

1 John also relates the Holy Spirit to the Father and the Son. In 2:20, 27 we read of the anointing of the Holy One, which most likely refers to the Holy Spirit. Significantly, the Holy One teaches believers all things, so there is no need to be taught by anyone else (e.g. the errors of the schismatics).[32] More specifically,

---

30. Bavinck, *Reformed Dogmatics*, vol. 2, pp. 259, 318–319.

31. Cf. Richard N. Longenecker, *The Christology of Early Jewish Christianity*, SBT 2.17 (London: SCM, 1970), pp. 136–141; Colin G. Kruse, *The Letters of John*, PNTC (Grand Rapids: Eerdmans, 2000), pp. 197–198; Robert W. Yarbrough, *1–3 John*, BECNT (Grand Rapids: Baker Academic, 2008), p. 319.

32. So Kruse, *Letters of John*, p. 153.

the Holy Spirit teaches about the realities of the Father and the Son (2:21–23), which are truths pertaining to salvation (cf. 5:11).

Another possible reference to the Holy Spirit comes in 3:9, which speaks of the seed (*sperma*) of God that abides in believers. The identity of this seed is debated, but a strong argument can be made that the Holy Spirit is in view since the seed appears to be the agent of new birth (cf. John 3:5–8), along with the operative principle enabling believers to walk in righteousness, in contrast to the schismatics (cf. 2:28 – 3:10).[33] If so, then the Holy Spirit would be viewed here as an anointing enabling sanctification, which would further comport with the sinlessness predicated of the Father and Son elsewhere in 1 John. Moreover, 1 John 3:4–9 would then evidence a triadic character: the Son of God appeared to destroy the works of the devil (3:8), God's Seed (Holy Spirit) enables true believers to practise righteousness (3:4–9), in order that they may be seen to be truly children of God (3:10).

An even clearer triadic pattern is seen in conjunction with the mention of the Holy Spirit in 3:24.[34] Those who keep God's commandments abide in God (3:24); God's commandment is to believe in his Son, Jesus Christ (3:23); we know God abides in us because of the Spirit he has given to us (3:24). We should abide in the Father (2:24; 3:24; 4:12) and the Son (2:6, 24, 27–28; 3:6), and it is the Spirit who provides the knowledge that we do (3:24). The role of the Spirit in this regard also points us to his role in providing assurance of salvation, which is an important concern in 1 John (5:13), since only a divine person can provide assurance of a divine salvation.[35]

We find a similar focus on abiding in conjunction with the Spirit in another triadic passage (1 John 4:7–21). In this context the love of God is particularly emphasized, and this love characterizes Father, Son and Spirit. Love is from God (4:7), and God is love (4:8). God demonstrates his love by sending his Son as a propitiation for our sins (4:9–10). If we love one another, then God's love abides in us, and we know this because of the Spirit God has given us (4:11–13). Again we get a glimpse into the profound unity of the triune God's works: God loved us, and sent his Son (4:9–10) – who also loves us (3:16; cf. 3:23) – as a sacrifice for sins, and God's Spirit provides assurance that we belong to God

---

33. See ibid., pp. 124–125, 153–154; Stott, *Letters of John*, p. 132; Christopher D. Bass, *That You May Know: Assurance of Salvation in 1 John*, NACSBT 5 (Nashville: B&H Academic), p. 114; contrast Yarbrough, *1–3 John*, p. 195.

34. Cf. Robert Letham, *The Holy Trinity: In Scripture, History, Theology, and Worship* (Phillipsburg, N.J.: P&R, 2004), p. 67.

35. Cf. Bavinck, *Reformed Dogmatics*, vol. 2, p. 312.

(4:13). Earlier the Spirit is associated with the truth of Jesus Christ (4:2, 6). The Spirit of God (4:2) testifies truly to God's children (4:4, 6) that Jesus Christ has come from God in the flesh (4:3). These verses underscore the agreement between Father, Son and Spirit, and therefore also exhibit a triadic shape.

Finally, we turn to 1 John 5:6–8. As is commonly known, in some translations and manuscript traditions 1 John 5:7 contains an explicit reference to the Trinity (the so-called Johannine comma). The AV phrases 5:7, 'For there are three that bear record in heaven, the Father, the Word, and the Holy Ghost: and these three are one.' As true as this statement may be, it is extremely improbable that it is original to 1 John. By way of illustration, in the early trinitarian controversies of the church this would have been a tailor-made passage for the church fathers to utilize as biblical evidence for the Trinity, but it is quoted by none of the Greek church fathers.[36] It is best explained as a later interpolation that probably derived from someone's marginal comment. However, to view the Johannine comma as secondary is not the same thing as saying that 1 John does not provide evidence for the Trinity. In fact, although I view the Johannine comma as spurious, I have argued throughout this section that we do find evidence for the Trinity in 1 John. Moreover, I believe we have good reason for reading 1 John 5:6–8, in its wider context, as evidence for a trinitarian understanding of God.

In 1 John 5:6 we read of Jesus Christ, who came by (or through) water and blood. We also read in 5:7–8 that there are three witnesses who agree: the Spirit, the water and the blood. This has historically been a tricky passage to understand, but the most probable interpretation in my view is that it refers to the entire ministry of Jesus, from his baptism (water) to his death (blood). The Spirit quite probably refers to the testimony of the Spirit at the baptism of Jesus (cf. John 1:29–34), and possibly the Spirit's presence throughout the entire ministry of Jesus.[37] This understanding recalls the Synoptic Gospels, in which the Father, Son and Spirit are all revealed at the baptism of Jesus.[38] Moreover,

---

36. Bruce M. Metzger, *A Textual Commentary on the Greek New Testament*, 2nd ed. (Stuttgart: Deutsche Bibelgesellschaft, 1994), pp. 647–649.

37. See D. A. Carson, 'The Three Witnesses and the Eschatology of 1 John', in Thomas E. Schmidt and Moisés Silva (eds.), *To Tell the Mystery: Essays on New Testament Eschatology. Festschrift for Robert H. Gundry*, JSNTSup 100 (Sheffield: JSOT Press, 1994), pp. 216–232.

38. Though the baptism of Jesus is not recorded in John, the testimony of John the Baptist regarding the Spirit's descent and remaining on Jesus probably refers to Jesus' baptism.

1 John 5:9 makes more explicit what is implicit in 5:6–8, namely that the Spirit (along with the water and the blood) provides testimony to Jesus Christ that God himself has given.[39] And in 5:10 we read that the testimony (from the Spirit) abides in those who believe in the Son of God, whereas those who do not believe God's testimony (through the Spirit) make God out to be a liar. Again we see the interplay between Father, Son and Spirit.

In sum, whatever one's view of the Johannine comma, it should be clear that the God of the Johannine epistles is described in triadic terms: Father, Son and Spirit, and this understanding is not limited to one contested verse.

Jude

Father and Son
Jude addresses his letter to those who are called, beloved by God the Father and kept for (or perhaps *by*) Jesus Christ (v. 1), indicating a shared divine status (the source of mercy, peace and love, v. 2), but a distinction in divine persons. This is confirmed throughout the letter, as the Father and Son are often mentioned in close proximity in relation to salvation. Thus in verse 4 Jude warns against those who pervert the grace of God into sensuality *and* deny our only Master and Lord, Jesus Christ, again placing Father and Son in close collocation in relation to salvation as he writes to contend for the faith that has been handed down (v. 3).

One of the most widely discussed verses in Jude is verse 5. Who was it that led the people out of Egypt? The twenty-eighth edition of the Nestle-Aland Greek text reads *Iēsous* (Jesus), whereas the twenty-seventh edition reads *kyrios* (Lord).[40] The text-critical arguments are complicated, and although either reading is possible, *Jesus* may be the best reading.[41] If so, then this would seem to be a rather clear indication of the pre-existence of Jesus, who was leading (and destroying) during the period of the wilderness generation in the Old Testament. However, even if *Lord* is the correct reading, the referent is quite probably still Jesus, in the light of Jude 4 and Jude's typical usage of *Lord* for

---

39. Stott, *Letters of John*, p. 181. Moreover, the *Spirit* also seems to testify to the reality that *Jesus Christ* was sent from *God* (4:1–6), further underscoring the trinitarian contours of 1 John.

40. The SBL Greek NT also reads *Iēsous*.

41. So several English translations, including ESV, NET, NLT. Alternatively, see NIV, NRSV, HCSB, NASB.

Jesus elsewhere.[42] If so, Jude 5 may be a reference to the pre-existence of the Son, similar to what we see elsewhere in the New Testament (e.g. 1 Cor. 10:4, 9). By speaking of Jesus as the Lord throughout his epistle (4, 14, 17, 21, 25) Jude demonstrates consistency with other New Testament authors, who view Jesus in glorious, exalted terms, which far exceeds the glory due to created beings.

Father, Son and Spirit

The Holy Spirit is also explicitly mentioned in Jude. In Jude 19 we read of scoffers who are devoid of the (Holy) Spirit, who cause divisions. In contrast, Jude's audience is to build themselves up in their holy faith, praying in the Holy Spirit (20). We should not miss the significance that our prayers are to be made in the Holy Spirit.[43] This fits with the traditional trinitarian understanding that the Spirit must be divine if he is to provide us genuine fellowship with the Father and the Son.[44] At this juncture in the epistle Jude moves seamlessly between persons of the Godhead, exhorting his audience to pray in the Holy Spirit (20), keep themselves in the love of God (21a) and wait for the mercy of the Lord Jesus Christ (21b). This is not an *argument for* a trinitarian understanding of God, but it reveals a deeper structure of thought in which salvation is triadically shaped.

Jude ends with one of the great benedictions of the New Testament (24–25). Again the emphasis is on the glory of God as Saviour, which comes through the Lord Jesus Christ. The glory, majesty, dominion and authority belong to God for ever and ever. It is also interesting that God as Saviour is able to present his people faultless before his glorious presence with great joy (24). Though the Holy Spirit is not mentioned in verse 24, the combination of God's glory and God's presence reminds one of the Holy Spirit's close relationship to God's glory elsewhere in Scripture (cf. 1 Peter 4:14). Jude's benediction, however, appears to focus on the glories of the Father and the Son. Nevertheless, we know from Jude's exhortations that we are to pray in the Holy Spirit, and by so doing can keep ourselves in the love of God as we await the return of the Lord Jesus Christ.

© Brandon D. Crowe, 2016

---

42. See variously Simon J. Gathercole, *The Preexistent Son: Recovering the Christologies of Matthew, Mark, and Luke* (Grand Rapids: Eerdmans, 2006), pp. 36–40; Bauckham, *Jude, 2 Peter*, p. 49; Tommy Wasserman, *The Epistle of Jude: Its Text and Transmission*, ConBNT 43 (Stockholm: Almqvist & Wiksell, 2006), pp. 262–266; Schreiner, *1, 2 Peter, Jude*, pp. 444–445.

43. See Bauckham, *Jude, 2 Peter*, p. 113.

44. Bavinck, *Reformed Dogmatics*, vol. 2, p. 312.

8. AN APOCALYPTIC TRINITARIAN MODEL: THE BOOK OF DANIEL'S INFLUENCE ON REVELATION'S CONCEPTION OF THE TRINITY

Benjamin L. Gladd

Many scholars deny the existence of the Trinity in the Old Testament, since they contend that it strikes at the heart of monotheism. Yet how could the Old Testament not speak of one of the most important doctrines of the Christian faith? Admittedly, the doctrine of the Trinity remains undeveloped in the Old Testament, but several passages are intentionally enigmatic and await a final, trinitarian interpretation that is in keeping with the original intention of the Old Testament author.[1] John 12:41 expresses one of the most tantalizing statements in this regard: 'Isaiah said this because he [Isaiah] saw Jesus' glory and spoke about him.' This statement, occurring in the midst of Jesus' interaction with an unbelieving crowd, claims that the prophet Isaiah somehow perceived the person of Christ in his heavenly vision in Isaiah 6. According to John's Gospel the prophet Isaiah had *some* inkling of Christ's pre-existence or 'glory'.[2]

---

1. For further discussion of this difficult issue see G. K. Beale and Benjamin L. Gladd, *Hidden but Now Revealed: A Biblical Theology of Mystery* (Downers Grove: InterVarsity Press, 2014), pp. 257–259.

2. Richard Bauckham rightly proposes that the background to Jesus' divinity is rooted in Jewish monotheism – Christ is to be identified with the unique person of the Lord himself (*Jesus and the God of Israel: God Crucified and Other Studies on the New*

The book of Revelation contains one of the most elaborate pictures of the Trinity in the New Testament. What is hinted at in other portions of the New Testament becomes explicit in John's Apocalypse. The Trinity in Revelation is so complex and developed that writing on the subject can easily become unwieldy. Due to the constraints of this chapter I will explore one aspect of the triune God in Revelation. I will argue that the book of Daniel provides a rough blueprint or model for John's conception of the Trinity.

In seed form Daniel sketches how the persons of the triune God relate to one another, particularly how God reveals mysteries, provides illumination to end-time revelations by the Spirit and executes them through the Son of Man. Some portions of Daniel are notoriously complex, even cryptic, but all the necessary ingredients remain for a robust understanding of the Trinity. The apostle John is indebted to Daniel's conception of God and further develops how the triune God communicates within the Godhead and how the triune God communicates to the church.

God as revealer of mysteries

Though it is tempting to skim past Revelation 1:1 and pursue the more dramatic portions of the book, we must not succumb to this temptation. The first verse of Revelation divulges with subtlety how God discloses the revelation to Christ. John opens his book with a 'chain' of revelation: 'The revelation from Jesus Christ, *which God gave him* [*hēn edōken autō ho theos*] to show his servants *what must soon take place* [*ha dei genesthai en tachei*]. He made it known [*esēmanen*] by sending his angel to his servant John' (1:1).[3] Though John does not explain in detail how God[4] reveals the content of the vision to Christ, he hints at what the content of the vision will entail. As a few commentators have argued, the expression 'what must soon take place' (*ha dei genesthai en tachei*) and the key verb 'made it known' or, better, 'signified' (*esēmanen*) probably recall the book of Daniel, particularly

---

Testament's Christology and Divine Identity [Milton Keynes: Paternoster; Grand Rapids: Eerdmans, 2008]). I augment this proposal in that the OT does indeed contain some enigmatic texts that anticipate what later biblical authors would develop into a robust doctrine of the Trinity.

3. Unless otherwise noted, all biblical references are from the NIV.

4. References to 'God', unless otherwise noted, refer to the 'Father', first person of the Trinity.

chapter 2.[5] But commentators have yet to capitalize on the phrase 'God gave him' (*edōken autō ho theos*) and apply it thoroughly to the book's prologue.[6] What is the significance of God's 'giving' the visions to Christ, especially in the light of the surrounding allusions to the book of Daniel? For us to comprehend this often overlooked clause, we will heed John's clues and consult the book of Daniel to determine the significance of God's 'giving' the revelation to Christ.

God as the source of revelation in Daniel

Much of the book of Daniel portrays God as the unrivalled source of wisdom. Each chapter relentlessly drives home this point, culminating in the symbolic portrayal of God as the 'Ancient of Days' with 'white' hair, probably a reference to his unsurpassed wisdom in 7:9 (cf. Lev. 19:32; Prov. 16:31; 20:29). *Central to the book of Daniel is God's ability to disclose his 'wisdom' or 'mysteries' to select individuals* (Nebuchadnezzar and Daniel). At its most basic level the term 'mystery' (*mystērion*) concerns God's *revealing* his wisdom.[7] This accounts for the high appropriation of revealing or disclosing vocabulary throughout the book of Daniel.[8]

In Daniel 2 God 'reveals' a 'mystery' to Daniel that concerns the destruction of hostile, pagan nations and the establishment of God's end-time kingdom (2:28, 44–45). Although revelatory language is lacking in chapter 4, it is still valid to call Nebuchadnezzar's dream in this chapter a revelation (cf. 4:9). The same characterization can be applied to Daniel's visions in chapters 7–12. Further-more, in 7:1 Daniel saw a 'dream, and visions' that are probably analogous to

5. E.g. G. K. Beale, *The Book of Revelation*, NIGTC (Grand Rapids: Eerdmans, 1999), pp. 181–183.

6. The term *didōmi* (to give) takes on a semi-technical use in Revelation, particularly in chs. 6–21. In most of the occurrences God is either the explicit or implicit subject of the verb. Oftentimes God's enemies are 'given' (implied subject with the passive voice) authority to execute some form of judgment (6:2, 4, 8; 7:2; etc.). This observation is significant in that the verb is connected to God's unmatched, sovereign power. Therefore the visions contained within the Apocalypse have been disclosed by God, who possesses unrivalled wisdom and power.

7. For more discussion of mystery in Daniel see Benjamin L. Gladd, *Revealing the Mysterion: The Use of Mystery in Daniel and Second Temple Judaism with Its Bearing on First Corinthians*, BZNW 160 (Berlin: de Gruyter, 2008), pp. 20–43.

8. The verb 'to reveal' (*glh*) appears eight times, referring to God's 'disclosing', 'mysteries' (2:19, 28–30), 'deep and hidden things' (2:22) and a visionary 'message' (10:1).

Nebuchadnezzar's dreams in chapters 2 and 4. Just as God delivers his wisdom to Daniel to know and interpret the dreams of Nebuchadnezzar in chapters 2–4, God directly discloses his wisdom to Daniel in chapters 7–12 and furnishes Daniel with wisdom to understand them.

God initially reveals wisdom, and also discloses the interpretative portion of the revelation. In chapter 2 Nebuchadnezzar dreams and desires to know the interpretation (2:1–13). God reveals both the dream and the interpretation – the mystery – to Daniel in a 'night' 'vision' (2:19), outlined in 2:31–45. This disclosure of God's wisdom is marked by the term 'interpretation' (*pešer*), a term used thirty-four times in Daniel. In Daniel 2 and 4 Nebuchadnezzar receives the mystery and Daniel interprets the visions, whereas in Daniel 7 – 12 the prophet Daniel receives the initial dream report and the angel interprets the visions. A distinctive, apocalyptic mark of Daniel is the nature of twofold revelation in contrast to other places in the Old Testament where the prophets directly receive God's revelation.

The upshot of this brief survey is that God, according to the book of Daniel, is the *source* of divine and hidden wisdom and chooses to disclose this wisdom to certain individuals. God also delivers the interpretative portion of the visions to other recipients.

God as the ultimate source of revelation in the Apocalypse

The model outlined above fits remarkably well here in Revelation 1:1, where God 'gave' the vision to Christ concerning 'what must soon take place'. Though the word 'mystery' is not found in the prologue (cf. 1:20; 10:7; 17:5, 7), it is probably implied, since the book fits within the genre of 'apocalypses'. Within apocalyptic literature the word 'mystery' (a previously hidden revelation that is subsequently revealed) is the means by which God discloses his message. God, according to Revelation 1:1, unveils his end-time mysteries to Christ, who then communicates them to the angel.

At the end of the Apocalypse, in the epilogue (22:6–21), God is once again described in an identical manner. The beginning of the epilogue reinforces and refines the themes introduced in 1:1. Here in the epilogue God is characterized as the ultimate source of revelation, a characterization that describes his interaction with other prophets. Moreover, John tightens this connection by alluding once more to Daniel 2:28, 45.[9]

---

9. Beale, *Revelation*, pp. 1124–1126.

Daniel 2:28, 45 (LXX [Theo])[10]	*Revelation 22:6*
'he has made known to King Nabouchodonosor *what must happen at the end of days [ha dei genesthai ep' eschatōn tōn hēmerōn]*' (2:28).	'The angel said to me, "These words are *trustworthy and true [pistoi kai alēthinoi]*. The Lord, the God who inspires the prophets, sent his angel to show his servants *the things that must soon take place [ha dei genesthai en tachei]*."'
'The great God has made known to the king *what must happen after this [ha dei genesthai meta tauta]*, and the dream is *true [alēthinon]*, and its interpretation *trustworthy [pistē]*' (2:45).	

Why does John weave these allusions to Daniel into the epilogue? Not only do they signal the initial fulfilment of the arrival of the eternal kingdom, as described in Daniel 2, but they also affirm God's character as the sole source of unveiled mysteries. In contrast to the 'beasts' in Revelation, who attempt to imitate God's truth through deception and 'blasphemies' (e.g. 13:5–18), God's revelation is without corruption and genuinely true. By framing the Apocalypse with God's ability to reveal mysteries in the prologue and epilogue John reinforces the authenticity of the revelation, so that the churches will be encouraged to persevere in the midst of deception.

Christ as the revealer of mysteries

Not only is God presented as the source of revelation in 1:1, but Christ too occupies a distinct yet crucial role. John opens the book with a somewhat ambiguous phrase *Apokalypsis Iēsou Christou* (1:1a). Commentators differ as to what type of genitive construction this. On the one hand, we could render this as 'a revelation *about* Jesus Christ' (objective genitive). On the other, it could be 'a revelation *from* Christ' (subjective genitive). For a number of reasons, the latter is probably most likely.[11] If the visions contained in John's Apocalypse are indeed 'from Christ', it forces the reader to pause and contemplate how the second member of the Trinity plays a unique role in disclosing revelation.

---

10. Unless otherwise noted, all quotations from the LXX are taken from the NETS.
11. Grant R. Osborne, *Revelation*, BECNT (Grand Rapids: Baker, 2002), p. 52.

Revelation 1:1 states, '*He made it known* [*esēmanen*] by sending his angel to his servant John.' The subject of the verb *sēmainō* (to make known) is not obvious and could be either God or Christ, but many commentators argue that Christ is indeed the subject.[12] Perhaps not coincidentally, according to the Old Greek translation of Daniel (with the exception of 2:15) God is the only one who 'signifies' or 'symbolizes' the visions (2:23, 30, 45 OG).[13] But here in Revelation 1:1 Christ communicates the symbolic visions to the angel(s).

One of the most riveting descriptions in the prologue occurs in 1:14, where John describes the Son of Man as embodying elements of the Ancient of Days, as found in Daniel 7:9: 'The hair on his [the Son of Man's] head was white like wool, as white as snow, and his eyes were like blazing fire.' By graphically describing the Son of Man as possessing 'white hair' John underscores Christ's inimitable wisdom, the same wisdom that God alone possesses.

A key distinctive of apocalyptic literature is mediation of revelation by angels. Typically, God issues a revelation, and a prominent angel communicates that revelation to an individual.[14] In Revelation 1:1 the 'chain' of communication is both traditional and unique. Not surprisingly, God is the ultimate source of the revelation, but Christ occupies a unique role in the sequence: 'God gave him [Christ] to show his servants what must soon take place. He made it known by sending his angel to his servant John.' The sequence of the chain is as follows:

God → Christ → angel → John → seven churches

In the following verse we read, '[John] who testifies to everything he saw – that is, *the word of God* [*ton logon tou theou*] and *the testimony of Jesus Christ* [*tēn martyrian Iēsou Christou*]' (1:2). Christ plays a unique role in the communication of the visions (a 'revelation from Christ', 1:1a). Christ is also the ultimate 'witness' of God's revelation in that he faithfully communicates it to the angels and ensures its truthfulness. The epilogue also touches on Christ's role as the supreme

---

12. David E. Aune, *Revelation 1–5*, WBC 52A (Dallas: Word, 1997), p. 15.

13. E.g. Dan. 2:45b says, 'The great God *has shown* [*esēmane*] the king what will be at the end of the days, and the vision is precise, and the meaning of it trustworthy' (NETS).

14. According to The Apocalypse Group at the Society of Biblical Literature, '*"Apocalypse" is a genre of revelatory literature with a narrative framework,* in which a revelation is mediated by an otherworldly being *to a human recipient, disclosing a transcendent reality which is both temporal, insofar as it envisages eschatological salvation, and spatial insofar as it involves another, supernatural world*' (John J. Collins, 'Introduction: Towards the Morphology of a Genre', *Semeia* 14 [1979], p. 9, italics original).

witness to God's revelation: '*He who testifies* [*ho martyrōn*] to these things says, "Yes, I am coming soon"' (22:20).

These observations suggest that the book of Daniel presents God as all wise and the supreme revealer of mysteries. By alluding to key portions of the book of Daniel in the prologue and epilogue John portrays the first member of the Trinity as functioning in an identical fashion: the great and sovereign Lord has revealed his wisdom once more to a select individual. But John also develops Daniel's configuration of the process of revelation by claiming that the revelation is 'from Christ' and giving Christ a prominent position in his chain of communication. Christ does more than simply mediate the revelation; he is the supreme 'witness' and plays some role in the source of God's revelation (1:2).[15]

The Spirit as illuminator of Revelation

The Spirit, the third member of the Trinity, is also introduced in the prologue and plays a remarkable role in the book of Revelation. John first mentions the Spirit in the trinitarian formula of 1:4–5: 'Grace and peace to you from him who is, and who was, and who is to come, and from *the seven spirits* [*tōn hepta pneumatōn*][16] before his throne, and from Jesus Christ' (cf. 3:1; 4:5; 5:6). The title 'the seven spirits' is unique, and commentators have good reason to ascribe Zechariah 4 as the background to this title ('seven lamps', 4:2; 'Spirit', 4:6; 'seven eyes of the LORD that range throughout the earth', 4:10; see Rev. 5:6).

The connection to Zechariah 4 in Revelation 1:4–5 is strong and is probably the dominant Old Testament passage; however, the book of Daniel could be considered as a secondary background to this unusual description in Revelation. The number 'seven' carries symbolic overtones within Daniel, particularly as it relates to a complete period of time. For example, 'seven times' will 'pass' until Nebuchadnezzar is restored (4:16, 23, 25, 32). Perhaps the most noteworthy occurrence of 'seven' is found in Daniel 9, where '*seventy "sevens"* [*šābuʿîm šibʿîm*] are decreed' (9:24). The remainder of the vision makes heavy use of this symbolic number: 'seven "sevens", and sixty-two "sevens"' (9:25), 'sixty-two "sevens"' (9:26) and 'one "seven" . . . "seven"' (9:27). Conceptually, the Spirit's

---

15. Richard Bauckham rightly adds, 'For John it seems that Jesus is the source, not the intermediary, of revelation . . . for John Jesus belongs with God as the giver [of revelation], while the angel belongs with John as instrument' (*The Climax of Prophecy: Studies in the Book of Revelation* [New York: T&T Clark, 1993], p. 135).

16. Cf. 4Q381 f76_77.13; *T. Reub.* 2.1–3; *T. Sol.* 8.1.

role in Revelation resonates within the book of Daniel, particularly the way in which the Spirit illuminates the meaning of God's end-time revelation.

The Spirit as illuminator in Daniel

Not only does the number 'seven' take on apocalyptic overtones in Daniel, but the Spirit also plays a key role in the book of Daniel, particularly *as the one who illuminates God's end-time revelation*. What makes Daniel unique in contrast to other prophetic literature (Isaiah, Jeremiah, Ezekiel, etc.) is the relationship between the presence of God's Spirit and the illumination of 'mysteries' or God's hidden wisdom. The book of Daniel coins the term 'mystery' and relentlessly insists that only the Spirit can impart understanding of the term. A careful reading of Daniel's narrative sheds light on the Spirit's work in furnishing understanding to the recipient of apocalyptic revelation.

A few commentators have recognized the significance of wisdom disputations or 'court narratives' in the book of Daniel. These court narratives in the book of Daniel, like Joseph and Esther, tell the story of a wise courtier whose wisdom far exceeds all others. This success story stands in direct opposition to the wisdom of their opponents.

Within these court narratives the person of Daniel, who possesses the Spirit, stands in contrast to the foolish Babylonians. In chapter 1 'wisdom' is used to characterize the young men exiled from Jerusalem, 'youths . . . showing intelligence in every branch of wisdom, endowed with understanding and discerning knowledge, and who had ability for serving in the king's court' (Dan. 1:4 NASB). It also appears once again in 1:17, describing Daniel and company, but here God is the source of such wisdom: 'God gave them knowledge and intelligence in every branch of literature and wisdom' (NASB). This verse is paradigmatic for the book of Daniel and prepares the reader for Daniel's role in chapter 2.[17] Daniel is much wiser than the Babylonians: 'he [Nebuchadnezzar] found them [Daniel and friends] ten times better than all the magicians and enchanters in his whole kingdom' (1:20).

In Daniel 2, verses 2–13 constitute the longest discourse on the futility of Babylonian wisdom. It is no coincidence that Daniel and his friends have received surpassing 'knowledge' and 'wisdom' in 1:17–20, a passage that immediately precedes the embarrassing situation of the so-called Babylonian wise men (Dan. 4:6; 5:8). Nebuchadnezzar, using his entire arsenal, beckons all of

17. John J. Collins, *Daniel*, Hermeneia (Minneapolis: Fortress, 1993), p. 144.

his wise men in 2:2: 'the king summoned the magicians, enchanters, sorcerers
and astrologers to tell him what he had dreamed'. The range of wise men is
extensive: magicians,[18] enchanters, sorcerers and astrologers, certainly representing the epitome of Babylonian wisdom.

The Babylonian wise men are left helpless. Unless they have dream
data they will not be able to issue an interpretation (they plead twice for the
king to relate the dream [2:4, 7]). A somewhat paradigmatic passage is 2:2–11,
when the diviners cry out, 'the king summoned the magicians, enchanters,
sorcerers and astrologers to tell him what he had dreamed . . . No one can
reveal it to the king except the gods, and they do not live among humans.'
The wise Babylonians declare that they are not privy to direct revelation. They
are incapable and ill equipped to relate and explain the dream.

Babylonian deities simply do not divulge such information to the wise men.
But Daniel's God is not like the gods; he is characterized by revealing. In direct
contrast to 2:10–11 Daniel states:

> As for the mystery about which the king has inquired, neither wise men, conjurers,
> magicians, nor diviners are able to declare it to the king. However, there is a God in
> heaven who reveals mysteries, and He has made known to King Nebuchadnezzar
> what will take place in the latter days. (2:27–28 NASB; see v. 47)

Therefore these two passages (2:10–11, 27–28) are significant for one's overall
interpretation of the book, for they establish the polemic between Daniel and
Babylon's wise men. The nature of the polemic between these two parties is
not primarily about Daniel's method over against Babylonian divination, but
Daniel's divinely revealed wisdom juxtaposed with the idolatrous wisdom of the
Babylonians. At this juncture, when Daniel clashes with the Babylonians,
the Spirit emerges as a key person in Daniel's narrative.

It is impossible for diviners to receive direct revelation to this extent, for
omens interpret what is already revealed. But Daniel's God does produce direct
revelation: 'there is a God in heaven who reveals mysteries' (2:28). Therefore
Daniel is truly wise because his wisdom comes directly from the true God. It
can thus be stated that Daniel is not wise on his own accord but because of his
God and the Spirit's work.

Nebuchadnezzar once more summons his wise men in chapter 4 to interpret the dream (4:6–7). But this passage differs from chapter 2 in that
Nebuchadnezzar does explicitly relate his dream. Now the Babylonians have

---

18. See Gen. 41:8, 24; Exod. 7:11, 22; 8:3, 14; 9:11.

their chance – the dream books are open and the interpreters are ready. But, to the king's great displeasure, the wise men have failed again, even after he gave them his dream. At this point the narrative points out the utter weakness of the Babylonian diviners. Finally, Nebuchadnezzar calls on Daniel in 4:8 [4:5 MT]: 'Finally, Daniel came into my presence and I told him the dream. (He is called Belteshazzar, after the name of my god, and *the spirit of the holy gods* [*rûaḥ-'ĕlāhîn qaddîšîn*] is in him.).' The LXX (Theo) translation tweaks this phrase a bit, by using the adjective 'holy' to modify 'spirit': 'who has a holy, divine spirit in himself' (*hos pneuma theou hagion en heautō echei*). The result is a clear reference to the person of the Spirit, and his role in Daniel's grasp of Nebuchadnezzar's dream.

Daniel and the diviners will collide once again in chapter 5, but this time under Belshazzar. The king celebrates a 'great feast' with sacred vessels, but 'Suddenly the fingers of a human hand appeared and wrote on the plaster of the wall' (5:5). Belshazzar beckons the 'enchanters, astrologers and diviners' (5:7), but this enigmatic writing proves too much for them: 'Then all the king's wise men came in, but they could not read the writing or tell the king what it meant' (5:8). Their wisdom fails once more, but Daniel again succeeds where the Babylonians faltered (5:25–28). Daniel can decipher the enigmatic writing because he has the 'spirit of the holy gods' (5:11). The Aramaic reads 'spirit of the holy gods' (*rûaḥ-'ĕlāhîn qaddîšîn*), and the LXX (Theo) renders this phrase as the 'spirit of God' (*pneuma theou*).

In the following verse the queen reminds Belshazzar why his father promoted Daniel: 'He [Nebuchadnezzar] did this because Daniel, whom the king called Belteshazzar, was found to have *a keen mind* [*rûaḥ yattîrāh*]' (5:12). Once again one version of the LXX removes the ambiguity here (the word *rûaḥ* here probably refers to Daniel's person or mind [cf. NIV, ESV, NJPS]). The OG translation reads 'holy spirit' (*pneuma hagion*).[19]

In the final vision of the book of Daniel this theme of understanding 'mysteries' continues, but is applied to many within Israel. Daniel 11:33 is the most explicit: '*Those who are wise* [*maśkîlê 'ām*] will instruct many, though for a time they will fall by the sword or be burned or captured or plundered' (cf. 11:34–35; 12:3, 10). Though enigmatic on several levels, we can at least

---

19. Note that the Theo version of the LXX reads 'extraordinary spirit' (*pneuma perisson*). The same formula appears once again in Dan. 6:3 [6:4 MT], 'he [Daniel] possessed *an extraordinary spirit* [*rûaḥ yattîrāh*]'. Both versions of the LXX follow suit; the OG reads 'holy spirit' (*pneuma hagion*) and Theo, 'extraordinary spirit' (*pneuma perisson*).

discern that a few within Israel, the 'wise', will inform the remnant within Israel (i.e. the 'many'). As some have recognized, the figure Daniel ought to be considered as one of the 'wise'.[20] The significance of this connection is that the righteous Israelites will all, in some way, be 'little Daniels' and understand God's wisdom concerning the events of the 'latter days'.

By unpacking in some detail the broader narrative of Daniel we have learned three items: (1) Daniel's God-given ability to understand 'mysteries' stands in contrast to the 'wise' Babylonians. He succeeds where they fail. (2) The Aramaic and Greek editions of Daniel explicitly attribute Daniel's acumen to understand wisdom to the third person of the Trinity. (3) In the latter days righteous Israelites will, like Daniel, understand God's apocalyptic wisdom, presumably through the Spirit's enablement.

The seven spirits of Revelation

As stated above, the introductory portion prologue of Revelation (1:1–4) is peculiar on a few fronts. Recall that only God and Christ are mentioned: 'The revelation from Jesus Christ, which God gave him' (1:1a). The Spirit is not mentioned until 1:4, within the salutation portion of the letter to the seven churches: 'To the seven churches in the province of Asia: Grace and peace to you from him who is, and who was, and who is to come, and from *the seven spirits* before his throne, and from Jesus Christ' (1:4–5a). The Spirit is found here in conjunction with God and Christ, a pattern found in introductory portions elsewhere in the New Testament (e.g. 1 Peter 1:1–2).

Remarkably, the Spirit plays a prominent role in Revelation 2 – 3 in a series of formulaic expressions: 'Whoever has ears, let them hear what the *Spirit* says to the churches' (2:7a; see 2:17, 29; 3:6, 13, 22). These references to the Spirit's role in the process of revelation are most peculiar in the light of the chain of communication in 1:1. Why does John omit the Spirit in the chain of communication in 1:1, yet prominently include him here in Revelation 2 – 3? Is not the Spirit a cardinal agent of revelation?[21] A bird's eye view of

---

20. E.g. Stefan Beyerle, 'Daniel and Its Social Setting', in John J. Collins and Peter W. Flint (eds.), *The Book of Daniel: Composition and Reception*, VTSup 83 (Leiden: Brill, 1993), pp. 205–228.

21. Note also that John appears to develop Matthew's expression ('whoever has ears, let them hear' [Matt. 11:15; 13:9, 43]) by explicitly inserting the Spirit's role (Beale, *Revelation*, pp. 236–239; Bauckham, *Climax of Prophecy*, pp. 92–117).

the Spirit in the book of Revelation causes us to pause once more. Explicit references to the Spirit tend to be clustered in Revelation. The term 'Spirit' (*pneuma*) is found a total of twenty times in Revelation, eight of which occur in chapters 2–3.

Determining the significance of these observations is not readily apparent. A clue is found, however, at the beginning and end of each letter to the churches. Each letter begins and ends in nearly identical fashion. For example, in the letter to the church in Ephesus the letter begins with 'To the angel of the church in Ephesus write: *These are the words of him* [Christ]' (2:1a) and ends with 'Whoever has ears, let them hear what the *Spirit* says to the churches' (2:7a).[22] The remaining six letters follow suit (2:8, 11–12, 17–18, 29; 3:1, 6). Each letter is prefaced with an introductory message from the Son of Man and culminates with the Spirit's role in the proclamation of the letter. The Spirit enables the reception of the Son of Man's prophetic message and aids in applying its truths to the congregations of the seven churches. We could thus synthesize this configuration with the chain of communication in 1:1: *the revelation originates from God, is mediated and borne witness to by Christ to an angel, then to John, and to the seven churches, which are dependent upon the Spirit's work to understand and apply the visions.* Without the Spirit's help the visions would fall upon deaf ears. 'The Spirit brings to the churches the powerful word of Christ, rebuking, encouraging, promising and threatening, touching and drawing the hearts, minds and consciences of its hearers.'[23]

One of the central themes in the book of Revelation is the admonition for the churches to understand the visions and its symbols. Revelation 1:3 programmatically reads, 'Blessed is the one who reads aloud the words of this prophecy, and blessed are those *who hear it* and *take to heart* what is written in it, because the time is near.' The words to 'hear' (*hoi akouontes*) and 'take to heart' (*tērountes*) refer to spiritual insight and thoughtful application of the book's truths. Moreover, Revelation generally divides humanity into two people groups: those who follow the lamb and those who follow the beast. Individuals who worship the lamb understand the truth about God and his plan for the cosmos, whereas those who worship the beast are beguiled and believe his lies. A dividing factor

---

22. In the letter to the church in Sardis the Son of Man is portrayed as 'him who holds the seven spirits' and the 'seven stars' (3:1). This indicates the close relationship between Christ's message and the Spirit's role in enabling the churches and their representatives (i.e. the 'stars') to understand and apply its message.

23. Bauckham, *Climax of Prophecy*, p. 161.

between these two groups is the Spirit's work in the lives of the believers.[24] Without the aid of the Spirit, believers are unable to perceive Revelation's mysteries.[25]

The effect of these observations from Revelation is clear enough: the Spirit functions in the same capacity in Revelation as he does in the book of Daniel. In both instances the Spirit gives individuals the ability to comprehend apocalyptic 'mysteries'. Much like the exchange between Daniel and the Babylonian 'wise' men, Spirit-filled believers in Revelation stand in stark contrast to those unable to perceive the truth. As mentioned above, Daniel 11 envisions the 'wise ones' as instructing the 'many' (i.e. the righteous Israelites). Revelation picks up on this pattern by considering John to be a 'wise' one and instructing the 'many' (i.e. the seven churches). *All* believers now possess the Spirit-enabled capacity to grasp the divine mysteries of Revelation (cf. 1 Cor. 2:6–16).

The Son of Man as the executor of Daniel's visions

Now that we have discussed the first and third persons of the Trinity, we will turn to the person of Christ and how he fits into Daniel's framework. We need not look very far. In the inaugural vision of Revelation Christ is explicitly identified as the 'Son of Man':

> I turned round to see the voice that was speaking to me. And when I turned I saw seven golden lampstands, and among the lampstands was someone like *a son of man*, dressed in a robe reaching down to his feet and with a golden sash round his chest. *The hair on his head was white like wool, as white as snow*, and his eyes were like blazing fire. His feet were like bronze glowing in a furnace, and his voice was like the sound of rushing waters. (1:12–15)

The combination of the title Son of Man and his 'white hair' clearly recalls Daniel 7. Without getting into the knotty details of Revelation 1:12–15, we need

---

24. In Rev. 13:18 John hints once more at the Spirit's role in understanding the visions: 'This calls for wisdom. Let the person who has insight calculate the number of the beast' (cf. 17:9). This resembles the book of Daniel's insistence that only those who possess God's 'Spirit' grasp divine wisdom.

25. The unique title the 'seven spirits' (1:4; 3:1; etc.) may also correspond to the seven letters of Revelation in chs. 2–3. The significance is that Revelation's message, as a whole, is tied to the Spirit's role in enabling and applying its truths to believers.

only to focus on a few particulars. First, the Son of Man is explicitly identified with the 'Ancient of Days', indicating that Christ is undeniably divine. Second, Christ is the executor of Daniel's end-time prophecy that God will one day establish his eternal kingdom. Verse 18 expresses the result of the Son of Man's death and resurrection: 'I am the Living One; I was dead, and now look, I am alive for ever and ever! And *I hold the keys of death and Hades.*' Christ's death and resurrection enable the triune God to defeat death and usher in the new creation – a central theme in John's Apocalypse. Without the Son of Man's death and resurrection, the triune God would not be in a position to judge evil decisively and establish the new heavens and earth in their fullness.

That much seems clear enough, but what must be kept in mind is that, according to Revelation, Christ executes his role in fulfilment of Daniel's prophecy of the Son of Man. *Much of Christ's work in Revelation, particularly chapters 1, and 4–5, is largely viewed through the lens of Daniel 7.*[26] The Son of Man figure looms large throughout all of John's visions, either explicitly or implicitly (cf. Rev. 1:7, 13; 11:15; 14:14–16). Before I unpack one particular role of the Son of Man in the Apocalypse, I will first turn to Daniel 7 and briefly sketch its immediate and broad contexts.

The Danielic Son of Man and the establishment of God's eternal kingdom

Daniel 7, with all of its complexity, is generally straightforward: the Ancient of Days (7:9) judges the earthly pagan kingdoms and establishes his eternal kingdom through the 'son of man' (7:13). Daniel 2 outlines four kingdoms (probably Babylon, Medo-Persia, Greece and Rome) that will consecutively emerge, but the fourth and final kingdom will give way to God's eternal kingdom. This same end-time blueprint continues into chapters 7–12. The central difference between chapter 2 and chapters 7–12 lies in the finer details of how the four kingdoms interact with one another and how, through the 'son of man', God's kingdom will vanquish the previous pagan kingdom. These four beasts in Daniel 7 should probably be identified with the four parts of the statue in chapter 2. They are here seen as devouring one another and 'winds of heaven churning up the great sea' (7:2). The sea is the embodiment of evil and rebellion. These kingdoms are symbolically grotesque, representing their arrogance and destructive nature.

---

26. G. K. Beale, *The Use of Daniel in Jewish Apocalyptic Literature and in the Revelation of St. John* (Lanham: University Press of America), pp. 154–228.

The vision then reverts to the heavenly throne, where an enigmatic figure, 'one like a son of man', travelled on clouds up to the Ancient of Days (7:13). The son of man then receives an inheritance: 'He was given authority, glory and sovereign power; all nations and peoples of every language worshipped him. His dominion is an everlasting dominion that will not pass away, and his kingdom is one that will never be destroyed' (7:14).

The second half of chapter 7 is devoted to the interpretation of the vision (7:15–27). The four beasts symbolize 'four kings' or kingdoms (v. 17). The final kingdom is discussed in some detail, particularly the 'little horn' (v. 8). The ten 'horns' refer to ten 'kings' (v. 24). This final 'horn' or king antagonizes other kings, persecutes and deceives the Israelites, and speaks against God (vv. 20–21, 24–25).

Identifying the 'son of man' figure with precision is notoriously difficult. The language is enigmatic, and 7:13–14 does not easily yield itself to interpreters. In the book of Daniel the phrase 'son of man' or 'sons of men' is a general reference to humanity (2:38; 5:21). The Greek translations of Daniel (Theo and OG) use the phrase as a reference to humanity (2:38), priests (3:84), the figure of Daniel (8:17) and angels (10:16). The phrase thus falls into two general categories: human and angelic.

Giving us deeper insight into the character is the way in which the 'son of man' approaches the Ancient of Days. The son of man rides on the clouds: 'I looked, and there before me was one like a son of man, *coming with the clouds of heaven*' (7:13). In the Old Testament, riding on the clouds is reserved for God alone (Exod. 19:9; Ezek. 1:4; Pss 18:11; 97:2; 104:3). Even angels are not privileged to do so. The book of Daniel symbolically casts the son of man as an enigmatic, divine figure.[27] How this figure relates to the Ancient of Days is

---

27. The LXX (OG) confirms that the son of man has divine qualities: 'I was watching in a vision at night, and, behold, as [*hōs*] a son of man came on the heavenly clouds, and as [*hōs*] the Ancient of Days he was present, and the attendants were with him [*autō*; {this figure}].' According to v. 9, Daniel sees the Ancient of Days taking his seat on the throne. A few verses later, in v. 13, the prophet sees another figure described 'as' or 'like' 'the son of man'. Is this figure angelic? The remainder of the verse answers in the negative, for another title is then given to this figure: 'like the Ancient of Days'. According to the OG there exists only one figure in v. 13; *the son of man is also 'like the Ancient of Days'*. Seyoon Kim rightly puts the pieces together: 'We must conclude that the heavenly figure "like a son of man" is described also as having been 'like the Ancient of Days' . . . That is, Daniel saw, besides the Ancient of Days, a heavenly figure "like a son of man and like the Ancient of Days" (*The 'Son of Man'*

unclear in the immediate context. The only hint we have is found in 7:13b, 'He [the son of man] approached the Ancient of Days and was led into his presence.' At the very least, the son of man enjoys a unique relationship to the Ancient of Days.[28]

Perhaps the reason why the heavenly figure is described as a 'son of man' stems from the close identification with true Israel. For example, the son of man receives 'authority, glory and sovereign power', 'an everlasting dominion' and a 'kingdom' (7:14). According to the 'interpretation' of the initial vision, the figure of the son of man is replaced by the remnant of Israel in 7:18, 22 and 27. The righteous remnant of Israel will 'receive the kingdom and will possess it for ever' (7:18; see 7:22, 27). The son of man and the remnant of Israel are to be identified with one another. The interpretative portion of the vision identifies the son of man as the 'holy people' of Israel. In the Bible, kings or prominent figures often represent the nation or a large group (Josh. 7:1–5; 1 Chr. 21:1–17; 2 Sam. 21:1). Here the son of man represents the righteous Israelites (hence the phrase 'son of *man*'). When he conquers the fourth and final beast, his actions are thus transferred to the group. The remnant is in a position to receive the kingdom, since the son of man, their representative, has vanquished their enemy. Conversely, what is true of the righteous Israelites is also true of the son of man. For example, Daniel 7:21 says, 'As I watched, this horn was *waging war against the holy people and defeating them*.' Here the remnant

---

as the Son of God, WUNT 30 (Tübingen: Mohr Siebeck, 1983], p. 23). *The inference is that the* OG *interpreted the son of man as a divine figure.* The identification of *autō* with son of man furthers this interpretation in that the LXX sees angels ministering or worshipping the son of man.

28. *1 Enoch* presents a Son of Man figure as pre-existent: 'he [the Son of Man] was concealed in the presence of (the Lord of the Spirits) *prior to the creation of the world, and for eternity*' (*1 En.* 48.6, emphasis added). This text and others like it (cf. *1 En.* 62.7–9) cast this son of man figure as existing before creation. Perhaps *1 Enoch* developed this notion by understanding that the son of man in Dan. 7:13 was a divine being (according to the OG and implied by 'coming with clouds', which elsewhere is a portrayal of God) who first had a heavenly existence before coming to earth to reign. Though this pre-existent figure is not largely developed in the OT or Judaism, there exist some general precedents for this notion. For further discussion of how Judaism in general and early Christianity developed a pre-existent notion of the coming end-time ruler (Son of Man, Son of God, Messiah, Lord) see Simon J. Gathercole, *The Preexistent Son: Recovering the Christologies of Matthew, Mark, and Luke* (Grand Rapids: Eerdmans, 2006).

is coming under severe persecution, suggesting that the son of man, too, will suffer intensely.

To summarize, the general thrust of Daniel 7 is the Ancient of Days' end-time judgment upon the pagan kingdoms and the establishment of his eternal kingdom. Although these rebellious kingdoms persecute God's people, even the son of man, God will deliver them and install his kingdom. The son of man's relationship to the Ancient of Days is unresolved, and it is not clear *how* the son of man will conquer the four kingdoms (through suffering?). But the son of man will emerge victorious and the saints will inherit the kingdom.

The Son of Man and the establishment of God's kingdom in Revelation

Now that we have briefly surveyed Daniel 7, we can appreciate John's description of the Son of Man in Revelation 1:12–14: 'I saw . . . someone like a son of man . . . The hair on his head was white like wool, as white as snow.' What was expressed enigmatically in Daniel 7 becomes explicit here in Revelation 1. In Daniel 7 it is difficult to determine the precise relationship between the Ancient of Days and the son of man, whereas in Revelation 1 this relationship is more clearly understood. The Son of Man in Revelation 1:12–16 is intimately identified *with* the Ancient of Days, particularly his unsurpassed wisdom and discernment ('white' 'hair' [cf. Prov. 16:31]). The Son of Man's identification with God is reinforced in 1:17b: 'Then he placed his right hand on me and said: "Do not be afraid. *I am the First and the Last*"' (see 22:13). The title 'First and the Last' recalls God's self-description in 1:8a ('I am the Alpha and the Omega'), recalling several salient texts from Isaiah (41:4; 44:6; 48:12). The Son of Man is indeed divine and enjoys an exalted status with the transcendent God, yet the Son of Man is distinct and found 'walking' among the lampstands (2:1).

Daniel 7 also plays a formative role in Revelation 4 – 5. G. K. Beale argues that the vision of Revelation 4 – 5 is literarily dependent upon two Old Testament texts: Ezekiel 1 – 2 and Daniel 7.[29] The latter text, however, dominates the backdrop of Revelation 4 – 5 more so than the former. By modelling the vision of Revelation 4 – 5 after Daniel 7, John demonstrates that the prophecy of Daniel 7 has indeed commenced with Christ's death and resurrection.[30] Through Christ's death and resurrection God has begun to install his end-time kingdom and rule over the nations.

---

29. Beale, *Revelation*, pp. 313–316.
30. Ibid., p. 368.

Daniel 7 – 8 and the satanic trinity

The book of Daniel not only forges John's understanding of the Trinity; it also contains the blueprint for his conception of the satanic trinity in Revelation 13. The three devilish figures in Revelation 13 (the dragon, the beast from the sea and the beast from the earth) are modelled after the Trinity.[31] Remarkably, John once again alludes to the book of Daniel to describe Satan's alliance with the two grotesque beasts.

The description of the first beast from the sea in Revelation 13:1–2 resembles the attributes from each of the four beasts in Daniel 7 (ten horns [13:1/7:24]; leopard [13:2/7:6]; etc.). The general sequence of events in Revelation 13 also recalls the events mentioned in Daniel 7 (see the table below):[32]

Daniel 7	Revelation 13
Four 'beasts' emerge from the 'sea' (7:3)	'Beast' emerges from the 'sea' (13:1)
The Son of Man receives 'authority' (7:14)	'Beast' receives 'authority' from the dragon (13:2)
The Son of Man is worshipped by the nations (7:14)	The dragon is 'worshipped' by the unbelievers (13:3–4)[33]
'Another king' will 'speak against' God (7:24–25)	The beast utters 'proud words' and 'blasphemies' (13:5–6)

The significance of John's framing the satanic trinity in the light of Daniel 7 is twofold: (1) Looking to the book of Daniel for a rough blueprint of how the triune God functions, albeit in seed form, remains valid. If Daniel is the basis for John's understanding of the satanic trinity, how much more does Daniel shape John's conception of the triune God? (2) The satanic trinity is bent on imitating the triune God. Where God reveals end-time truth to God's people,

---

31. Bauckham, *Climax of Prophecy*, pp. 434–435; Beale, *Use of Daniel*, pp. 229–248.

32. For further allusions to Dan. 7 see Bauckham, *Climax of Prophecy*, pp. 424–425.

33. Unbelievers 'worshipped' the beast by exclaiming, '*Who is like the beast*? Who can wage war against it?' (13:4). The first rhetorical question is an allusion to Exod. 15:11, where Moses and the Israelites celebrate Yahweh's inimitable act of delivering them from the chaotic waters of the Red Sea and destroying the Egyptians. Here in Rev. 13:4 unbelievers mimic this adoration, thus underscoring the corrupt worship of a false god.

Satan divulges lies and deception. Whereas God and the Son of Man possess 'authority' to conquer evil, the beast from the sea enjoys 'authority' to wage war against the church. Eventually, the devilish trinity will collapse within itself (17:5–18) and be unable to sustain its imitation.

Conclusion

The book of Revelation's presentation of the Trinity is not a recent development in early Christianity but ultimately finds its roots in the Old Testament, albeit in an undeveloped form. John presents God as the ultimate source of revealed mysteries, in keeping with Daniel's portrayal of God. But the book of Revelation uniquely includes Christ as the source of wisdom and revelation in a number of prominent passages, suggesting that the second person of the Trinity plays a key role in the formulation of divine revelation. The Spirit effects the revelation in the lives of the saints, enabling its reception and the ability to perform its requirements. The Spirit's role, within the book of Revelation, closely resembles the Spirit in Daniel, who enables the figure Daniel to understand the divine wisdom. Lastly, the person of Christ not only functions as a source of apocalyptic revelation, but is also the executor of it. Christ, as the Son of Man from Daniel 7, actualizes the content of revelation. The one who aids the Father in formulating the visions performs them. Though the satanic trinity attempt to mirror the triune God in their behaviour, such actions will eventually lead to their demise.

9. THE TRINITY AND THE OLD TESTAMENT: REAL PRESENCE OR IMPOSITION?

Mark S. Gignilliat

Introduction

The identification of YHWH as the God Christians name Father, Son and Holy Spirit remains a challenging subject matter for several reasons. One primary reason is the governing hermeneutical norms for modern criticism collapse the *sensus literalis* with the historical sense of Scripture.[1] Evangelical scholars tend to limit the historical sense to the named author of Scripture, where such applies or can be responsibly reconstructed. Critical scholarship expands the historical sense to include various levels of tradition and redaction-critical analysis. Despite the differences, evangelical and critical hermeneutical approaches share the interpretative instincts inherited from the rise of historical consciousness in the early eighteenth century.[2]

---

1. See Brevard Childs, 'The Sensus Literalis of Scripture: An Ancient and Modern Problem', in Herbert Donner (ed.), *Festschrift für Walther Zimmerli zum 70. Geburtstag* (Göttingen: Vandenhoeck & Ruprecht, 1977), pp. 80–93.
2. See Thomas Albert Howard, *Religion and the Rise of Historicism: W. M. L. De Wette, Jacob Burckhardt, and the Theological Origins of Nineteenth-Century Historical Consciousness* (Cambridge: Cambridge University Press, 2000).

The previous claim is not intended as a pejorative comment per se. The benefits of modern criticism for the lexical and historical contextualization of Scripture aid modern readers in multiple ways. Scripture's so-called depth dimension, a textual phenomenon valorized in the modern period, is not necessarily at odds with a confessional understanding of Scripture because it reflects the dynamically present character of the divine word to subsequent generations of readers/hearers. This textual dynamic is present within the Scripture's own self-witness. Jeremiah, for example, appeals to Micah's prophecy for the sake of bolstering his own claims (Jer. 26:18). The *middôt* (attributes) of God heralded in Exodus 34:6–7 weave their way through the Minor Prophets at critical, interpretative junctures.[3] While compositional history and textual reception are related but distinct matters, the fact remains that Scripture listens to Scripture in its own compositional history. These insights into Scripture's own internal cross-association – intertextuality is the term *de jour* – help the modern reader in multiple ways, the least of which is an appreciation for how Scripture's tradition-building process reveals a canon consciousness in the texts themselves. On this account, canon is not an extrinsic imposition of later doctrinal formulae onto Scripture's self-witness but emerges from the text's own internal forces.

All the historical advances of modernity notwithstanding, trinitarian readings of the Old Testament run into hermeneutical brick walls. How can texts written before the incarnation refer to metaphysical realities beyond the conceptual horizons of the human authors and tradents of the Old Testament? For example, was Moses a trinitarian? These kinds of questions are not new, raising their heads at various moments in the church's struggle to name its God. The hermeneutical question is straightforward. Is the Old Testament's trinitarian character grounded in the exegesis of Scripture itself or does it amount to a homiletical or hermeneutical palimpsest imposed onto rather than drawn from Scripture's own self-witness? Moreover, if as Christians we affirm the triune character of our God, then a question regarding the identity of YHWH in the Old Testament follows. Is YHWH a *persona* of the divine essence or the *ousia* itself? Put in other terms, is YHWH the Father or the divine essence of three *personae*?

Admittedly, these questions are enormous and of some consequence. The present chapter does not portend towards an exhaustive answer, but will make initial steps towards clarifying what it means to understand YHWH as triune

---

3. See Raymond C. Van Leeuwen, 'Scribal Wisdom and Theodicy in the Book of the Twelve', in L. G. Perdue, B. B. Scott and W. J. Wiseman (eds.), *In Search of Wisdom: Essays in Memory of John G. Gammie* (Louisville: Westminster John Knox, 1993), pp. 31–49.

and to read the Old Testament witness accordingly. Our attention turns first to the identity of Israel's God, YHWH.

Who is YHWH? Exodus and the divine name

The question 'Who is God?' registers somewhere near the heart of the Old Testament's theological subject matter.[4] When Moses encounters God at the burning bush, the matter of identifying his name comes to the fore (Exod. 3:13–14, my tr.). 'When they ask for your name, how shall I answer them?' God's reply to Moses' straightforward question remains a disputed matter to this day. *'ehyeh 'ăšer 'ehyeh*. Tell them *'ehyeh* ('I am' or 'I will be') has sent you.

Coming to terms with the significance of this encounter and the connotative force of the name is no mean task. Along with the LXX and the majority of the Christian interpretative tradition – for good measure I will add Maimonides's name to the list – the revelation of God's name in Exodus 3 speaks of his essence or being, his pure existence or his eternal presence where future and past enfold into God's eternal present.[5] Existence resides at the heart of God's 'godness'.[6] He is.

This essentialist reading of God's nature has come under critical scrutiny in twentieth-century theology, but it is beyond the purview of this chapter to chase this rabbit too far. Put simply, essentialist categories for answering the 'Who is God?' question have had to make room for narrative approaches where God's identity and relationship to his creation are more closely linked with the divine economy itself: a bottom up approach, if you will. The lines dividing God's eternal self (immanence) from his creative/redemptive revelation of himself in time (economic) blur in this narratival move. But all are not persuaded by the recent trends. The title of a recent monograph makes the point sharply: *God Is Not a Story*.[7]

---

4. The hesitation to identify *the* centre of the OT's theological witness is warranted.

5. Moses Maimonides, *The Guide of the Perplexed*, vol. 1, tr. S. Pines (Chicago: University of Chicago Press, 1963), vol. 1, p. 61.

6. In classical trinitarian terms God's essence and existence are coterminous. For creaturely realities where the two are distinguished, existence occurs because of an external cause. Such cannot be the case with God because no external agent brings about his existence. See Thomas Aquinas, *Summa Theologiae*, *Prima Pars*, q. 3, art. 4.

7. Francesca A. Murphy, *God Is Not a Story: Realism Revisited* (Oxford: Oxford University Press, 2007).

A close reading of Exodus 3 within the larger frame of Exodus's name theology may help chart a course between these alternatives. Or, put more precisely, Exodus 3 may bring essentialist and narratival concerns into a reciprocal relationship. God's relating to his creatures in acts of creation, revelation and redemption – the stuff of God's economy – flows from the essential character of his being. In Aquinas's frame of understanding, the eternal processions of God (immanence) are revealed, even if analogically, in the temporal mission (economy) of God. These two facets remain distinct for an important theological reason, to wit the maintaining of the Creator–creature distinction. Yet they remain distinct in an insoluble and reciprocating relation to one another. Gilles Emery frames the matter as follows: 'In the mission or temporal processions, explains Saint Thomas, the divine person who is sent forth impresses on the soul of the saints a likeness of his eternal property.'[8]

I will leave the fine-tuning of these theological categories to those whose pay grade matches the subject matter.[9] Notwithstanding, these categories emerging from speculative theology or Christian dogmatics provide helpful, even necessary, hermeneutical keys. Within Exodus's theological movement as a book, God's revelation of his name emerges from the complex dynamic of God's will to redeem his people. God's revealed self takes a particular clarifying turn in Exodus as God's eternal identity is enmeshed with his redemptive, covenantal relation to his people.

At the wrestling match on the banks of the Jabbok River, a narrative I will look at closely in due course, Jacob asks for the name of his supernatural

---

8. Gilles Emery, O. P., 'Trinity and Creation', in R. Van Nieuwenhove and J. Wawrykow (eds.), *The Theology of Thomas Aquinas* (Notre Dame: University of Notre Dame Press, 2005), p. 68. Emery also states, 'The procession of the Word and that of the Spirit are not only the source of creation; they extend their influence to the entire divine economy' (p. 67).

9. The secondary literature on this subject is voluminous. Readers may find helpful the essays in M. T. Dempsey (ed.), *Trinity and Election in Contemporary Theology* (Grand Rapids: Eerdmans, 2011). Especially instructive is the interlocution between Matthew Levering and Bruce McCormack in their respective readings on Aquinas and the relation between the processions and missions of the Trinity. Matthew Levering, 'Christ, the Trinity, and Predestination: McCormack and Aquinas', in Dempsey, *Trinity and Election*, pp. 244–276; Bruce L. McCormack, 'Processions and Missions: A Point of Convergence Between Thomas Aquinas and Karl Barth', in B. L. McCormack and T. J. White, O. P. (eds.), *Thomas Aquinas and Karl Barth: An Unofficial Catholic–Protestant Dialogue* (Grand Rapids: Eerdmans, 2013), pp. 99–126.

opponent (Gen. 32). The response is sharp: 'What is that to you?' Admittedly, the episode is strange on multiple fronts. But the unfolding of the divine name within the Pentateuch is specifically linked to the exodus event. While the Jabbok narrative may have a complex religious-historical backstory regarding some of its enigmatic elements, the Pentateuchal context of the story renders the divine reticence to give his name a theological significance. The connotative significance of the name YHWH is linked with the exodus episode, and Jacob is not privy to such knowledge yet.

In a similar vein to the Jacob narrative at Jabbok is Exodus 6:2–3, a text that is central to the name theology of the book of Exodus:

> God also spoke to Moses and said to him, 'I am the LORD [YHWH]. I appeared to Abraham, Isaac, and Jacob as God Almighty [El Elyon], but by my name "The LORD" I did not make myself known to them.' (Exod. 6:2–3)[10]

This verse persists as a source critic's darling. The rationale goes something like the following: the patriarchs knew only the name El or Elohim, with YHWH appearing later in Israel's religious-historical development; the Canaanite religious instincts became borrowed capital for Israel's own developing religion or Yahwism. This religious-historical narrative is told often enough to resist full repeating here.[11] In brief, however, Abraham had no concept of the name YHWH.

While elements of this religious-historical narrative may ring true, the canonical presentation differs at crucial points. The patriarchal history is rife with references to YHWH. One need only recall Abraham's encounter at the oaks of Mamre in Genesis 18 to problematize an account of the divine name as presented in certain quarters of critical theory. According to the canonical presentation, Abraham knew YHWH. So what is Exodus 6:3 claiming?

The revealing of the divine name in Exodus 3 and 6 locates God's self-determination to reveal himself within the nexus of his redemptive actions. It is not that Abraham did not know the Semitic phonemes of the divine name. Nevertheless, Abraham's position within the divine economy before the exodus event limits his knowledge of the name's soteric significance, especially given

---

10. Unless stated otherwise, Bible quotations in this chapter are from the NRSV.

11. See Rainer Albertz, *A History of Israelite Religion in the Old Testament Period*, vol. 1: *From the Beginnings to the End of the* Monarchy, OTL (Louisville: Westminster John Knox, 1994), pp. 27–32.

this crucial and defining episode in Israel's covenantal history.[12] This moment
in the divine economy renders the divine name and its significance in a fuller,
redemptive frame particular to this moment of divine self-unveiling. By way of
extension a similar claim may be made about the last verse of Jesus' high priestly
prayer in John 17:26, 'I made your name known to them, and I will make it
known'.[13] The disciples were not unaware of the divine name. But this singular
moment in the divine economy of redemption attaches a significance to the
divine name unknown till this moment of self-unveiling.

It comes, then, as little surprise to find discourse pertaining to the divine
name towards the end of the Exodus narrative as well (Exod. 32 – 34). The
golden calf episode marks another crucial turning point in the divine economy.
The either/or character of the Decalogue and God's covenantal claims on Israel
are now tested: 'I will take you as my people, and I will be your God' (Exod.
6:7). Israel's worship of the golden calf breaks the covenantal claim 'You shall
have no other gods before me.' When God interrupts his conversation with
Moses midstream on Sinai's heights, the reader of Exodus realizes the stakes
are high. God makes use of the cold and distant second person possessive
pronoun and tells Moses to go to '*your* people' because they have offended
against my law (Exod. 32:7). The either/or moment arrives. Yet, Moses intercedes. God in his mercy relents. Immediately following God's relenting,
Moses asks the unthinkable: he asks to see the glory of God. YHWH then in
theophanic glory passes by and in the next chapter gives a detailed exposition
of the significance of his own name:

---

12. Benno Jacob's classic commentary on Exodus claims, 'The two periods of history
    were not distinguished through the knowledge of one or another Name of God,
    but through two distinct aspects of God revealed in each period' (Benno Jacob,
    The Second Book of the Bible: Exodus, tr. W. Jacob [Hobokon: KTAV, 1992], p. 146).
    Similarly, Francis Turretin asserts, 'In this sense, he says that he had not been known
    to the patriarchs by his name Jehovah (Ex. 6:3), not as to the signifying word (for
    the contrary is evident from the book of Genesis), but as to the thing signified'
    (Francis Turretin, *Institutes of Elenctic Theology*, tr. G. M. Giger, ed. J. T. Dennison Jr.,
    3 vols. [Phillipsburg, N.J.: P&R, 1992–7], vol. 1, p. 185). See also Christopher Seitz,
    'The Call of Moses and the "Revelation" of the Divine Name: Source-Critical
    Logic and Its Legacy', in C. Seitz and K. Greene-McCreight (eds.), *Theological
    Exegesis: Essays in Honor of Brevard S. Childs* (Grand Rapids: Eerdmans, 1999),
    pp. 145–161.
13. The NIV unfortunately leaves *onomos* untranslated in its rendering of the text's
    dynamic sense.

The LORD passed before him, and proclaimed,

The LORD, the LORD . . .
        (Exod. 34:6)

YHWH's proclamation of his own name *is* the revelation of his glory. The thirteen *middôt* of God listed by YHWH himself (Exod. 34:6–7) reveal the character of the divine name, and in so doing reveal the character of YHWH. He is merciful and severe. Moreover, his mercy far outweighs his severity. The name of YHWH entails existence, but does so in a redemptive and revelatory context where his being is made available by his own unveiling. Moreover, this self-unveiling locates God's being as merciful and severe, the two necessarily conjoined with God's mercy shaping our understanding of his severity. By way of extension the intertextual appeal to Exodus 34:6–7 that runs throughout the Minor Prophets reveals Israel's continual struggle to come to terms with YHWH's mercy and severity. Like Jacob at the Jabbok River, Israel's covenantal existence endures as a wrangling with their merciful and severe God, even till the break of day (Hos. 12:1–6).

The revealing of the divine name and the redemptive context of this self-unveiling are of some consequence when coming to terms with the Trinity and the Old Testament. YHWH's mission to create and redeem does not exhaust the scope of God's being. As various episodes within the Old Testament attest, the being of God resists domestication of any sort. Moses' fearful encounter with YHWH in Exodus 4:24–26 is a case in point. Nevertheless, God's revealed being remains ensconced within a salvific context where his mercy and severity come to the fore.[14] As mentioned above, the

---

14. Richard Muller recounts Calvin's comments on Ps. 8, where he prioritizes the relational/revelational character of the divine name over subtle speculations regarding God's essence. For Calvin, God is known primarily by his works. 'It [God's name] ought rather to be referred to the works and properties by which he is known than to his essence.' Calvin's prioritization of the relational/revelational emerges from a Reformed emphasis on the applicability of doctrine and exegesis. Calvin is happy enough to affirm, for example, the traditional metaphysical understanding of the inseparability of God's essence and his existence. But he does so when such claims flow organically from the exegesis of Scripture itself, i.e. Calvin's comments on the name Jehovah in Ps. 83:18 (Richard Muller, *Post-Reformation Reformed Dogmatics: The Rise and Development of Reformed Orthodoxy, ca. 1520 to ca. 1725*, 2nd ed., 4 vols. [Grand Rapids: Baker Academic, 2003], vol. 3, p. 251).

missions of God in time (creation and redemption) reveal the eternal processions of God in his subsisting relations. The two remain distinct yet
inseparable.

YHWH: the one and the many

A peculiar facet of the identity of YHWH, merciful and severe, emerges in the
Old Testament's textual witness. In certain streams of tradition YHWH has
the ability to differentiate himself from himself without fragmenting his deity
or divine being. Benjamin Sommer identifies this feature of YHWH as 'the
divine fluidity model'.[15] For example, YHWH's location at Teman or Hebron
may be particular to that place so that YHWH's presence there differs somewhat
from YHWH at Jerusalem. Absalom's trek back to Hebron to make vows to
YHWH there when Jerusalem was just around the corner may make some sense
of this religious dynamic (2 Sam. 15:7).[16] The evidence in the Old Testament
for the distinction between YHWH's self at various locations is scant. Therefore,
building theological or metaphysical conclusions on this basis remains thin. The
relationship between YHWH and his *mal'āk* (messenger/angel), however, is
another matter.

The relationship between YHWH and the Angel of YHWH is of material
consequence when attending to the trinitarian character of the Old Testament.
In some instances the Angel of YHWH resists any identification with YHWH's
being (cf. 2 Sam. 24:16–18). In these cases the Angel of YHWH exists as a
messenger or herald sent at YHWH's bequest to do his bidding. In other
instances, however, differentiating between YHWH and his *mal'āk* becomes
more problematic and, one should add, more interesting. As Gerhard von Rad
claimed:

> The most interesting are those which are not really able to distinguish between Jahweh
> and his angel, and which therefore do not take the angel as only a messenger, but as a
> manifestation of Jahweh himself. The angel of Jahweh is Jahweh himself, appearing to
> human beings in human form.[17]

---

15. Benjamin Sommer, *The Bodies of God and the World of Ancient Israel* (Cambridge:
    Cambridge University Press, 2009), p. 38.
16. Ibid., p. 39.
17. Gerhard von Rad, *Old Testament Theology*, vol. 1, tr. D. M. G. Stalker (San Francisco:
    HarperSanFrancisco, 1962), p. 287.

In line with Sommer's 'divine fluidity model' certain traditions within the Old Testament narrate the *mal'āk*'s identity in such a way that differentiating him from YHWH becomes difficult, if not impossible. Herman Bavinck states:

> So much is clear: that in the *Mal'akh Yahweh* who is pre-eminently worthy of that name, God (esp. his Word) is present in a very special sense. This is very evident from the fact that though distinct from Jehovah this Angel of Jehovah bears the same name, has the same power, effects the same deliverance, dispenses the same blessings, and is the object of the same adoration.[18]

The plurality of persons within a unified divine essence remains an Old Testament problem, leaning against the notion that such trinitarian logic is foisted onto the text rather than drawn from it.

The texts supporting the plurality of persons within a unity of divine being are the usual suspects. Rublev's notable icon of the Trinity depicts Abraham's encounter with YHWH in Genesis 18. In the narrative movement of this text the three visitors become a single *persona* as one figure emerges who speaks directly with Abraham as YHWH embodied. Later in the Abrahamic narratives the Angel of YHWH halts the sacrificial knife and commences to speak to Abraham in YHWH's first person voice (Gen. 22:16). A similar dynamic between the *mal'āk* and YHWH occurs in the calling of Gideon (Judg. 6:17–40). The blessing of Jacob in Genesis 48:15–16 links together *mal'āk* and *'ĕlōhîm* [God] in synonymous parallelism. Along this line of enquiry one fascinating text emerges as central to the discussion at hand because of its own reception in the compositional history of the Old Testament itself – Jacob's wrestling match with a 'man' (*'îš*) in Genesis 32:22–32.

The wrestling match at the river Jabbok continues to bewilder and capture the imagination of readers because the text is fraught with enigmatic elements. Jacob sends his family and servants across the southern banks of the river to its northern side. 'Jacob was left alone' (32:24). Why? One practical reason is the thwarting effect such a herd of folks might have had on Esau's violent anger. From a narrative standpoint, Jacob's remaining behind and alone provides the opportunity for this providential sparring match with 'a man'.[19] Von Rad makes much of the mental strain and focus Jacob suffered because of his unavoidable

---

18. Herman Bavinck, *The Doctrine of God*, tr. W. Hendriksen (Edinburgh: Banner of Truth, 1997), p. 257.

19. Luther understands Jacob's desire to be alone as indicative of his pressing need to pray.

future engagement with Esau.[20] And yet out of nowhere on the riverbanks of the Jabbok a man appears, and this event is far more dangerous than any encounter with Esau.

The two men begin to wrestle. Again we are left in enigmatic territory. Why did they begin to wrestle? We are not told. Nevertheless, Jacob (*ya'ăqōb*) wrestles (*yē'ābēq*) with a man by the river Jabbok (*yabbōq*) until the break of dawn. The assonance of the Hebrew words has the poetic effect of emphasizing the centrality of this episode as it pertains to Jacob's name and its alteration. For Jacob, the defining moment of his life was going to happen the next day when he met Esau. For YHWH, however, the defining moment of Jacob's life is this encounter by the Jabbok. Here Jacob strives with God, prevails/perseveres and receives a blessing, for ever altering his identity and his gait. No longer is he the 'heel-grabber'. Now he is Israel, one who has striven with God. He has a limp for the rest of his life to prove it.

The details of this text necessitate critical and creative enquiry. For example, how can Jacob strive with God and prevail? Certain Jewish interpreters identify this man as the protective angel of Esau for obvious theological reasons – prevailing over God is inconceivable and theologically offensive. Other interpretative questions emerge. Why does 'the man' need to depart before the breaking of dawn? Why does the man refuse to give his name? Interpretative questions such as these remain the material of scholarly discussion and disagreement. Pursuing their answers removes us from our enquiry, but, admittedly, the text is riddled with enigmatic elements. Despite these uncertain textual elements, the interpretative framework provided by Hosea 12:4–6 is of some consequence to our trinitarian investigation.

Hosea 12:4 identifies 'the man' with whom Jacob wrestles as a *mal'āk*. This identification comes as no surprise because it is not out of the ordinary for an angel to be predicated with the term *'îš* (man).[21] The 'confusion' arises in verse 6 when the prophet also identifies the figure with whom Jacob wrestled as YHWH. As Sommer clarifies:

> The reason for the apparent confusion between God and angel in these verses from Hosea is simply that both passages, Hosea 12 and Genesis 32, reflect a belief that the selves of an angel and the God YHWH could overlap or that a small-scale fragment of YHWH can be termed a *mal'akh*.[22]

---

20. Gerhard von Rad, *Genesis: A Commentary*, OTL (Philadelphia: Westminster, 1972), p. 320.
21. Sommer, *Bodies*, p. 41.
22. Ibid.

The Hosea text understands the figure of Genesis 32 as at the same time both an angel and YHWH.[23]

Perhaps Hosea's interpretation of Jacob at Jabbok hovers in the material world of speculative, Christian theology with its distinction between *person* and *essence*. I am not claiming Hosea was thinking in these terms. Therefore, I am not basing the argument on human, authorial intentionality. Nevertheless, ontology and epistemology or the being of God and our understanding of God's being are related but distinct matters. One should not expect Hosea, Moses or David, for example, to be conceptually aware of the full ontological implications of their prophetic words regarding the divine being. Put positively, the ontological dimension of Scripture's witness allows the *signa* to be fitted properly to Scripture's *res significata*, a subject matter made available by the total witness of a two-testament canon. Moreover, the distinctions made within the speculative, theological traditions of the church are made for the sake of coming to terms with the claims of Scripture's total witness, a point Lewis Ayres and others have made persuasively.[24] Distinguishing between *person* and *essence* remains at the heart of trinitarian theology and biblical interpretation.

The relation between YHWH and his *mal'āk* – and by extension his Spirit and Word/Wisdom – indicates an overlap of identities and a simultaneous distinction between persons.[25] This biblical description reinforces the tendency of classical trinitarian thought to identify YHWH with the divine essence or being rather than with a particular *hypostasis* or *persona* of the Godhead; that is,

---

23. The incommunicability of the Tetragrammaton to creatures became a matter of some consequence in Protestant orthodoxy's reaction to Socinianism. If the Tetragrammaton is predicated on the *mal'āk* of the OT, then by necessary conclusion the angel must be an uncreated angel and not a created one, a 'prelude to [Christ's] incarnation' (Turretin, *Institutes*, vol. 1, p. 185). See also, Muller, *Reformed Dogmatics*, vol. 3, pp. 259–260, 264.

24. Lewis Ayres, *Nicaea and Its Legacy: An Approach to Fourth-Century Trinitarian Theology* (Oxford: Oxford University Press, 2004), pp. 31–40; see also David Yeago, 'The New Testament and Nicene Dogma: A Contribution to the Recovery of Theological Exegesis', *ProEccl* 3 (1994), pp. 152–164.

25. Well worth pursuing is YHWH's special provenance as it pertains to creation and redemption and the 'fittingness' of the Word and the Spirit as agents of YHWH's single will to create and redeem. I thank my colleague Carl Beckwith for making this point clear. On this point see Boris Bobrinskoy, *The Mystery of the Trinity: Trinitarian Experience and Vision in the Biblical and Patrisitic Tradition*, tr. A. P. Gythiel (Crestwood: Saint Vladimir's Seminary Press, 1999), pp. 31–49.

YHWH is not identified as the Father *simpliciter*. Richard Muller describes the Protestant Orthodox view in the following way:

> Given, moreover, that the name 'Jehovah' belongs to God *essentialiter, absoluté,* and *indistincté* apart from an identification or determination of the persons of the Godhead, Scripture can also apply the name and the texts in which it occurs to individual persons, namely, to Christ. The threefold glory of Isaiah 6:3 is, thus, applied to Christ by the evangelist John.[26]

YHWH as God's personal name refers to the divine Godhead in its fullness, the divine essence equally shared by the three persons. As such, YHWH can be predicated on any of the divine persons without remainder. And at the same time, the name YHWH is not the sole possession/indicator of any one person. YHWH *is* the Father, Son and Holy Spirit in their co-equal sharing of the divine essence in its fullness.[27]

Concluding reflections

The rise of historical consciousness in modernity brought with it many positive results for the engaging of the biblical material. Such a claim resists easy disputation. On the other hand, the reducing of the biblical material to its historical/literary origin – original author, original audience, immediate circumstances giving rise to the subject under discussion, and/or the complex tradition-building

---

26. Muller, *Reformed Dogmatics*, vol. 4, p. 303.

27. The danger of identifying YHWH as the divine essence is the introduction of the fourth member into the Trinity, to wit, the essence as an independent transcendent agent. Paul Hinlicky identifies this danger and rightly steers clear of it when he claims, 'I would argue that there is no divine essence existing apart transcendentally causing things in general, which may or may not be connected to its own real presence in the Son and blessing in the Spirit as the eternal Father. If that is so, the divine essence *is* the Father of the Son and breather of the Spirit' (emphasis original). To speak of YHWH as the divine essence *is* to speak of the divine essence as Father, Son and Holy Spirit in their eternal processions (Paul R. Hinlicky, 'Quaternity or Patrology', *ProEccl* 23 [2014], p. 52). Aquinas's understanding of the persons of the Trinity as 'subsisting relations' avoids the danger of isolating the divine essence from the personal relations in their distinction. Relation in God *is* the divine essence (Aquinas, *Summa Theologiae, Prima Pars*, q. 29, art. 4).

process leading to the text's final form – runs the danger of cutting Scripture from its ontological subject matter. The hermeneutical backbone of modern criticism, in the oft-repeated phrase of Brevard Childs, altered Scripture's status from a witness of divine revelation into a source for critical reconstruction: literary, historical or otherwise. Once the historical excavation of the text ends, whether in reconstruction of the historical or literary-critical background, attendance to the text's literal sense concludes as well. The Christian interpreter must strain to affirm the trinitarian character of the Old Testament with these governing hermeneutical instincts deployed. YHWH's triune identity, on this account, is a homiletical extra, not a close reading of the text itself.

The church's interpretative tradition, on the other hand, keeps the verbal character of Scripture and its divine subject matter insolubly linked when attending to Scripture's literal sense. To affirm the Old Testament's trinitarian character or to identify YHWH as the Father, Son and Holy Spirit are attempts at allowing the Old Testament's own idiom to have a constraining role in the characterization of God as one in essence and three in persons. The language of Nicaea would be foreign to the intellectual horizons of Moses or Isaiah. Such formulations are waiting in time for reflection and clarification. But what must be maintained is that the formulations of Nicaea are exegetically grounded attempts to provide a theological and hermeneutical framework for Scripture's own total witness regarding the identity of the one God with whom we have to do.

The distinction between essence and person arises in speculative theology for the sake of allowing Scripture's total witness regarding the divine being to have his say.[28] Hermeneutical assumptions governed by the anteriority of faith's confession and commitments are present from beginning to end. Such a claim need not be denied in a feigned effort at hermeneutical neutrality. At the same time, the verbal character of the Old Testament itself is fertile soil for a trinitarian hermeneutic where the unity of the divine essence and diversity of the divine personae are affirmed, as Genesis 32:22–32 and Hosea 12:1–6 attest. In fact, the Old Testament's own self-presentation regarding YHWH's singularity and diversity of personae constrains the faithful reader towards this interpretative conclusion.

© Mark S. Gignilliat, 2016

---

28. See Gilles Emery, 'Essentialism or Personalism in the Treatise on God in St. Thomas Aquinas?', in idem, *Trinity in Aquinas* (Ann Arbor: Sapientia, 2003), pp. 165–208.

PART 2:

PRACTICAL RELEVANCE

10. THE MYSTERY OF THE TRINITY[1]

Scott R. Swain

Introduction

The doctrine of the Trinity is the most sublime truth of the Christian faith and its supreme treasure. Christian teaching concerning one God in three persons flows from the revelation of the high and holy name of the Lord God Almighty, 'the name of the Father and of the Son and of the Holy Spirit' (Matt. 28:19).[2] This glorious name identifies the true and living God and, because it is the name into which we are baptized, constitutes our only comfort in life and in death. Not only does the doctrine of the Trinity identify God; it also illumines all of God's works, enabling us to perceive more clearly the wonders of the Father's purpose in creation, of Christ's incarnation and of the Spirit's indwelling. All

---

1. An earlier version of this chapter appeared in *Credo Magazine* (Apr. 2013), pp. 26–33. See http://www.credomag.com/the-magazine/archives/the-trinity-and-the-christian-life-why-a-triune-god-makes-all-the-difference (accessed 21 Nov. 2015). For more detailed elaboration of the doctrine of the Trinity see Scott R. Swain, 'Divine Triunity', in Michael Allen and Scott R. Swain (eds.), *Christian Dogmatics: Reformed Theology for the Church Catholic* (Grand Rapids: Baker Academic, forthcoming).
2. All translations in this chapter are from the ESV.

things are from the Trinity, through the Trinity and to the Trinity. And so, seen in the sublime light of the Trinity, we see all things in a new light.

Sublime and supreme, the doctrine of the Trinity is also singular and self-interpreting. The doctrine is singular in so far as the truth about God as Trinity cannot be categorized among or explained by comparison with other 'trinities' in creation (e.g. the threefold form of ice, water and vapour). The Lord asks in Isaiah 40:18:

> To whom then will you liken God,
>   or what likeness compare with him?

And the desired response is 'no one'. The triune God is and acts in a class by himself. For this reason the Trinity is self-interpreting, a mystery that faith comes to grasp only in so far as the triune God interprets his identity and action to us in holy Scripture. 'No one knows the Father except the Son', Jesus declares in Matthew 11:27, 'and anyone to whom the Son chooses to reveal him'. The good news of course is that the triune God does interpret himself to us, presenting to Christian theology the delightful and demanding task of bearing witness to the supreme and singular reality that is the Lord our God, the reality of the Father, the Son and the Holy Spirit.

The purpose of this chapter is to provide a brief overview of the doctrine of the Trinity, following the Lord's teaching in Matthew 11:25–27 as our primary guide, but also attending to ways in which this teaching is echoed throughout the Bible and summarized in the church's creeds and confessions. In the doctrine of the Trinity, as in all other doctrines, the Lord Jesus Christ is our only teacher (Matt. 23:8). He alone knows the Father (again Matt. 11:27) and he, with the Father, gives us the Spirit that we may know the things freely given to us by God (1 Cor. 2:11–12). Therefore, if we would learn of the Trinity, we must learn from Jesus (Matt. 11:29). We must direct our attention to the place where he speaks, Holy Scripture, and we must submit our minds to the obedient pattern of thinking that he demands. Only then will we know the doctrine of the Trinity as we ought to know it. Only then will we share the mind of Christ.

Learning of the Trinity, learning from Jesus: Matthew 11:25–27

> At that time Jesus declared, 'I thank you, Father, Lord of heaven and earth, that you have hidden these things from the wise and understanding and revealed them to little children; yes, Father, for such was your gracious will. All things have been handed over to me by my Father, and no one knows the Son except the Father,

and no one knows the Father except the Son and anyone to whom the Son chooses
to reveal him.'

The revelation of the Trinity causes Jesus to rejoice. This revelation is not
a puzzle we are called to solve or a conundrum devised to confound us. It is a
source of joy: first in Jesus, then in those who come to know this revelation
through Jesus. Unveiled at the Father's sovereign behest, 'such was your gracious
will' (11:26), and to an unlikely audience, 'to little children' (11:25), the mystery
of the Trinity makes known the supreme life of communication and communion
that is God's life as Father, Son and Spirit. The Father, the Son and the Spirit,
official church teaching says, are 'consubstantial' in one divine life, one divine
action, one divine right to our faith and worship.

Jesus' teaching about the Trinity begins with teaching about the Father. Note
the twofold description of God that Jesus acclaims: 'I thank you, Father, Lord of
heaven and earth' (11:25). The first description 'Father' takes up the Old Testament
characterization of God as the father of Adam (Gen. 5:1–3; Luke 3:38), Israel
(Exod. 4:22; Deut. 32:6) and the Davidic king (2 Sam. 7:14), and gives it a new and
unique significance by applying it to God's relation to Jesus. (We will return to
this new and unique sense of God's fatherhood in a moment.) The second
description 'Lord of heaven and earth' signifies the Father's supreme sovereignty.
God is the Father who reigns 'in heaven' (Matt. 6:9), with whom 'all things are
possible' (Matt. 19:26), from whom every blessing in nature and in grace flows
(Matt. 6:25–34) and to whom belongs eternal dominion and glory (Matt. 6:13).

Jesus' teaching about the Trinity begins with teaching about the Father, but
continues with teaching about his identity as the Son. Here we have a twofold
description of the Son that parallels the twofold description of the Father. First,
Jesus has received 'all things' from the Father. This description indicates that,
with the Father, the Son shares supreme divine sovereignty. Jesus has sovereign
authority on earth to forgive sins (Matt. 9:6), an authority that belongs to God
alone (Matt. 9:3; Mark 2:7). Jesus exercises sovereign authority over the wind
and the waves (Mark 4:35–41), an authority that belongs to God alone (Ps.
107:23–32). Jesus exercises 'all authority in heaven and on earth' (Matt. 28:18)
– again an authority that belongs to God alone (Ps. 135:6). Second, Jesus stands
in a unique relation to the Father, the relation of '*the* Son' (Matt. 11:27). Jesus
is not just one son of God among many, not even in the Davidic sense of being
the messianic king appointed by God to rule on earth as God rules in heaven
(see Matt. 22:41–46). He is the Son of God in the full and proper sense (John
5:18), a sense that distinguishes him from all other creaturely sons of God. He
is God's lordly Son, who has received all things from the Father (Matt. 11:27),
who with the Father reigns on God's sovereign throne (again Matt. 22:41–46),

and who with the Father reveals the mystery of the Trinity to us (Matt. 11:25, 27). Jesus is God's divine Son.

Common and personal properties

The twofold description of the persons exhibited in Matthew 11:25–27, and also in many other biblical texts, constitutes the fundamental biblical basis for the doctrine of the Trinity. The Bible identifies the persons with characteristics each person holds in common with the other persons ('common properties'), and with characteristics each person holds in distinction from the other persons ('personal properties').

With respect to the first type of description, the Bible identifies each person as the one true and living God. The three persons share a single divine 'name' (Matt. 28:19): the Father is the one Lord God (e.g. Matt. 11:25), the Son is the one Lord God (e.g. John 20:28; 1 Cor. 8:6) and the Spirit is the one Lord God (e.g. Acts 5:3–4; 2 Cor. 3:17–18). Furthermore, the Bible identifies each person as an agent of God's uniquely divine acts of creation, providence, redemption, and so forth (Gen. 1:1–2; Ps. 33:6; John 1:1–3; Gal. 4:4–6; etc.). These 'common properties' reveal that the multiplication of persons in the Trinity does not amount to the multiplication of gods (see Eph. 4:4–6). The doctrine of the Trinity is a species of monotheism (cf. Deut. 6:4 with 1 Cor. 8:6). The three distinct persons are in common, and completely in themselves one supreme Lord and God. Again, to borrow creedal terminology, the Son and the Spirit are 'consubstantial' with the Father.

With respect to the second type of description, the Bible indicates that each person is truly distinct from the other persons. What is the nature of this real distinction? The distinction does not involve the deity of the persons – these three are one Lord God. Nor does it involve a distinction in their power, wisdom or will – in God all these things are 'one' (Deut. 6:4). The nature of the real distinction between the persons is revealed in their personal proper names: 'Father', 'Son' and 'Holy Spirit'. As these names indicate, the persons are distinguished by their *relations*: the Father is Father to the Son ('paternity' is thus his unique 'personal property'), the Son is Son to the Father ('filiation' is thus his unique personal property) and the Spirit is the Spirit of the Father and the Son ('spiration' is thus his unique personal property). These personal properties are not interchangeable. The Father is not the Son. The Son is not the Father. And the Spirit is not the Father or the Son.

What more can be said about these personal properties? Again, attentive to the personal names themselves, the church has recognized that these names indicate *communicative relations*. That is to say, the personal names reflect the distinctive ways in which the persons share or communicate (i.e. 'make common') the one divine essence they hold in common. The Father is Father in that he eternally communicates the one divine essence to the Son through eternal generation: 'All things have been handed over to me by my Father' (Matt. 11:27). 'As the Father has life in himself, so he has granted the Son also to have life in himself' (John 5:26). As Adam begot Seth in his likeness, communicating human nature to him (Gen. 5:3), so the Father has eternally begotten the Son, eternally communicating the divine nature to him.

To be sure, the Adam–Seth relation is but a creaturely analogue of the Father–Son relation. Consequently, we should not measure the latter divine relation by the standard of the former creaturely relation. Adam begot Seth *in time* and in so doing became a father. However, the Father has *eternally* begotten the Son and so has always been a Father. Furthermore, when Adam begot Seth, communicating human nature to him, that human nature was *divided* into two human beings. However, in eternally begetting the Son, and communicating the divine nature to him, the divine nature is not divided into two divine beings. The Father eternally communicates the *simple, undivided* divine essence to the Son, constituting him a second divine person but not a second God.

The Son, accordingly, is Son in that he eternally receives the one divine essence from the Father in eternal generation. He is the radiance of the Father's glory and the exact representation of his person (Heb. 1:3). In terms of the Nicene Creed the Son is 'God of God, Light of Light, true God of true God.' As the preceding discussion suggests, the point of eternal generation is not that the Son is a derivative deity. The point is only that his distinctive way of being the one God is as the true Son of the Father: the Father's eternal offspring, one God with his Father in every way.

Eternal generation is not something our minds can comprehend, so determined is our thinking by the categories of time and finitude. According to Martin Luther, the doctrine of eternal generation 'is not even comprehensible to the angels', and 'those who have tried to grasp it have broken their necks over it'.[3] Nevertheless, Luther also insists, eternal generation is a doctrine 'given to us in the gospel' and glimpsed 'by faith'. The doctrine is, furthermore, beautiful teaching, for it indicates the kind of perfection that characterizes the Father as an eternally radiant, communicative perfection, and it indicates the kind of perfection that characterizes the Son: when we see the Son, we see deity shining forth in its full brilliance, supreme over all creaturely lights.

---

3. See Martin Luther, *The Three Symbols or Creeds of the Christian Faith*, in *LW*, vol. 34, pp. 216–218.

What about the Spirit? The Spirit is the Spirit of the Father (Matt. 10:20) and of the Son (Gal. 4:6). The Spirit is Spirit in that he eternally receives the one divine essence from the Father and the Son by 'spiration' or by being 'breathed out'. In classical Augustinian terms the Spirit proceeds from the Father and the Son as from one spirating source. The Spirit's 'communicative relation' is even more difficult to describe than that of the Son. But this difficulty should not discourage us; for in fact the difficulty in perceiving his mode of procession follows from the way he reveals himself: the Spirit sovereignly 'blows were he wishes' (John 3:8), characteristically directing us away from himself to the person of the Son (see John 16:13–15). When it comes to the divine light that is the Holy Spirit, proceeding from the Father and the Son, we do not typically look *at* that light but *through* that light to the glory of God that shines in the face of Jesus Christ (see 1 Cor. 2:9–16; 2 Cor. 3:18; 4:4, 6; Eph. 1:17–18). In his light we see light (Ps. 36:9).

One further point about the personal properties is worth making. The personal properties of the Father, the Son and the Spirit not only teach us about the distinctive ways in which the persons *are* God but also about the distinctive ways in which the persons *act* as God. While all three persons cooperate in all divine actions because they are one Lord God, their unified divine action nevertheless exhibits an order that corresponds to their distinctive personal properties. As the Father is the first person of the Trinity, neither begotten nor breathed, so he initiates all divine action. All things are 'from him' (1 Cor. 8:6). As the Son is the second person of the Trinity, eternally begotten of the Father, so he acts from the Father. All things are 'through' him (1 Cor. 8:6). As the Spirit is the third person of the Trinity, eternally breathed out by the Father and the Son, so he acts from the Father and the Son:

> When the Spirit of truth comes, he will guide you into all the truth, for he will not speak on his own authority, but whatever he hears he will speak, and he will declare to you the things that are to come. He will glorify me, for he will take what is mine and declare it to you. All that the Father has is mine; therefore I said that he will take what is mine and declare it to you. (John 16:13–15)

All things are brought to completion 'in him'.

Trinitarian heresies

In the light of the Bible's twofold description of the divine persons, and the doctrine of the Trinity that arises therefrom, we can better identify the root of several trinitarian errors that have plagued the church throughout history. The error of 'Sabellianism' or 'modalism' rightly recognizes the common properties of the persons – the properties that identify the persons as one God, but fails to recognize the personal properties of the persons – the properties that distinguish the persons from each other. The error of 'Arianism' or 'subordinationism' makes the opposite mistake, rightly recognizing the personal properties that distinguish the persons from each other but failing to recognize the common properties that identity each person as the one Lord God. This error not only occurs among those who deny the full deity of the Son and the Spirit; it also occurs among those who fail to appreciate that the common properties not only identify the persons as *equally* divine but also as *identically* divine – as *one* Lord God. This is the error of tritheism, an error that many contemporary 'social trinitarians' come dangerously close to making.

Space forbids lengthy reflection on these errors. It is nevertheless instructive to observe their common root: each of these trinitarian mistakes arises, to some degree, from a failure to consider what the whole counsel of God teaches regarding the persons of the Trinity. That is to say, each of these trinitarian mistakes arises from a partial, selective reading of the Scriptures. Of course, these errors exhibit other methodological mistakes as well; for example, the attempt to measure the unlimited being of the Trinity by the limited standard of creaturely being. Still, it is their failure to consider *all* of God's wonderful names, both personal and common, that constitutes the root of their idolatries.

Conclusion

When it comes to the mystery of the Trinity, Francis Turretin says we are dealing with a topic 'which neither reason can comprehend nor example prove', but which 'the authority of divine revelation alone proposes to be received by faith and adored with love'.[4] This is the goal of trinitarian doctrine: that we may rejoice in the Father, the Lord of heaven and earth (Matt. 11:25), that we may rejoice in the Son, to whom the Father has given 'all things' (Matt. 11:27) and through whose death and exaltation the Father has granted us every spiritual blessing (Rom. 8:32; Eph. 1:3) and

---

4. Francis Turretin, *Institutes of Elenctic Theology*, vol. 1, ed. James T. Dennison Jr. (Phillipsburg, N.J.: P&R, 1992), p. 253.

that we may rejoice in the Spirit (Luke 10:21), who fills our hearts with the fullness of love that characterizes God's eternal, sublime life as Father, Son and Spirit.

11. THE TRINITY AND PRAYER

Carl R. Trueman

Introduction

While all Christians believe in the doctrine of the Trinity, it is often the case that somewhat fewer are confident about the difference it makes. If they are members of a church where the Bible is consistently expounded in a manner that self-consciously connects to the historic creedal tradition, then they will no doubt have seen how the Trinity connects to the narratives and the theology of the Scriptures. Yet they may still be somewhat unclear about the present, practical difference the doctrine makes to their everyday lives.

The irony of this is that the doctrine is, in fact, one of the most immediately practical for Christians. The Trinity is far from being an abstract doctrine, and is not to be relegated to a virtual appendix in Christian theology. On the contrary, trinitarianism shapes everything, from Christian doctrine to Christian practice. If the Christian is one who is adopted by the Father through being united to Christ by the Holy Spirit, then to be a Christian is to have an identity that is trinitarian at its very core. Thus everything the believer is and everything the believer does has to be understood at some level in trinitarian terms.

Even some of the elements of trinitarianism that seem at first glance somewhat abstract are of immense existential and practical significance. It is surely no coincidence that the development of the classical doctrine of the Trinity is inextricably connected to the development of liturgies and patterns of worship in the ancient church.[1] Further, when Athanasius refused to compromise on the issue of the consubstantiality of the Father and the Son, this was for reasons vital both to salvation and to the heart of the Christian's worship and life: prayer. Prayer is, after all, the most intimate point of practical communion between the believer and God, and that intimacy is itself rooted in the action of God in Christ towards God the Father through the Holy Spirit. As salvation is trinitarian, so inevitably is prayer.[2]

When questions of the Trinity and prayer typically arise, they tend to focus on issues of the object of prayer. Do we pray to the Father alone, or to each of the persons of the Trinity? Is it legitimate to pray to Jesus? Do we pray by ascribing different roles in creation and salvation to each of the three persons? All of these are legitimate concerns and reflect a desire to allow the trinitarian economy of salvation to shape the believer's devotional life. But there is more to trinitarian prayer than the question of to whom prayer is to be directed and for what. The Trinity is first significant not so much for the shape of our prayers as for their very foundation. Trinity and Christology establish prayer as part of the economy of salvation itself. In fact, if God were not Trinity, then specifically Christian prayer would not exist in any form, for there would be no means of addressing God. Thus in this chapter we will look first at the foundation of prayer in the Trinity and then at how the trinitarian work of salvation shapes the practice of prayer.

---

1. See Robert Daly, S. J., 'Eucharist and Trinity in the Liturgies of the Early Church', in Khaled Anatolios (ed.), *The Holy Trinity in the Life of the Church* (Grand Rapids: Baker Academic, 2014), pp. 15–38.

2. 'For if there were no unity, nor the Word the own Offspring of the Father's Essence, as the radiance of the light, but the Son were divided in nature from the Father, it were sufficient that the Father alone should give, since none of originate things is a partner with his Maker in His givings; but, as it is, such a mode of giving shews the oneness of the Father and the Son. No one, for instance, would pray to receive from God and the Angels, or from any other creature, nor would any one say, "May God and the Angel give thee;" but from Father and the Son, because of Their oneness and the oneness of Their giving. For through the Son is given what is given; and there is nothing but the Father operates it through the Son; for thus is grace secure to him who receives it' (Athanasius, *Against the Arians* 3.12 [*NPNF*[2] 4:400]).

The Trinity and the foundation of Christian prayer

Central to understanding the connection of the Trinity to prayer is Christ's role as priest. Prayer is an integral part of his priestly role, and it is this that provides the objective basis for the prayers of the saints. It is because Christ is the great intercessor on behalf of his people that his people's own intercessions are heard by the Father.

The Westminster Shorter Catechism summarizes Christ's priesthood well:

> Q. 25. How does Christ execute the office of a priest?
> A. Christ executes the office of a priest, in his once offering up of himself a sacrifice to satisfy divine justice, and reconcile us to God, and in making continual intercession for us.

Here the Catechism summarizes an important strand of biblical teaching. The New Testament makes a clear connection between the prayers of the saints and the intercession of Christ before the Father. The argument of the book of Hebrews makes this a central point: the divine–human mediator is central to the Christian's status before God and to understanding the ongoing nature of divine activity in our salvation. Intercession is an integral part of Christ's priestly action that continues in the present. As he died on Calvary as a sacrifice for sin, so he now lives before the Father to offer that sacrifice on behalf of his people.

There are a number of observations we can make about this priesthood in relation to the Trinity.

First, we should note that Christ's priesthood points clearly to God's sovereignty in salvation. The Lord chooses who is to be a priest (Lev. 8). Specifically, we are told that he appointed Christ as priest (Heb. 5:4–6). This is demonstrated in the historical narrative of the virgin birth and the Spirit's anointing of Christ at his baptism. This sets all of the actions of Christ's priesthood, including his intercession within the context of God's sovereign will. Thus the definitive act of prayer – that of Christ to his Father – is an act of the sovereign God.

Second, we should note that Christ's priesthood in general reveals the trinitarian nature of God. As Christ declares in his high priestly prayer in the Gospel of John, he has been sent by the Father. He is also one who is empowered by the Spirit at his baptism. There is no other God than that God who has revealed himself in the actions of Father, Son and Holy Spirit. They are all bound together in the economy of salvation in a manner that exhibits a perfect harmony of intention and execution. Thus all of Christ's actions, including his intercession are to be set within the context of a trinitarian understanding of God.

Indeed, the New Testament makes it quite clear that the human act of prayer is intimately connected to the trinitarian actions of God and is in fact enfolded and subsumed within that larger divine action. Thus in Romans 8:26 Paul declares that the Spirit intercedes for believers in their weakness, when they do not know what they should pray for. The personhood of the Spirit is important here: intercession is a personal activity. Furthermore, Paul is stirring up the believer to confidence by placing human prayer within the divine economy of salvation relating to the persons of the Trinity. Thus the human act of prayer is clearly to be understood against the background of a more profound reality: the intercession of the Spirit for the saints. This places the believer's prayers within the very trinitarian life of God himself and is both a doctrinal truth and a practical reality

Third, given this we should observe that this trinitarian economy of salvation serves to make the accomplishment of salvation by Christ itself an act of devotion and prayer. Christ's earthly life was marked by prayer, and that was also closely connected to his obedience and suffering (Heb. 5:7–8). This also places love at the centre of salvation: Christ offers himself through his prayer to God the Father as an act of love towards both him and those on whose behalf he prays.

Furthermore, while we should never reduce the work of Christ to that of mere moral example, it is clear from Christ's own life that his intercession is in part paradigmatic for the believer. As Christ prayed to the Father, so he instructs his followers to do the same (Matt. 6:9; 26:39). As Christ prayed for strength from the Father, and for the Father's will to be done, so he instructs his followers to do the same (Matt. 6:10–11; 26:39). And even in the practice of drawing aside to pray, Christ makes it clear that he is setting his disciples an example to follow (Matt. 6:6; Mark 6:46).

This then brings us to the first practical point about prayer and the Trinity: Christ's trinitarian priesthood should fill Christians with confidence and be an encouragement to all those who fear God to approach him. This is because in Christ we have the perfect example and the perfect intermediary. While there can be a tendency to understand Christ's intercession as something that cajoles the Father into granting something he is not immediately keen to do, such a view rests upon a failure to understand the significance of that which Athanasius saw so clearly: God the Father, God the Son and God the Holy Spirit are one God and all desire the same things. Thus Christ as the God-man asks the Father only for that which the Father desires to give him, and he does so as one who perfectly understands what it is to be human. When Christ prays to the Father for us, the Father will grant him what he asks, for it is only what he himself desires anyway.

Yet the very fact that in Christ human nature has been brought into communion with the Godhead also has profound significance. Human beings instinctively like intermediaries in difficult situations, even trivial ones. When we move into the spiritual realm and address the matter of a holy God and a sinful people, the desirability of an intermediary is dramatically increased. When Adam fell, he feared God because he knew he was naked and thus incapable of standing before God in his own strength. There was no intermediary, so he covered himself and hid from the Lord's presence. At Sinai the people of Israel were terrified by the noise and storm surrounding God's presence and thus Moses acted on behalf of them on the mountain, an arrangement later formalized in the rituals surrounding the Tent of Meeting. Most significantly, in the Old Testament the priest entered the Holy Place alone to make atonement and to offer intercession on behalf of the people.

Against this background the incarnation takes on specific importance with regard to prayer. Typically, of course, the incarnation has often been construed as necessary with reference to the death of Christ. The influence of the Anselmic argument has undoubtedly exerted huge influence here. Yet it is also clear that a similar argument for the incarnation can be derived from Christ's intercession, which is hardly surprising given that sacrifice and intercession are both aspects of his priesthood.

First, Christ's humanity makes him an appropriate person to intercede on our behalf, for he knows what it is like to be human and is from our perspective an approachable intermediary (Heb. 4:14–16). He is human like us; he has been tempted in every way like us except he is without sin. He understands what it is like to be us, and approaches his Father on that basis. In Christ God does not merely stoop down to the level of humanity: human nature is carried up into an intimate relation with the divine.

Second, his divine nature makes his intercession not merely something of power but something that has an absolute guarantee of success. Our prayers are powerful because they rest upon his status as both sacrificer and sacrifice. As the Levitical priests both sacrificed and then offered that sacrifice to God, so Christ is both sacrificed on the cross and then presents that sacrifice before his Father as he intercedes for his people in heaven. The unity of the priestly action of Christ is thus effective and powerful and now finds its location at the very heart of God.

This is one very practical reason why the fourth-century debates about the consubstantiality of the Father and Son – the fights over the *homoousion* – were so practically vital. While contemporary scholarship has demonstrated the complexity of the fourth-century debates and effectively undermined the old taxonomy that pitted clearly defined parties against each other, the practical importance of the *homoousion* (of *same* substance) can still be shown by comparing it with one of the alternative terms that emerged in the 360s: *homoiousion* (of *similar* substance). Similarity seems to offer a reasonable alternative to the options of radical difference or absolute identity. Yet the compromise is fatal to the economy of salvation. Similarity supposes difference and, as Athanasius and his allies argued, if the Son is not God as the Father is God, he cannot save. Such a Christ could not draw humanity up into the full communion with God that salvation involved.

When reflecting on the importance of the Trinity for prayer, we may make the same point from the perspective of Christ's intercession. If Father and Son are only of similar substance, then a potential gap always exists between that which the Father wills and that which the Son desires. As noted above, that which guarantees the efficacy of the Son's intercession is that he asks for that which the Father desires to give. We may add the Spirit to this and say that the Spirit's intercession as described in Romans 8 is also effective only because he too acts at all times in accordance with the divine will because he too is fully God. The power of the intercessions of Christ and the Spirit rests on the fact that they desire from God the Father only that which he himself delights to grant. If that is undermined by any gap between the nature of their being and that of the Father, then the confidence we can have in our prayers is effectively shattered.

In fact, we can conclude this summary understanding of the relationship between Trinity and intercession by noting that it is simply one specific element in the larger trinitarian economy of salvation. Father, Son and Holy Spirit all play their part in creation and providence, and all play their part in salvation too.

Practically speaking, therefore, a healthy, vibrant prayer life depends to a large extent upon a good understanding of trinitarian doctrine. Only then will we both understand what it is we are doing and have confidence that it will be effective and powerful. A correct doctrine of God as Trinity does not guarantee a healthy prayer life, but a defective doctrine of the Trinity guarantees a prayer life that will be much less than it should be.

Given this, we now need to address the second aspect of the trinitarian understanding of prayer. If the doctrine of the Trinity explains the foundation of prayer in the person and work of Jesus Christ, Son of the Father, through the Holy Spirit, then how practically should this shape the human act of prayer?

On trinitarian communion

Given what we noted above, it is perhaps strange that very few theologians have ever attempted to articulate an understanding of the practice of prayer that is decisively rooted in understanding the Trinity. One notable exception to this is the English Puritan John Owen (1616–83). His *On Communion with God in Three Persons* (1657) is a masterful account of how the three persons interact on the economy of salvation and of the implications this has for how believers should frame their devotional life.

Before outlining Owen's arguments, it is worth noting that it is no coincidence that he produced such a treatise. Reformed orthodoxy, the tradition of theology that stemmed from the Reformed wing of the Reformation, was in part driven by the desire to understand the connection between an anti-Pelagian understanding of salvation, which placed a high premium on the sovereignty of God's grace, and the fact that God is Trinity. Thus Reformed orthodoxy was occupied to a significant extent with working out the implications of trinitarianism for salvation in all its aspects. This operated at both the strictly dogmatic level, where theologians developed concepts such as the covenant of redemption, and the practical level, where such questions as 'To whom should I pray to give thanks for particular elements of my salvation?' arose.[3]

Thus Reformed orthodoxy at its best was profoundly trinitarian, setting redemption within a trinitarian structure and thus the identity of redeemed men and women within a trinitarian context. The believer is the one who has communion with God the Father by union with God the Son through the Holy Spirit. Prayer, as a central act of the believer's life, is thus to be understood in trinitarian terms.

Many Christians, of course, instinctively acknowledge the identity of God as Trinity and the significance of this for their prayer life by ending their prayers with a formulaic reference something akin to 'to you, God our Father, in the name of your Son, Jesus Christ, by the power of His Holy Spirit'. This is good as far as it goes, for it acknowledges the fact that each person of the Trinity is involved in some way in our salvation and in our action of prayer, which derives from that salvation. Yet, as with all such formulas, we need to make sure that the words we use lead us into a deeper understanding of what we do.

Owen's argument rests upon the assumption that, in their natural state, human beings live in darkness, cut off from God, who is, by way of contrast, light.[4] Thus any discussion of communion with God or of prayer to him is

---

3. For more detail on this general development see Carl R. Trueman, *The Claims of Truth: John Owen's Trinitarian Theology* (Carlisle: Paternoster, 1998). Owen's works are available from Banner of Truth, ed. W. Goold, in 16 vols. (Edinburgh, 1965–8). Hereafter *Works*.

4. *Works* 2.6.

predicated upon the saving action of God in Christ and on the believer's union with him. Owen divides this communion in two. There is the perfect communion that will be enjoyed only in eternity; and there is an initial, incomplete communion we have here and now. The former is to be seen as the perfection of the latter and thus, in a very deep sense, as being continuous with it.[5] This is consistent with what we have already noted about the foundation of our intercession and salvation: the work of Christ before the Father by the Spirit.

Owen then moves from this foundation to state that the believer has distinct communion with Father, Son and Holy Spirit. Owen's primary text for this is 1 John 5:7, the so-called Johannine comma. Taken by itself, of course, this would be extremely weak as support for Owen's argument, given its status as a later interpolation. Yet Owen's argument does not depend upon this verse. Clearly, there is the larger trinitarian structure of salvation that lies behind his thinking at this point and that he elaborates at great length elsewhere.[6] There are also other texts to which he points, for example Ephesians 2:18, which distinguish economic roles of Father, Son and Holy Spirit in the believer's communion with God.

Worship is also key to the foundation of Owen's trinitarian understanding of prayer. For him worship involves making God the object of the graces of the soul, faith, love, trust, joy, and so on. And Scripture ascribes each of these to each member of the Godhead. For example, the Father is the object of faith because he testifies to the Son, and in believing his testimony we show faith in the Father (1 John 5:9). The Son too is an object of faith (John 14:1). And the sin of unbelief is characterized as opposition to the Holy Spirit. A similar arrangement applies to the matters of love and joy as well.[7]

The same basic distinction of persons in the one economy of salvation can be noted relative to actions. Thus the Father teaches the promise of salvation (John 6:45), but so does the Son (Matt. 17:5) and the Spirit (John 14:26). In each case Scripture attributes acts in the economy of salvation to the different persons of the Godhead, even when the same act is being ascribed to each of them.

For Owen this has implications for the practice of prayer. It is not enough for the believer to ascribe salvation to God as an undifferentiated *one*. The nuances of Scripture reflect nuances in the economy of salvation and these are to be reflected in the act of prayer. We may observe, therefore, that the standard trinitarian close to prayer, from Owen's perspective, fails to do justice to the

5. Ibid., p. 9.

6. See Trueman, *Claims of Truth, passim.*

7. *Works*, vol. 2, pp. 11–14.

richness of the trinitarian content of salvation. Those who do not allow trini-tarianism to permeate the content and structure of their prayer are not allowing Scripture to regulate their prayer in a truly Christian way.

Communion with the Father

As a good trinitarian, Owen is aware that one can never talk exclusively about one person of the Godhead without including at some level the other two. Failure to understand that leads inexorably towards tritheism. Owen holds to the standard patristic axiom, that external works of the Godhead are works of the whole God. There is also a concurrence of each of the persons in every act.[8] Thus when Owen talks of distinct communion with each of the persons, he is speaking of the 'order in the dispensation of grace which God is pleased to hold out in the gospel'.[9] In other words, he believes that Christians should frame their prayers to God in a manner that takes specific account of the foun-dation, execution and application of salvation.

Thus when Owen addresses the matter of communion with the Father, the central point he wants the believer to understand is that the economy of salva-tion reveals the Father as a God of love. Unlike creation and fall, which show God the Father as sovereign and powerful, and then righteous and wrathful against sin, under the gospel the Father is pre-eminently revealed as loving.[10]

Owen here adopts the standard distinction between the love of good pleasure and the love of friendship, both of which he says should be ascribed to the Father.[11] The distinction is important, particularly in a day like ours, where love has been reduced to something sentimental or even merely sexual. Love is biblically and historically a much richer concept than the attenuated idea presented in a myriad soap operas and sitcoms.

The love of good pleasure is God the Father's determined will to do good. Thus the whole of the economy of redemption, rooted in the love of God as articulated in John 3:16, is thus rooted in this. Yet there is more to divine love than this basic loving purpose. There is also a more intimate, personal love, expressed in texts such as John 14:23, that binds the Father together with the individual Christian.

---

8. Ibid., p. 18.
9. Ibid., p. 19.
10. Ibid.
11. Ibid., p. 21.

Owen correctly sees that mistakes at this point are often the source of pastoral difficulties for Christians. For example, there is the idea that Christ's atonement is somehow an offering made by a Son who loves sinners to a Father who is angry with them and who thus needs to be cajoled into changing his mind. This kind of theology is predicated on a view of God the Father that is likely to cause problems, as the believer's mind is filled with concerns about the attitude of God the Father towards her. Indeed, we may even press it further and say that it is ultimately lethal to any understanding of prayer: if the believer's prayer is powerful because of the intercession of the Son and Spirit, but these two are at odds with the Father, then how can the Christian have any confidence that prayer will be answered? Owen puts forward the contrary, stated in a powerful and beautiful way:

> Few can carry up their hearts and minds to this height of faith, as to rest their souls in the love of the Father; they live below it, in the troublesome region of hopes and fears, storms and clouds. All here is serene and quiet. But how to attain this pitch they know not. This is the will of God, that he may always be eyed as benign, kind, tender, loving, and unchangeable therein; and that peculiarly as the Father, as the great fountain and spring of all gracious communications and fruits of love. This is that which Christ came to reveal.[12]

We can draw some obvious practical results that flow from this. First, prayer is to be confident because we approach a God who loves us. That we are praying to God the Father as *our* Father is itself evidence that he first loved us, for it is predicated upon a relationship he has sovereignly established. The opening of the Lord's Prayer is full of theological significance upon which the believer should meditate. She does not approach a distant deity or a God who relates to her simply as a lord relates to a vassal or a master to a servant. The Lord is our Father and that sets the tone both of respect and intimacy that come from paternal love.

Second, if God loves us as Father, then prayer is to be understood as a responsive act of love on our part. If God's love to us is one of bounty, to use Owen's phrase, one that flows out to us from his being, then our love to him is one of duty. Yet this duty is to be understood in affiliative terms. It is not a duty that is the foundation for our relationship with God, but it is a response to that relationship. Prayer is thus part of our loving response, framed by love and rooted in our understanding God the Father as love.

---

12. Ibid., p. 23.

The result of this is that Owen regards reflection upon the love of God the Father as central to Christian piety. It encourages us to delight in God, to respond to him in love and to have exalted thoughts of him. All of these are important elements of a healthy prayer life and also indicate that doctrine, so often decried as the enemy of piety, is actually central to piety and foundational to a proper attitude in prayer. Correct doctrine in itself, of course, does not guarantee piety; but it is a precondition to it. When believers come before God in prayer, it is vital that they have a clear understanding that the God to whom they pray is loving, and that requires a solid understanding of the role of God the Father in the economy of salvation. It also drives believers towards God the Son.

Communion with God the Son

The centrality of love to Owen's understanding of God the Father is connected to his understanding of God the Son. God the Son reveals the love of God the Father. Yet the Son also has a distinct role to play in the believer's communion with God: he is the mediator and as the principle distinct act of God the Father is his love, so that of the Son is grace. This section of Owen's work is by far the longest, and reflects the fact that Owen's theology is Christological at its very core: the mediation of Christ is the supreme revelation of God and the dynamic centre of salvation.

Owen divides grace into three. First, there is the grace of Christ's person, in terms of his personal excellence; there is the grace of free favour; and there is the grace of the fruits of the Spirit.[13] As to the first, Owen sees Christ's grace as involving his incarnation, which was a free act of the Godhead, the complete sufficiency of the incarnate Christ to save, and his complete suitability to meet all of the real needs of fallen human beings.[14]

This communion of the believer with Christ ties in with the Father because it is only in Christ that God is revealed as loving and merciful. Other attributes, such as justice, patience and wisdom are revealed elsewhere and then more perfectly in Christ.[15] But only in Christ is love revealed. Of course, as noted above, love is an attribute of the Father, but that love of the Father is made manifest exclusively in the sending of the Son. Thus the Son reveals the love

---

13. Ibid., pp. 47–48.
14. Ibid., pp. 51–52.
15. Ibid., pp. 83–91.

of the Godhead for sinners.[16] The same is also true of his mercy.[17] Again we can see the immediate significance of this for prayer. To thank God the Father for his love is to reflect upon the mission of Christ; and knowing that the mission of Christ arises out of the love of God the Father reinforces our confidence that our intercessions will be heard because Christ's intercession is itself part of the Father's loving will. Only in Christ, Owen believes, do we find all the attributes of God perfectly manifested and set forth in a way that brings comfort, rather than fear or darkness.[18]

In fact, Owen sees Scripture as going further than simply presenting Christ as comfort. Communion with God the Son is to be understood in conjugal terms, as a marriage between Christ and the believer. While much of Owen's textual support for this is rooted in a traditional allegorical reading of the Song of Songs, which some modern readers may find unpersuasive, at least in isolation, he is of course also building on clear New Testament teaching as found, for example, in Ephesians 5. In this context it is interesting that Owen explores the idea in a slightly unusual way. Whereas the tendency is often to focus on the unitive aspect in the analogy of Christ and the church to human marriage, he focuses primarily on the mutual self-revelation that takes place between husband and wife. Christ in taking the church as his bride reveals his thoughts to the saints, and the saints in turn reveal their thoughts to him. This is at the heart of the mutual delight that Christ and the saints have in each other.[19] The Christian approaches God in Christ as if Christ were a loving husband. Love and delight are to characterize the relationship.

In addition to the conjugal relation Owen also identifies adoption as providing another guiding motif for understanding communion with God the Son. In Christ the believer is adopted as a child of the Father and thus approaches the loving God as Father. Again this is to have a profound impact upon the way we pray, especially giving us boldness in our approach.[20] One might also add that

---

16. Ibid., pp. 81–82.

17. Ibid., pp. 82–83.

18. Ibid., p. 92.

19. 'It is only a bosom *friend* unto whom we will *unbosom* ourselves. Neither is there, possibly, a greater evidence of delight in close communion than this, that one will reveal his heart unto him whom he takes into society, and not entertain him with things common and vulgarly known. And therefore have I chose[n] this instance, from amongst a thousand that might be given, of this delight of Christ in his saints' (ibid., p. 119, emphases original).

20. Ibid., p. 221.

it offers us a framework for praying about suffering: nothing is more important to a loving earthly father than both appropriate loving discipline for his children, which may be experienced by them at times as a form of suffering, and alleviating their unnecessary suffering. Our status in Christ as sons and daughters of God the Father should shape how we address the matter of suffering in our supplications and intercessions.

Thus when we think of God and approach him in prayer, Owen would argue that the love of the Father is manifested through the forgiveness and adoption we have through Jesus Christ the Son. That gives us confidence in our approach because it gives us confidence in our status and in God's disposition towards us. Again doctrine is central, not in a dry way but as that which shapes and suffuses the believer's devotions with appropriate and affective thoughts of Christ.

Communion with God the Spirit

Owen stands in the sound biblical and theological tradition of seeing the Holy Spirit as the agent of God's work in creation. In this context Owen draws first upon the biblical notions of the Spirit as Comforter. Of course, by this point in Owen's argument it should be clear that the comfort the Spirit provides is itself trinitarian: the comfort of knowing personally the love of the Father as revealed in the Son. This is why Jesus' ascension was a good thing, because then the Spirit came in fullness and Jesus was, we might say, present everywhere.[21]

For Owen the primary significance of the Spirit is that he draws attention to Christ. Thus he brings to the believer's mind the words of Christ, something that is constitutive of the comfort the Spirit provides: the promises of Christ and the revelation of God the Father's love are the foundation of the believer's comfort and assurance.[22] The Spirit also sheds abroad the love of God in our hearts and assures us of our adoption. Again we can see the obvious trinitarian context of this.[23]

Owen is aware, however, that the ministry of the Spirit has historically been subject to two errors. First, there are those who effectively ignore and practically despise the ministry of the Spirit. Owen is a man – and a Puritan – of his time,

---

21. Ibid., p. 226.
22. Ibid., p. 237.
23. Ibid., pp. 240–241.

and sees this to be the error of conformist Anglicans with a high view of formal liturgy.[24] On the other side, Owen notes those who talk up the Spirit without reference to Word or ordinance. This was the error of radicals.[25] For Owen, in contrast to both, prayer is to be *in the Spirit*. That means it is to be rooted in the Word and the word, as both reveal God to us. Second, prayer is to glorify God, for that is what the Spirit is meant to do. And as Christians are those in whom the Spirit dwells, then our lives, and especially perhaps our prayers, are to do the same. The trinitarian function of the Spirit spills over into the purpose of our prayers.[26]

Further, there is the fact that the Spirit is the Spirit of adoption.[27] It is through the Spirit that the believer cries out to God as Father. Again this ties in with the basic trinitarian structure of salvation and of the Christian's identity: the Spirit enables us to call out to God as Father as we have been adopted by him through the Son.

Praying to God as a Trinity

Because God is a Trinity and because we commune with him as a Trinity, Owen believes that we are to be conscious of how each person works within the economy of salvation. Thus in each section of the discourse he highlights specific things the believer is to understand about each of the persons. At the end of the treatise, however, he addresses specifically the nature of prayer and the Godhead.

He makes it clear that the divine essence is to be the object of worship. Thus as Father, Son and Holy Spirit all partake of the divine essence, so all are to be objects of worship and invocation. Owen sees this taught, for example, in Ephesians 2:18, where we have access to God the Father through the Son by the Holy Spirit. Yet Owen also believes each person is to be worshipped individually.

This touches on a question sometimes raised with regard to prayer: Can one address prayer only to God the Father or also to the Son and the Holy Spirit? Scripture, after all, seems to give explicit sanction only to the first. Yet Owen makes the eminently reasonable point that both Son and Spirit are divine, which

---

24. Ibid., p. 255.
25. Ibid., p. 257.
26. Ibid., pp. 257–258.
27. Ibid., p. 249.

fact should provoke our adoration, and that both do saving works, which should provoke our gratitude.[28]

Trinitarian prayer today

It is clear from the above that trinitarianism is vital to a confident prayer life, that a solid trinitarianism is vital for a healthy Christian life. There is nothing more distinctive and personal about Christianity than prayer; and here at the heart of prayer lies the doctrine of the Trinity. At a theological level trinitarianism is the basis upon which – to put it rather bluntly – prayer works. It is because we have an advocate with the Father who is of the same substance as the Father that we can be confident our prayers will be heard and answered. It is because the Spirit is God and intercedes for us in ways which transcend our comprehension that we can be confident our prayers will be heard and answered. Any teaching on prayer, and any encouragement to pray, needs to be rooted in this great doctrinal truth.

The first step to encouraging trinitarian prayer is, therefore, to cultivate a robust understanding of the Trinity in our congregations. While the world of academic theology may be said to have had something of an embarrassment of riches in terms of studies of the Trinity over the last fifty years, it seems that this has yet to make a profound impact at the local level. Thus pastors and elders need to be very self-conscious in their approach to this issue. It is only as Christians are exposed to the importance of the Trinity week by week that they will come to see the doctrine's crucial importance for understanding the identity of Christ, the economy of salvation and the trinitarian dimensions of their own identity in Christ. The elements in this are the elements of worship itself: sermons, hymns and prayers that advocate and model trinitarianism and highlight the significance of the Trinity for the Christian life.

Of course, ours is an anti-dogmatic age, at least when those dogmas happen to be those of traditional Christian theology and seem at first glance to be rather complicated and perhaps abstract. Yet we must remember that from the role of liturgy in the formation of trinitarian dogma through to Owen's elaborate exposition of communion with God, the church regarded the Trinity as something of huge practical, doxological importance. Pastors need to be well versed in trinitarianism and to teach it to their congregations. And that not simply as an abstract truth, but as something with obvious, vital, practical significance.

---

28. Ibid., pp. 269–270.

Though Owen disliked formal liturgy intensely, it is arguable that one of the best ways to cultivate and reinforce trinitarianism in worship is to recite the Nicene Creed, the definitive church statement of the doctrine, as part of regular worship. In addition, careful attention to the selection of hymns and praise songs is important. People learn from everything that happens in a worship service, not just the sermon. Indeed, there are probably many Christians who imbibe more of their theology, for good or ill, from what they sing than from what they hear taught. Not all hymns are explicitly trinitarian but we should take time to make sure that those which are trinitarian are used regularly and to good effect. Those with the gift of writing hymns and praise songs should consciously strive to make them trinitarian, both as exercises in doxology and as examples of pedagogy.

It also requires a revival in the habit of well-thought-out public prayer. Evangelicalism has tended to emphasize spontaneity as a hallmark of spiritual authenticity and vitality. While this is no doubt intended for good – nobody wants dry formalism, after all – it has nonetheless always been a somewhat specious criterion. How spontaneous can even the most contemporary praise song really be, given it is already a set form of words by the time it is used in worship? In fact, to lead in public prayer in church is not only to lead the congregation into the presence of God but it is also to influence the way the congregants themselves will pray. Such prayers are to model reverence and should also model the theology of prayer: approaching God as triune and ascribing to each person the work that Scripture specifically allocates to each one.

Finally, individual Christians must take responsibility for understanding what they do when they pray. As with so many tasks we do on a regular, routine basis, prayer is something that many of us rarely reflect upon as a theological act. Yet it is clear that prayer must be understood theologically if it is to be done confidently and joyously. And understanding how it connects to the doctrine of the Trinity is one vital – perhaps the most vital – aspect of that.

12. THE TRINITY AND REVELATION

Mark D. Thompson

In conversation with his disciples Jesus said, 'no one knows the Son except the Father, and no one knows the Father except the Son and anyone to whom the Son chooses to reveal him' (Matt. 11:27). When, a little later, Simon Peter confessed, 'You are the Christ, the Son of the living God', Jesus responded, 'Blessed are you, Simon Bar-Jonah! For flesh and blood has not revealed this to you, but my Father who is in heaven' (Matt. 16:16–17).[1] God has a deep, personal and eternal investment in knowing and being known. As an expression of this, he gives himself, by an act of sovereign grace, to be known by his creatures in the created arena of space and time. The trinitarian God's eternal self-knowing and the activity of making himself known in the economy of creation and redemption are, therefore, distinct but inseparable, just as more broadly the eternal processions and the temporal missions of the Trinity are distinct but inseparable.[2] So too all true human knowledge of God is in reality

---

1. English translations are taken from the ESV.
2. The classic treatment of the distinction between eternal processions and temporal missions is Augustine's *De Trinitate*, bks. 5 and 15. For modern discussion of the relation between the two see Travis E. Ables, *Incarnational Realism: Trinity and the Spirit in Augustine and Barth* (New York: Bloomsbury T&T Clark, 2013), pp. 180–185; Scott R. Swain, *The God of the Gospel: Robert Jenson's Trinitarian Theology* (Downers Grove: InterVarsity Press, 2013), pp. 191–193.

a subset of the triune God's knowledge of himself: partial and subject to our epistemological limitations, but nonetheless real and true.[3] Our knowledge of God is dependent on both his nature and his will. The apostle Paul would spell this out further. It is the Spirit who enables the believer to cry, 'Abba! Father!' (Rom. 8:15–16), the same Spirit without whom it is impossible to confess 'Jesus is Lord' (1 Cor. 12:3). So a trinitarian consideration of God's activity of revealing himself is not a novelty: the New Testament itself binds together the doctrine of the Trinity and the doctrine of revelation.

Without revelation there could be no doctrine of the Trinity. That is almost self-evident. The doctrine of the Trinity is not a conclusion from natural theology. This description of God's eternal being and nature does not ordinarily arise from our meditation upon the world around us. Aquinas's unmoved mover, uncaused cause, unconditioned conditioner of all things, and all the rest, need not be triune.[4] Despite the 'vestiges' or echoes of God's triune nature in the world he has created, suggested by Augustine and others through the ages, no one has seriously suggested that the doctrine arises from our reflection upon them. They are faint, partial and imperfect confirmations of what we have heard from elsewhere.[5] The knowledge of the one God as eternally Father, Son and Holy Spirit is not something that comes naturally to us. We had to be told and shown that this is what God is like. In other words, this doctrine is given to us, not achieved by us.

---

3. Reformed theology, since at least the time of Franciscus Junius' *De vera theologia* (1594), has employed a distinction between *theologia archetypa* and *theologia ectypa* to make an important point about God's knowledge of himself and our knowledge of God: 'This [true] theology is either archetypal, i.e., the wisdom of God himself, or ectypal, i.e., wisdom informed by God' (W. J. van Asselt, 'The Fundamental Meaning of Theology: Archetypal and Ectypal Theology in Seventeenth-Century Reformed Thought', *WTJ* 64 [2002], p. 327). Archetypal theology is original, direct, infinite and exhaustive. Ectypal theology, on the other hand, is finite, derivative and mediated, and so always partial and incomplete (see 1 Cor. 13:12). F. Junius, *A Treatise on True Theology*, tr. D. C. Noe (Grand Rapids: Reformation Heritage, 2014), pp. 103–120. It is most likely, as Amandus Polanus suggested, this distinction is a variation of the distinction between *theologia in se* and *theologia nostra* used by Duns Scotus in his *Lectura librum primum sententarium, Opera Omnia XVI* (Civitas Vaticana, 1950–), prol., q. III, lec. iv (Van Asselt, 'Fundamental Meaning', p. 322).

4. Aquinas, *Summa Theologiae*, Ia, q. 2, art. 3.

5. Augustine himself admitted this (Augustine, *De Trinitate* 15.6 [10]).

But to what extent might the opposite be true: that without the Trinity there could be no genuine doctrine of revelation? At one level, of course, this is nonsense. Both Judaism and Islam have doctrines of revelation while refusing to countenance any suggestion that the God who reveals himself and his will is triune. There seems no prima facie reason why a solitary monad could not make himself known just as effectively as the triune God of Christian faith. That is, until we start to examine more closely the issues surrounding a transcendent God's making himself known within the structures of a world created and at every point sustained by him. To use the terminology of the philosophers, how can the finite possibly contain or even comprehend the infinite? Questions emerge about the necessity or otherwise of mediation when it comes to revelation. Can a transcendent God be known directly and in an unmediated fashion? Does the Creator–creature distinction, recognition of which prevents us falling into pantheism or even panentheism, have consequences for our knowing? Are Jesus' words 'No one comes to the Father except through me' (John 14:6) a reference to a covenantal decision on the part of God, or do they reflect something about God's very nature and the way he has always related to creation?

The two questions that provide the basic structure of this chapter then are these: first, how necessary is God's eternal triune nature to divine revelation in general and the Christian doctrine of revelation in particular? Then, what shape does God's eternal triune nature give to the Christian doctrine of revelation?

The necessity of God's triune being and nature for true and effective revelation

The biblical answer to my first question is evident in the quotation with which I began: 'no one knows the Son except the Father, and no one knows the Father except the Son and anyone to whom the Son chooses to reveal him' (Matt. 11:27). A similar conviction is found in the prologue to John's Gospel: 'No one has ever seen God; the only God, who is at the Father's side, he has made him known' (John 1:18). Most direct of all are the words of Jesus already mentioned, 'No one comes to the Father except through me' (John 14:6). As one contemporary commentator has put it, 'There is a self-enclosed world of Father and Son that is opened to others only by the revelation provided by the Son.'[6] The eternal Father remains unknown and unapproached apart from the ministry of

---

6. D. A. Carson, 'Matthew', in F. E. Gaebelein (ed.), *The Expositor's Bible Commentary*, 12 vols. (Grand Rapids: Zondervan, 1984), vol. 8, p. 277.

Jesus Christ, the eternal Son. More than that, our knowledge of God is firmly anchored in this eternal relation of the Father and the Son.[7] Once again that picture is filled out in a more explicitly trinitarian direction when Jesus speaks of the coming of the Spirit later in John's Gospel. On the night of his betrayal and arrest Jesus comforted his disciples:

> When the Spirit of truth comes, he will guide you into all truth, for he will not speak on his own authority, but whatever he hears he will speak, and he will declare to you the things that are to come. He will glorify me, for he will take what is mine and declare it to you. All that the Father has is mine; therefore I said that he will take what is mine and declare it to you. (John 16:13–15)

Further precision is called for at this point. We are not asking whether *the doctrine of* the Trinity is necessary for effective divine revelation. In such a case the revelation of the Lord to faithful Israelites under the old covenant would be called into question. The *doctrine* of the Trinity is the result of that progressive revelation of the living God in Scripture, which comes to its culmination in the resurrection of Jesus and the donation of the Spirit, and is expounded more systematically in the face of the challenges of others over the first four centuries of the Christian church. Rather, the question is whether an effective revelation of God, the one who made all things and upon whom all things that exist depend, is in fact made possible by who he is as Father, Son and Spirit. Just how deep does the claim 'no one comes to the Father except through me' go? What is it about the relation of Father, Son and Spirit that makes the knowledge of God possible, and not just possible but *only* possible at this point?

We are face to face here with theological categories such as the transcendence and incomprehensibility of God. In terms of the first of these the universe is not an extension of God's being, providing us with a route to travel back from the creation to the Creator. God created the universe *ex nihilo* and as something genuinely other than himself. Creation was an act of love entirely consistent with God's eternal character as love, but it was also itself an act of grace in which God remains sovereignly free. So care is needed in affirming the words of John of Damascus from the eighth century:

---

7. 'The Son is not only the organ of revelation but is himself a mystery to be revealed; the knowledge of the Father and the knowledge of the Son are two sides of the same mystery, which is now revealed, and so the Father and the Son in fellowship with one another are both subject and object of revelation' (Ned B. Stonehouse, *The Witness of Matthew and Mark to Christ* [London: Tyndale, 1944], p. 212).

Since, then, God, who is good and more than good, did not find satisfaction in self-contemplation, but in his exceeding goodness wished certain things to come into existence which would enjoy his benefits and share in his goodness, he brought all things out of nothing into being and created them, both what is visible and what is invisible.[8]

These words may be taken to suggest some kind of deficiency in God, something that makes his eternal existence apart from creation unsatisfactory. Yet this was not the Damascene's intention at all. The sovereign, self-sufficient God does not need creation to fill some lack in his eternal triune life. However, he chose to go beyond himself and create a genuine other, one that did not and could not continue to exist apart from his will and yet remains distinct at the level of being.

The ancient doctrine of God's aseity addresses precisely this point, affirming as it does both God's perfect self-sufficiency in his eternal relations as Father, Son and Spirit and the fullness of life that grounds his movement beyond himself to creatures.[9] The doctrine has its biblical warrant in both the name pronounced to Moses from the bush that did not burn 'I AM WHO I AM' (Exod. 3:14), and the words of Jesus 'For as the Father has life in himself, so he has granted the Son also to have life in himself' (John 5:26). Just so, the Spirit is life and the giver of life (John 6:63; Rom. 8:10–11). The concept of aseity has sometimes been narrowed simply to indicate God's independence or his absolute lack of contingency. However, when this attribute is understood in trinitarian terms it is much more than a contrastive concept. John Webster explains:

It is as Father, Son, and Spirit that God is of himself, utterly free and full, in the self-originate and perfect movement of his life; grounded in himself, he gives himself, the self-existent Lord of grace. God *a se* is the perfection of paternity, filiation and spiration in which he is indissolubly from, for, and in himself and out of which he bestows himself as the Lord, Savior, and partner of his creature. This triune character is the distinguishing feature of the Christian confession of God's aseity.[10]

---

8. John of Damascus, *The Orthodox Faith* 2.2 (PG 94:864–865; *NPNF²* 9:18).

9. 'For God is said to have life in Himself, not only because He alone lives by His own inherent power, but because He contains in himself the fulness of life in Himself and quickens all things' (John Calvin, *Commentary on John*, in D. W. Torrance and T. F. Torrance [eds.], *Calvin's New Testament Commentaries*, 12 vols. [Grand Rapids: Eerdmans, 1961], vol. 4, p. 131).

10. John Webster, 'Life in and of Himself: Reflections on God's Aseity', in Bruce L. McCormack (ed.), *Engaging the Doctrine of God* (Grand Rapids: Baker, 2008), p. 113.

Far from being a barrier to revelation, God's aseity, trinitarianly considered, is its essential presupposition. Precisely because God is life in himself and sufficient in himself, and because this life and sufficiency has an *ad extra* as well as *ad intra* dimension, the free act of revelation is possible without any compromise of his essential nature and character. Here we may appreciate the contribution of Karl Barth:

> The biblical witness to God sees His transcendence of all that is distinct from Himself, not only in the distinction as such, which is supremely and decisively characterised as His freedom from all conditioning by that which is distinct from Himself, but furthermore and supremely in the fact that without sacrificing His distinction and freedom, but in the exercise of them, He enters into and faithfully maintains communion with this reality other than Himself in His activity as Creator, Reconciler and Redeemer.[11]

A monistic concept of transcendence renders any suggestion of revelation problematic. How can one who is entirely distinct and ontologically remote from all else make himself known in the created order? Where would be the point of connection that makes genuine self-communication possible?[12] However, the trinitarian concept of aseity allows transcendence to be understood as relational rather than merely contrastive and to that extent isolating. If the fullness of life in God is most fundamentally relational and carries with it his freedom and determination to be the life-giver, then by analogy the fullness of God's self-knowledge may carry with it his capacity and determination to make himself known and so to be known by his creatures through revelation. Transcendence speaks of lordship at every point, not distinction to the point of isolation. Yet God's lordship, like everything else about him, must be understood in a trinitarian fashion and so is given content by the dynamic of knowing and being known, loving and being beloved, which is a feature of God's eternal relations.

---

11. *CD*, II/1, p. 303.

12. 'Historically, terrible problems have developed with concepts of transcendence and immanence. The transcendence of God (His exaltation, His mysteriousness) has been understood as God's being infinitely removed from the creation, being so far from us, so different from us, so "wholly other" and "wholly hidden" that we can have no knowledge of Him and can make no true statements about Him. Such a god, therefore, has not revealed – and perhaps cannot reveal – himself to us' (John M. Frame, *The Doctrine of the Knowledge of God* [Phillipsburg: P&R, 1987], p. 13).

This in turn causes us to think again about the related doctrine of divine incomprehensibility. Classically, the divine transcendence carries with it some notion of incomprehensibility. This ought not to be confused with divine ineffability, the suggestion that God is 'completely unknowable, completely beyond all human comprehension, completely beyond all human language and conceptions' and which in its strongest forms is self-referentially incoherent.[13] In contrast, incomprehensibility acknowledges a genuine knowledge of God, but within limits generated not just by our finitude and fallibility but by God's own perfection. God's person, character and will remain inexhaustible (Job 11:7–9; Rom. 11:33–36). Not only are his thoughts and ways higher than those of his creatures (Isa. 55:8–9), but he alone dwells in unapproachable light (1 Tim. 6:16). Nevertheless, he is still truly known by the means he has chosen (Isa. 55:10–11; 1 Tim. 6:11–15) and there will come a day when I will 'know' even as I am 'known' (1 Cor. 13:12; cf. 1 John 3:2). The doctrine of incomprehensibility is misused when it becomes the basis for agnosticism, either about God's person or his revealed will. Rather, particularly when it is put in a trinitarian frame, it presents to us an important aspect of God's being and character that is genuinely known. Incomprehensibility is in the end an *affirmation* made about God's nature.

One contemporary writer has put it this way:

> It is important to note that the warning implied in asserting the incomprehensibility of the divine essence does not arise because we do not know enough about God, or dare not speak of God the Trinity. Rather, it is because we know God in God's trinitarian self-revelation, and so feel compelled to invoke God by no other name, that the incomprehensibility of God must be emphasized. All we know and all we can say about God does not give us a comprehending take on God, but points us back to the divine self-communication, which we cannot but receive as a gift that constitutes the Christian faith.[14]

Incomprehensibility functions then as another expression of the lordship of the triune God. He is neither contained nor constrained by our knowledge

---

13. R. T. Mullins, 'An Analytic Response to Stephen R. Holmes, with a Special Treatment of His Doctrine of Divine Simplicity', in T. A. Noble and J. S. Sexton (eds.), *The Holy Trinity Revisited: Essays in Response to Stephen Holmes* (Carlisle: Paternoster, 2015), pp. 88–91.

14. Christoph Schwöbel, 'Where Do We Stand in Trinitarian Theology? Resources, Revisions, and Reappraisals', in Christophe Chalamet and Marc Vial (eds.), *Recent Developments in Trinitarian Theology: An International Symposium* (Minneapolis: Fortress, 2014), p. 70.

of him. Not only is it true that 'God's revelation does not totally exhaust his being and activity', a point made acutely by Carl F. H. Henry, but God remains the sovereign redeemer who determines how he is known.[15] T. F. Torrance spells out what this means:

> [E]ven when God draws near to us and draws us near to himself on the ground of the atoning sacrifice of Christ, and gives us access to himself through Christ and in his Spirit to know him, in some real measure, as he is in the inner relations of his eternal Being as Father, Son and Holy Spirit, he does not surrender (in Irenaean terms) his invisibility in the visibility, his incomprehensibility in the comprehensibility, of the incarnation, or therefore reduce knowledge of himself to what we can completely grasp or articulate.[16]

This idea of a true knowledge of God read against the backdrop of his inexhaustible perfection was articulated in a slightly different, and less overtly trinitarian, way by Martin Luther, who famously spoke of the hidden and revealed God (*Deus absconditus* and *Deus revelatus*). Taking a distinction he had previously used of God's acts (he acts in a hidden way under the form of the opposite: strength revealed in weakness, life-giving in death, etc.[17]), Luther turned to speak about the hiddenness of God himself:

> God must therefore be left to himself in his own majesty, for in this regard we have nothing to do with him, nor has he willed that we should have anything to do with him. But we have something to do with him insofar as he is clothed and set forth in his Word, through which he offers himself to us and which is the beauty and glory with which the psalmist celebrates him as being clothed.[18]

The inexhaustible perfection of God does not end up with silence or apophatic negations (limiting ourselves to saying only what God is not) for the reason that this perfection is ultimately relational in a way that makes his

---

15. Carl F. H. Henry, 'The Hidden and Revealed God', in idem, *God, Revelation and Authority*, vol. 2: *God Who Speaks and Shows. Fifteen Theses, Part One* (1976; repr. Wheaton: Crossway, 1999), p. 47.

16. T. F. Torrance, *The Christian Doctrine of God, One Being Three Persons* (Edinburgh: T&T Clark, 1996), p. 81.

17. 'Lectures on Romans' (1515–16), in *LW*, vol. 25, p. 366.

18. 'The Bondage of the Will' (1525), in *LW*, vol. 33, p. 139 = *WA*, vol. 18, p. 685.14–17.

movement towards his creatures in love and light a proper reflection of who he is. Revelation is a free and sovereign activity of God but it is also an entirely appropriate activity. Recognizing this, our attention is drawn not so much to the unfathomable depths of God's being and character but to what has been revealed: 'The secret things belong to the LORD our God, but the things that are revealed belong to us and to our children for ever, that we may do all the words of this law' (Deut. 29:29). What is revealed is true and truly known, yet we do not, and cannot, know God as he knows himself. As Jerome put it in the fourth century, 'It is one thing to know by equality of nature, and another by the condescension of him who reveals.'[19]

The eternal relation of the persons of the Trinity makes clear that God's nature is to be self-disclosing.[20] His giving of himself to himself as Father, Son and Holy Spirit is the prior condition of his giving of himself to creatures. Put another way, 'God's perfection is his communication *ad intra;* God's presence is his communication *ad extra.'*[21] Communion and communication are interwoven on both levels and so qualify the theological statements about transcendence, aseity and incomprehensibility. Yet care is needed at this point too. As Scott Swain reminds us, the distinction and relation of these two levels or vantage points both need attention:

> [T]he triune life of communication and communion must be considered from two
> vantage points, one internal to God (the divine life *ad intra*) and one external to
> God (the divine life *ad extra*). The triune life of communication and communion
> *ad intra* is necessary, fully actualized, and eternal – the triune God always is as he is
> in the full splendor of his blessed life (Exod. 3.14; Ps. 102.26–27; Heb. 13.8). The
> triune work of communication and communion *ad extra,* however, is contingent,
> in the process of being completed, and temporal – it is 'an economy for the fullness
> of time' (Eph. 1.10). A lot hangs on the *distinction* between these two modes of divine
> self-communication. Fail to preserve the distinction and one fails to honor the deity
> of God and the creatureliness of the creature. But a lot hangs on the *relation* between
> these two modes of self-communication as well. Fail to consider the relation and one
> fails to appreciate the wonder of the gospel: that the one who is 'the *eternal* Father of

19. Jerome, *Commentary on Matthew,* tr. Thomas P. Scheck, Fathers of the Church 117 (Washington, D.C.: Catholic University of America Press, 2008), p. 137.

20. Gabriel Fackre, *The Doctrine of Revelation: A Narrative Interpretation* (Edinburgh: Edinburgh University Press, 1997), p. 29.

21. Kevin J. Vanhoozer, *Remythologizing Theology: Divine Action, Passion, and Authorship* (Cambridge: Cambridge University Press, 2010), p. 260.

our Lord Jesus Christ' is *also* 'for the sake of Christ his Son *my* God and *my* Father' [Heidelberg Catechism Q. 26].[22]

This leads us to consider the critically significant theological category of mediation. Such mediation seems required if God is to engage the world without jeopardizing its integrity as something other than himself. But by what means does the triune God relate to the world that is other to himself and yet always and at every point dependent upon him, no less in the field of revelation as in any other sphere? The unfolding narrative of the Bible points us to significance of the word of God as his means of bringing the creation into existence, sustaining it and directing it towards the goal he has purposed for it. The psalmist rejoices that

> By the word of the LORD the heavens were made,
>   and by the breath of his mouth all their host . . .
> For he spoke, and it came to be;
>   he commanded, and it stood firm.
>
> (Ps. 33:6, 9)

This mediation is critical because it allows the created order to exist as genuinely the creation of God and yet as a genuine other, rather than as an emanation or extension of God's own being. It further secures our appreciation of God's freedom and sovereignty with respect to creation. 'The otherness of creation consists not only in its being called into existence by God's word, but also in its being capable of being addressed by God and of being called into communion with God.'[23]

It is the word spoken by God and heard by those to whom it is addressed that provides the impetus for the biblical story: from the word of blessing and then of promise in the midst of judgment in the garden, to the call of Abraham, the commissioning of Moses, the voice from the mountain after the redemption

---

22. Scott R. Swain, *Trinity, Revelation, and Reading: A Theological Introduction to the Bible and Its Interpretation* (London: T&T Clark, 2011), p. 6, emphases original.

23. Christoph Schwöbel, 'God as Conversation: Reflections on a Theological Ontology of Communicative Relations', in J. Haers and P. De Mey (eds.), *Theology and Conversation* (Leuven: Leuven University Press, 2003), p. 51. See also Colin E. Gunton, *The Christian Faith: An Introduction to Christian Doctrine* (Oxford: Blackwell, 2002), p. 10: 'In the theology of creation, therefore, language of mediation by God's Word enables us to speak both of God's free involvement with his creation and, ultimately, in Christ, of his equally free and sovereign identification with a part of it.'

from Egypt, the words given to the prophets, and finally the coming of the one who is himself the Word:

> Long ago, at many times and in many ways, God spoke to our fathers by the prophets, but in these last days he has spoken by his Son, whom he appointed the heir of all things, through whom also he created the world. (Heb. 1:1–2)

The entire biblical account of God's dealings with his creatures is framed by his words: from 'Let there be light' in Genesis 1 to 'Surely I am coming soon' in Revelation 22. 'No activity is as characteristic, or as frequently mentioned in the Bible, as God's speaking.'[24]

To give words a prominent place in my discussion of divine mediation is fitting given my reflection on divine communication and communion *ad intra* as well as *ad extra*. Communication is not alien to God's nature but integral to it. Christian trinitarian theism is, to borrow Kevin Vanhoozer's phrase, communicative theism. Such a description gives appropriate prominence to the way the living God differentiates himself from the idols that are merely the projections of human religiosity: they have mouths but cannot speak (Ps. 115:5); they are like scarecrows in a cucumber field and cannot speak (Jer. 10:5); 'Woe to him who says to a wooden thing, Awake; / to a silent stone, Arise! / Can this teach?' (Hab. 2:19). In contrast God 'having spoken . . . spoke' (Heb. 1:1–2). Christoph Schwöbel has put it well:

> The conversation about God and with God is itself rooted in the fact that God engages in conversation with his creation, from creation until the consummation of God's conversations with his creation in the Kingdom of God. Furthermore, that God engages in conversation with his creation is rooted in God's own being as conversation so that the being of the world has its ground in the conversation that God is.[25]

It is against this broad canvas of mediation through speech that the incarnation of the Son is described in John's Gospel as 'the word became flesh and dwelt among us, and we have seen his glory, glory as of the only Son from the Father, full of grace and truth' (John 1:14). The words spoken throughout

---

24. Vanhoozer, *Remythologizing*, p. 212. Karl Barth challenged the tendency to rush too quickly to a view of speaking that is more personal or powerful than acting: 'The Word of God does not need to be supplemented by an act. The Word of God is itself the act of God' (*CD*, I/1, p. 143).

25. Schwöbel, 'God as Conversation', p. 45.

the history of Israel provide the interpretative framework for understanding God's living and acting within his creation as the man Jesus Christ.[26] Conversely, as that to which those words have always been pointing, the incarnate life, death and resurrection of Jesus Christ both confirms and clarifies them. In Jesus this mediation between God and human creation in particular is seen in greater depth. As one who is genuinely God, 'in Jesus Christ God has given us a Revelation that is identical with himself',[27] while at the same time genuinely human and so part of the created order itself, he is uniquely suited to be the 'one mediator between God and men' (1 Tim. 2:5). This is a point driven home by T. F. Torrance in a variety of contexts: 'the incarnation of the Son or Word constitutes the epistemological centre in all our knowledge of God, with a centre in our world of space and time and a centre in God himself at the same time'.[28] More fulsomely:

> Because Jesus Christ is God of God and man of man in himself, in Christ we who are creatures of this world may know God in such a way that our knowledge of him rests upon the reality of God himself. It is not something that is thought up and devised out of ourselves and mythologically projected onto God, but it is grounded and controlled by what God is in himself.[29]

Torrance may well be right to say 'everything hinges on the reality of God's *self*-communication to us in Jesus Christ',[30] but what of the Holy Spirit? Just as the Son was sent into the world, was not the Spirit sent too? If the Spirit mediates God's purpose and presence in the created order, how is this coordinated with the mediating role of the Son? The most direct biblical testimony to this role of the Spirit is found in the Farewell Discourse of John's Gospel (John 14 – 16). Jesus promised his disciples that he would ask the Father and that the Father would give another helper 'to be with you for ever' (14:16). This helper is the Spirit of Truth who proceeds from the Father and 'he will bear witness about me', Jesus said (15:26). He will come to guide Christ's disciples into all

---

26. T. F. Torrance, *The Mediation of Christ*, 2nd ed. (Edinburgh: T&T Clark, 1992), p. 19.

27. Ibid., p. 23.

28. T. F. Torrance, *The Ground and Grammar of Theology: Consonance Between Theology and Science*, 2nd ed. (Edinburgh: T&T Clark, 2001), p. 165.

29. Ibid., p. 40.

30. T. F. Torrance, *Reality and Evangelical Theology: The Realism of Christian Revelation* (Downers Grove: InterVarsity Press, 1999, repr.), p. 23, emphasis original.

truth and 'take what is mine and declare it to you' (16:14). Jesus will continue to be present among his disciples after his death, resurrection and ascension through the ongoing presence of the Spirit. The correlation between Jesus' mediation and that of the Spirit is clear: the Spirit is present in the world as the one sent by the Father and the Son (14:26; 15:26; 16:17), just as the Son came into the world as the one sent by the Father (14:24; 16:5; 17:3). Luke's Gospel provides a complementary perspective that enables us to see the Spirit's mediation not as subsequent to or as a replacement for the Son's mediation, since the Spirit is intrinsically and necessarily involved in the incarnation of the Son. Not only does the Spirit overshadow the virgin, enabling her to conceive, but the Spirit rests upon the incarnate Son throughout his ministry (Luke 3:21–22; 4:16–21; 11:20). The Spirit is 'the divine agent who locates the Messiah in space and time'.[31] In particular, in Luke's Gospel, this is done through the identification of Jesus as the son of David, with all the messianic promises attached to that identification.[32] Climactically, as the writer to the Hebrews observes, it is 'through the eternal Spirit' that Christ 'offered himself without blemish to God' (Heb. 9:14). The mediation of Christ and the mediation of the Spirit are not two separate mediations but inextricably bound together. There is a deep basis in reality, in God's eternal triune life, for Calvin's insistence that word and Spirit belong together:

> For by a kind of mutual bond the Lord has joined together the certainty of his Word and of his Spirit so that the perfect religion of the Word may abide in our minds when the Spirit, who causes us to contemplate God's face, shines; and that we in turn may embrace the Spirit with no fear of being deceived when we recognize him in his own image, namely, in the Word.[33]

Apart from God's eternal triune nature, with his deep personal investment in knowing and being known that shapes the reality of his transcendence, aseity and incomprehensibility, the whole idea of divine revelation would begin to unravel. Revelation by a solitary divine being, utterly distinct from all he has made and with no need of the creation he has brought into existence is, as I

---

31. David A. Höhne, *Spirit and Sonship: Colin Gunton's Theology of Particularity and the Holy Spirit* (Farnham: Ashgate, 2010), p. 46.

32. Ibid., p. 45.

33. *Institutes* 1.9.3. Translation from John Calvin, *Institutes of the Christian Religion*, ed. John T. McNeill, tr. Ford Lewis Battles, 2 vols., LCC 20 (Louisville: Westminster John Knox, 1960), vol. 1, p. 95.

have said, deeply problematic. However, the true mediation of God's person and his purpose to us and our created existence, with all its contingency and limitations, is given in the Son who is both God and man, identified and anointed by the Spirit in the world as the Christ. In him necessary existence and contingent existence come together, as do eternity and time. The eternal self-giving of God within his own triune life is given free, sovereign expression in his reaching out to human beings to give a knowledge of himself and his purposes for us and for all of his creation. It is the dynamic relational nature of God that lies at the heart of the Christian confession of the Trinity that makes revelation possible and enables us to see that God makes himself known as he actually is:

> Through the incarnation of his Son or Word, and in the Holy Spirit mediated through him God the Father does not remain closed to us but has opened himself to our human knowing. Through Christ Jesus – as Paul expressed it – and in one Spirit we have access to the Father (Eph 2.18).[34]

Revelation shaped by God's triune being and nature

The revelation of the triune God has a particular character precisely because it is *his* activity. The direction of the disclosure is from God to creatures, whether the revelation be what is commonly described as General Revelation (the limited revelation addressed to all human beings in every place and across time through the structures of the created order, Ps. 19; Rom. 1) or Special Revelation (a more direct and focused phenomenon, addressed to specific people at particular times and in particular places: the prophets in Israel, Jesus to his disciples, and the apostles to followers of Christ throughout the last days, Heb. 1:1–3). God makes himself and his purposes known in a variety of ways and through a variety of means. However, since it is God who is making himself known, and he really is whom he has shown himself to be, we can discern a pattern in his revelatory activity. Similarly, while God's revelation of himself radiates throughout the whole creation, its central address is to human beings, whom God created to be his conversation partners, so we can expect human language, words and concepts to have a critical role.[35]

---

34. Torrance, *Reality*, p. 23.

35. 'Only God's word disambiguates God's deed' (Vanhoozer, *Remythologizing*, p. 213). On this issue see also John M. Frame, *The Doctrine of the Word of God* (Phillipsburg, N.J.: P&R, 2010), pp. 3–11; Samuel G. Craig, 'Benjamin B. Warfield', in B. B. Warfield,

The trinitarian shape of divine revelation has been a particular interest of Christian thinkers since the 1950s. Very largely this has been under the impress of the work of Karl Barth, who remains the Protestant theologian most responsible for a renaissance in trinitarian thinking since the mid-twentieth century. Barth famously emphasized that

> the Christian concept of revelation already includes within it the problem of the doctrine of the Trinity . . . we cannot analyse the concept without attempting as our first step to bring the doctrine of Trinity to expression.[36]

Why is this so? Barth's answer occurs just a few pages earlier: '*God* reveals Himself. He reveals Himself *through Himself.* He reveals *Himself.*'[37] God is the subject, object and means of revelation. This is why we must affirm that revelation is essentially *personal* and not a matter of theoretical knowledge that can be accessed or understood apart from the person of God. The goal of revelation is not just knowledge *about* God but the knowledge *of* God. Yet while Barth was certainly emphasizing the personal character of God's revelation – it is God's self-revelation at root – he was insisting on more than that. Divine revelation has a threefold character as a direct correlate of God's eternal triune nature. God is the one doing the revealing. God is the one revealed. God is himself the only means by which this revelation can happen.[38] He speaks. He joins himself to us through the mediation of the Son. He draws us to himself through the ministry of the Spirit.

At this point it is helpful to compare Barth's emphasis with that of his old protagonist Emil Brunner.[39] Brunner tended to overplay the personal character

---

Biblical and Theological Studies, ed. Samuel G. Craig (Philadelphia: P&R, 1968), p. xx; D. B. Knox, 'Propositional Revelation the Only Revelation', *RTR* 19 (1960), pp. 1–9.

36. *CD*, I/1, p. 304.

37. Ibid., p. 296 (emphases original).

38. 'God Himself in unimpaired unity and also in unimpaired distinction is Revealer, Revelation and Revealedness' (*CD*, I/1, p. 295). 'The question of revealer, revelation and being revealed corresponds to the logical and material order both of biblical revelation and also of the doctrine of the Trinity' (ibid., p. 314).

39. Barth and Brunner clashed dramatically in the mid 1930s over the issue of Natural Theology and just how much of God's purposes can be read off the structures of creation and human society without direct recourse to Christological categories. In 1934 Brunner published a little booklet entitled 'Nature and Grace' (*Natur und Gnade* [Tübingen: Mohr, 1934]). Later that year Karl Barth published his reply, 'No!' (*Nein! Antwort an Emil Brunner* [Munich: C. Kaiser, 1934]).

of revelation to the exclusion of propositional content (as if personal and propositional are two mutually exclusive forms of revelation):

> what God wills to give us cannot really be given in words, but only in manifestation: Jesus Christ, God himself *in persona* is the real gift. The Word of God in its ultimate meaning is thus precisely not 'a word from God', but God in person, God Himself speaking, Himself present, Immanuel.[40]

The problem lies with what he denied rather than what he affirmed. He was certainly right to warn against an abstract analytical approach to revelation. Revelation is indeed a revelation of the triune God and his purposes, and while revealing himself necessarily involves revealing the truth about himself, it is always deeply and unavoidably personal. Here he and Barth were in complete agreement: 'What God speaks is never known or true anywhere in abstraction from God Himself. It is known and true in and through the fact that He Himself says it, that He is present in person in and with what is said by Him.'[41] However, Barth would also insist

> God does reveal Himself in statements, through the medium of speech, and indeed of human speech. His word is always this or that word spoken by the prophets and apostles and proclaimed in the Church. The personal character of God's Word is not, then, to be played off against its verbal or spiritual character.[42]

We are taken further towards the heart of the matter when we speak of divine revelation as irreducibly *relational*. Colin Gunton drew attention to the way John's Gospel makes use of the idea of mutual indwelling when speaking about the knowledge of God that derives from revelation: 'The knowledge of which he speaks is first of all the knowledge by acquaintance that is a function of the interrelatedness of persons.'[43] Is it not because Jesus Christ, 'the only God', is 'at the Father's side' (John 1:18) that he is able to 'exegete' him? At the other end of the Gospel, in Jesus' high priestly prayer, does he not talk about 'those who will believe in me through their [the apostles'] word' that 'they may all be one, just as you, Father, are in me, and I in you, that they also may be in us, so that the

---

40. Emil Brunner, *The Divine–Human Encounter*, tr. A. W. Loos (London: SCM, 1944), p. 53.

41. *CD*, I/1, p. 137.

42. Ibid., p. 138.

43. Colin E. Gunton, *A Brief Theology of Revelation* (Edinburgh: T&T Clark, 1995), p. 118.

world may believe that you have sent me' (John 17:20–21)? Put another way, 'communication in its deepest sense is a matter of self-giving, a "making common" of one's life ... it is the basis of interpersonal fellowship and communion'.[44] God's self-revelation arises out of his eternal relatedness and is the means by which he is known by his creatures. It is as he makes himself known that these creatures are able, from their side as creatures, to enter into relationship with him.

In more explicitly trinitarian terms God's revelation is a revelation of the Father by the Son in the Spirit. Of course, this is fully articulated only in the New Testament, where Jesus speaks of no one coming to the Father except through him (John 14:6), and Paul writes of how it is the 'Spirit of his Son' sent by God himself, who enables us to cry 'Abba! Father!' (Gal. 4:6). However, from this vantage point we are able to look back to God's dealings with Israel as the work of him who is eternally Father, Son and Spirit. The God whom faithful Israelites came to know, and in whose promises they came to trust, is none other than the Father of our Lord Jesus Christ, who with his Father gave the Spirit so that the prophets might speak the word of God. 'For no prophecy was ever produced by the will of man, but men spoke from God as they were carried along by the Holy Spirit' (2 Peter 1:21). We are brought back again to the words of Jesus with which we began (Matt. 11:27) and the realization that revelation arises in the context of the Father–Son relation and is perfected in our experience by the work of the Holy Spirit.

Yet revelation is essentially relational when viewed from another angle as well. It is relational in its goal. Once again it is John's Gospel that gives us warrant for describing revelation in this way. With reference to the Old Testament Jesus could say to the Jews who opposed him, 'You search the Scriptures because you think that in them you have eternal life; and it is they that bear witness about me, yet you refuse to come to me that you may life' (John 5:39–40). The goal of God's revelation in those Scriptures was to announce his promise and so prepare the way for the coming of the Christ in order that men and women might find life in him. This too is the purpose behind John's Gospel itself:

> Now Jesus did many other signs in the presence of the disciples, which are not written in this book; but these are written so that you may believe that Jesus is the Christ, the Son of God, and that by believing you may have life in his name. (John 20:30–31)

God's revelation of himself to creatures does not have as its goal self-actualization or autonomy. Instead it calls for a response to the one who has made himself

---

44. Swain, *Trinity, Revelation and Reading*, p. 8.

known and on whom our very life depends at every point. It calls for faith and acknowledgment, obedience and worship. John Owen drew revelation, response and God's divine nature together in his discourse on the Holy Spirit:

> His Being, absolutely considered, as comprehending in it all infinite, divine perfections, is the formal reason of our worship; but this worship is to be directed, guided, regulated by the revelation he makes of that being and of those excellencies unto us. This is the end of divine revelation, – namely, to direct us in paying that homage which is due unto the divine nature.[45]

One further consideration is crucial. Precisely because it is the decision of the triune God whose self-sufficiency and transcendence are intrinsic and inviolable, revelation is an expression of God's lordship. This has been a concern of theologians as diverse as Karl Barth and John Frame. Barth insisted:

> In terms of the doctrine of the Trinity, knowledge of revelation as it may arise from the witness of Scripture means, in all three moments of the event, knowledge of the Lord as the One who meets us and unites Himself to us.[46]

God always remains one 'who does not need us but who does not will to be without us'.[47] Frame's four-volume magnum opus is entitled *A Theology of Lordship* and he justifies summarizing Scripture's teaching on God under the concept of divine lordship in this way:

> throughout redemptive history, God seeks to identify himself to men as Lord and to teach and demonstrate to them the meaning of that concept. 'God is Lord' – that is the message of the Old Testament; 'Jesus is Lord' – that is the message of the New.[48]

Once more it is the work of the Spirit that identifies Jesus as the Christ (Rom. 1:4) and enables us to confess him as Lord (1 Cor. 12:3).

The essential correlate of the lordship of God is that the revelation God provides of himself is authoritative. God never ceases to be Lord and what he

---

45. John Owen, *Pneumatologia or A Discourse Concerning the Holy Spirit* (1674) reprinted in *The Works of John Owen*, ed. W. Goold, 16 vols. (Edinburgh: Banner of Truth, 1965–8), vol. 3, p. 65.

46. *CD*, I/1, p. 383 (punctuation added).

47. Ibid., p. 140.

48. Frame, *Knowledge of God*, p. 12.

makes known about himself and his purposes stands over and judges all human thought. In contrast to Paul Ricœur's vision of a 'non-heteronomous dependence',[49] the revelation of God comes to us from outside us and reshapes our thinking. It has a claim on us. As others have noted, this is what lies at the heart of the modern offence with the appeal to revelation.[50] To come to such a conclusion would seem to violate one of the cherished principles we have inherited from the Enlightenment, namely the autonomy of the individual. Nevertheless, if this is what God has made known about himself and everything else, then it carries his authority and such authority stands over any claim we may have to discern the truth, to distinguish good from evil, for ourselves. What matters most is not our thoughts about God, but God's thoughts about God, and us, and all things.[51]

Revelation and the triune God of the gospel

Revelation that takes its shape from the triune nature of God's eternal life finds its focus in the Son as the one who truly makes the Father known, but who is known as Lord and as the Son of God only by the ministry of the Spirit. In this way the centrepiece of God's revelation is the gospel (Rom. 1:1–6). It is a message that can never be viewed apart from the one in whom it is embodied and who remains in every way the 'one mediator between God and men, the man Christ Jesus' (1 Tim. 2:5). In him we truly know God. In him *alone* we truly know God. By means of his Spirit, the Spirit of God, who searches even the depths of God, we have been given a glimpse of 'what God has prepared for those who love him' (1 Cor. 2:9–10). Our knowledge of God now is not exhaustive. God cannot be contained or mastered by us since he remains the Lord in every sense: transcendent, self-sufficient and incomprehensible. Yet he can be truly known because it is in his eternal nature to give of himself and in his sovereign, loving freedom he has determined to give of himself to men and women. As he spoke the world into being in the beginning, so he still speaks. 'No longer do I call you servants,' Jesus told his

49. Paul Ricœur, 'Toward a Hermeneutic of the Idea of Revelation', *HTR* 70 (1977), pp. 1–37.

50. Gunton, *Revelation*, pp. 21, 31.

51. An expanded paraphrase of Barth's early challenge to the liberal theology in which he was raised (Karl Barth, 'The New World in the Bible, 1917', in idem, *The Word of God and Theology*, tr. A. Marga [London: T&T Clark, 2011], p. 25).

disciples, 'for the servant does not know what his master is doing; but I have called you friends, for all that I have heard from my Father I have made known to you' (John 15:15).

13. THE TRINITY AND WORSHIP

Robert Letham

Biblical basis

Nature of worship

In the New Testament *proskyneō*, the most commonly used verb for worship, refers to an expression of devotion by which a person prostrates himself or herself, perhaps kissing the feet of the object of worship. On most such occasions in the Bible the worshipper falls to the ground. It is 'an expression of devotion and subservience',[1] 'to express by attitude and possibly by position one's allegiance to and regard for deity'[2].

In Revelation 4:9–11, 11:16, 19:4 the twenty-four elders and the four living creatures fall down and worship God, who is seated on the throne, while in Revelation 7:11 the angels, besides the elders and living creatures, follow suit. Paul refers to the putative convicted unbeliever's falling down and worshipping

---

1. William F. Arndt and Wilbur A. Gingrich. *A Greek-English Lexicon of the New Testament and Other Early Christian Literature* (Chicago: University of Chicago Press, 1957), pp. 723–724.
2. Johannes P. Louw and Eugene A. Nida, *Greek-English Lexicon of the New Testament Based on Semantic Domains*, 2 vols. (New York: United Bible Societies, 1988), vol. 1, p. 540.

(1 Cor. 14:25). In each case there is willing subservience and adoration in the presence of the supreme Creator.

These are characteristics of the act of worship. However, does worship include the whole of life? Certainly, our life is to be an expression of our worship, a congruity existing between the two. Indeed, it is necessary to be reconciled to others before we appear before God (Matt. 5:23–24). Worship of God must be in harmony with the way we live, so that Paul urges us, in so far as it is possible, to live at peace with all people (Rom. 12:14–21). However, references to worship in the New Testament denote actions distinct from the rest of life. Is there a good reason why one should fall on one's face while serving God as an airline pilot, university professor or business person? The Ethiopian had travelled to Jerusalem for the express purpose of worshipping God there (*hos elēlythei proskynēsōn eis Ierousalēm*); his destination was to worship at Jerusalem, while the travelling was a distinct prelude and postlude (Acts 8:27).

Object of worship

The Bible commends and requires only one object of worship, Yahweh, the God and Father of our Lord Jesus Christ. In the Old Testament this was enshrined in the first commandment (Exod. 20:2–3), reiterated in Deuteronomy (Deut. 6:4–5, 13–15) and cited by Jesus in his wilderness temptations (Matt. 4:10; Luke 4:8). This was a central theme, and a corresponding problem for Israel, who continually dabbled in idolatry until eventually being cast out of the land at the exile for worshipping pagan deities.

In the New Testament worship is directed to Jesus. The Magi visit Bethlehem for that purpose (Matt. 2:2, 11), falling down and worshipping when they find him. There are ascriptions of praise, and confession that Jesus is the Son of God (Matt. 14:33). The man healed from congenital blindness worships Jesus (John 9:38). After the resurrection, the disciples worship the risen Jesus (Matt. 28:9, 17), and the apostles worship the ascending Christ (Luke 24:52). Jesus presents himself as coordinate with God the Father as the object of faith (John 14:1).

In contrast, John unthinkingly falls at the angel's feet and worships him, only to receive a stiff rebuke and a reminder that God alone is the one to receive adoration (Rev. 19:10; 22:9). Paul writes of the futility and perversity of angel worship, improper for the church and its members (Col. 2:18).

Worship is not only to be directed to God alone but is a duty incumbent on all people. God calls his church to worship him. We worship because we must and because we may. It is our responsibility as creatures; it is our privilege as those united to Christ and given access to the communion of the life of God.

Settings of worship

The Bible speaks of worship as occurring in a variety of settings. There is individual worship, frequently found expressed in the book of Psalms, some attributed to David as king of Israel in his representative capacity, but some from other authors. Daniel prays to Yahweh at set times during the day as his regular discipline (Dan. 6:1–15). Beyond this, family worship is stressed (Deut. 6:4–9); since this is in a covenantal context (Moses reiterating the terms of the Sinaitic covenant) it assumes dominant focus. It is restated in the New Testament (Eph. 6:1–3), reinforced by the covenantal promise of long life. However, the defining feature is the corporate worship of the covenant community, expressed in the feasts of Israel, the sacrificial system and latterly the synagogue. In the New Testament it occurs in the gatherings of the church. It is a meeting of the living triune God with his covenant people.

Who is God?

Only God can make God known and determine how we relate to him

Naming in the ancient Near East denoted the sovereignty of the one who named over the one named. Thus Adam names the animals (Gen. 2:19–20) in fulfilling the creation mandate of Genesis 1:28–30 to exercise dominion over the animal world. However, only God ever names God. Only he has the right to name himself, for he as the Creator is not subject to any other being. Moreover, the covenant community is to have no other gods than him (Exod. 20:1–3). Contemporary human attempts to reimagine God or to name him as Mother or the like are simply figments of the imagination, idols made in a human image, without validity.

It follows that God is sovereign in his self-revelation. This is clear in Exodus 33:18 – 34:7, where Yahweh refuses Moses' request to see his glory. Instead, he affirms his utter authority, placing Moses in a cleft in the rock while granting him a new revelation of his name.[3] Further, God is sovereign in granting us knowledge of himself by the Holy Spirit. Sin places us in total reliance on God to make himself known. Paul insists we were dead in sin, helpless to do anything to put right our rebellion against God, unwilling to do so, for the dead can will and do nothing (Eph. 2:1–2). He also says unbelievers are incapable of repentance since they are blinded by the god of this age and unable to see the light of the gospel of the glory of God in Christ (2 Cor. 4:4). As Jesus taught,

---

3. See Thomas F. Torrance, 'The Christian Apprehension of God the Father', in Alvin F. Kimel Jr. (ed.), *Speaking the Christian God: The Holy Trinity and the Challenge of Feminism* (Grand Rapids: Eerdmans, 1992), pp. 120–143.

we trust him only as we are drawn by the Holy Spirit (John 6:44). Hence human-ity's predilection for new objects and forms of worship is rebellion against the true and living God. Only by the gracious action of God, breaking into our darkness and death and arousing us to new life, can we truly know him. This was extensively and graphically portrayed by Calvin, in his treatment of the knowledge of God,[4] idolatry and superstition,[5] creation as the means of knowing God,[6] but a knowledge given only through the Scriptures,[7] which must be confirmed by the witness of the Holy Spirit.[8] This was Calvin's teaching through-out his career.[9]

The new covenant name of God

The God who has made himself known for our salvation has revealed himself to be triune. He unfolds progressively his revelation in covenant history. At each stage he names himself, in the Abrahamic covenant as El Shaddai (God Almighty, Gen. 17:1), in the Mosaic covenant as 'ehyeh (Exod. 3:14; cf. yĕwāh, 6:3).[10] At the apex of redemptive history Jesus came to fulfil the promises of the Old Testament. Matthew records how Jesus inaugurates the kingdom of heaven, promised to Abraham. The covenant, no longer restricted to Israel, extends to the whole world. Indeed, many Israelites would be cast out while Gentiles were now to be included (Matt. 8:11–12). As the Mosaic covenant was inaugurated with the sprinkling of covenantal blood, so the new covenant is founded on the blood of Jesus (Matt. 26:27–29). Finally, Matthew recounts how the nations are to be made disciples, with the new covenant sacrament of baptism. This baptism is into *the one name of the Father, and the Son, and the Holy Spirit* (Matt. 28:19–20). Jesus the Son names God as the one God who is the Father, the Son and the Holy Spirit, in connection with the new covenant sacrament, baptism. By naming the one God he affirms his equality with and identity to Yahweh.

---

4. John Calvin, *Institutes of the Christian Religion* 1.1.1 – 1.3.3.

5. Ibid. 4.1–4.

6. Ibid. 5.1–14.

7. Ibid. 6.1–4.

8. Ibid. 7.1–5.

9. See I. John Hesselink, *Calvin's First Catechism: A Commentary. Featuring Ford Lewis Battles' Translation of the 1538 Catechism* (Louisville: Westminster John Knox, 1997), pp. 44–53, whose discussion of this early writing of Calvin demonstrates its congruity with his more developed expression in the 1559 *Institutes*.

10. Robert Letham, *The Holy Trinity: In Scripture, History, Theology, and Worship* (Phillipsburg, N.J.: P&R, 2004), pp. 59–60.

This is God's crowning self-revelation. Retrospectively, it casts light on all that led up to it, like a detective mystery discloses in the final scene the clues that make sense of the entire story.[11]

So the triune God alone grants us access to himself and determines how we are to relate to and approach him. In the Mosaic covenant Moses was required to construct the paraphernalia of Israel's worship exactly as Yahweh told him (Exod. 25:1–40; 40:1–38). Latterly, Jesus announced that no one comes to the Father except through him (John 14:6). Access to the Father is exclusively through the mediation of the Son.

Therefore Christian worship is distinctively trinitarian. This has been recognized by the church from its earliest days. In the fourth century Gregory of Nazianzus, instrumental in the resolution of the trinitarian crisis, wrote:

> When we look at the Godhead . . . that which we conceive is One; but when we look at the persons in whom the Godhead dwells, and at those who timelessly and with equal glory have their being from the first cause[12] – there are three whom we worship.[13]

Later, in the eighth century, John of Damascus wrote that

> one essence, one divinity, one power, one will, one energy, one beginning, one authority, one dominion, one sovereignty, *made known in three perfect subsistences and adored with one adoration* . . . united without confusion and divided without separation.[14]

The basis of worship

The church's worship is grounded on who God is and what he has done. The Father has sent the Son 'for us and our salvation'. This is prominent in John,

---

11. Ibid., pp. 59–60; Kevin J. Bidwell, *The Church as the Image of the Trinity: A Critical Evaluation of Miroslav Volf's Ecclesial Model*, WEST Theological Monograph (Eugene, Ore.: Wipf & Stock, 2011), p. 239.

12. Here is the characteristic Cappadocian teaching on the Father as the fountain of deity, although it was not confined to the Greeks; see e.g. Augustine, *De Trinitate* 2.1.3, 4.20.T; Lewis Ayres, *Augustine and the Trinity* (Cambridge: Cambridge University Press, 2010), pp. 178–187; Calvin, *Institutes* 1.13.18, 20, 25.

13. Gregory Nazianzen, *Oration* 31.14 (tr. from *NPNF*² 7:322).

14. John of Damascus, *On the Orthodox Faith* 1.8 (tr. from *NPNF*² 9:2:6), emphasis added.

chapters 5, 10 and 17, but Paul also directs our attention to it in Romans 8:32. In turn, the Father together with the Son has sent the Holy Spirit to indwell the church. The focus of the Spirit's ministry is to speak of Christ the Son. This is summarized clearly in Galatians 4:4–6:

> When the fullness of time had come God sent forth his Son, born of woman, born under the law, to redeem those under the law, that we might receive the inheritance of sons. And because you are sons, God sent forth the Spirit of his Son into our hearts, crying 'Abba, Father.'[15]

Here lies the basic premise of all God's actions – *from the Father through the Son by the Holy Spirit*. As Cyril of Alexandria states in his *Commentary on John*, 'all things proceed from the Father, but wholly through the Son in the Spirit'.[16] These words of Paul, and this order that is so evident in the church fathers, encapsulates the whole of redemptive history. Not only is our salvation a work of God, not only is it trinitarian through and through, but it is initiated by the Father, accomplished by the Son and applied by the Holy Spirit. Of course, Augustine was right in that all aspects of this great drama of redemption are put into effect by all three persons of the Trinity working together in harmony – *opera trinitatis ad extra indivisa sunt*. The Trinity is indivisible and the works of the Trinity are inseparable. However, Calvin's description holds true both as a general principle and as a reflection of what has actually happened in human history, that to the Father 'is attributed the beginning of activity, and the fountain and wellspring of all things; to the Son, wisdom, counsel, and the ordered disposition of all things; but to the Spirit is assigned the power and efficacy of that activity'.[17] The Father sent the Son; then, following the Son's death and resurrection, he sent the Spirit of his Son.

---

15. My tr. The words *abba* (Aramaic) and *patēr* (Greek) both mean 'Father'. Hence Jew and Gentile are on the same footing. That *abba*, contrary to popular preaching stemming from the influence of Joachim Jeremias, does not mean 'daddy' has been established by James Barr, 'Abba Isn't Daddy', *JTS* 39 (1988), pp. 28–47.

16. Cyril of Alexandria, *Commentary on the Gospel According to St. John (IX–XXI)*, tr. T. Randell, LFC 48 (London: Walter Smith, 1885), p. 481; cf. 484 (PG 74:477).

17. Calvin, *Institutes* 1.13.18, tr. from John Calvin, *Institutes of the Christian Religion*, ed. John T. McNeill, tr. Ford Lewis Battles, 2 vols., LCC 20 (Louisville: Westminster John Knox, 1960), vol. 1, pp. 142–143. Hereafter 'Battles'.

New Testament pattern of trinitarian worship
Ephesians 2:18

Paul has pointed out that Christ made reconciliation by the cross (Eph. 2:14), tearing down the dividing wall between God and ourselves due to sin, and between Jew and Gentile due to the ceremonial law. He goes on to say that both Jew and Gentile have identical means of access to God in Christ. 'Through him [Christ] we both [Jew and Gentile] have access in one Holy Spirit to the Father' (ESV). Access to God is ultimately access to the Father. This is through Christ, the one mediator between God and man (1 Tim. 2:5). It is the Spirit who gives us life in place of death (Eph. 2:1), raising us in Christ (2:6–7) and graciously granting faith (2:8–10). Calvin held that the principal work of the Holy Spirit is to give us faith.[18] It is a cardinal teaching of Scripture that saving faith is the gift of God, given by the Spirit (John 6:44; 1 Cor. 12:3; Eph. 2:1–10). Here is the reverse movement to that seen as the ground of the church's worship – *by the Holy Spirit through Christ to the Father*. This encompasses our entire response to, and relationship with, God – from worship through the whole field of Christian experience.

From this it follows that prayer is distinctively trinitarian. The Christian faith exists in an atmosphere saturated by the Trinity. At its most basic level every Christian believer experiences in a tacit, unarticulated form communion with the holy Trinity. The Holy Spirit creates a desire to pray and to worship God, brings us to faith and sustains us in a life of faithful obedience. In turn, our access to the Father is exclusively through his Son, Jesus Christ. No one comes to the Father except through him (John 14:6). Now that he has offered the one perfect sacrifice for sins for all time, we have access to the holy place, the presence of God (Heb. 10:19–20), and so can approach with confidence the throne of grace, knowing that our great high priest is there to intercede for us, he who has experienced to the full the struggles of human life in a fallen world and so can sympathize with us in our weakness (Heb. 4:14–16). Indeed, Jesus introduces us to the same relation he has with the Father. He is the Son by nature; we are children by grace. We now call on God as 'our Father'. Moreover, the Spirit brings us into his own intercession for us (Rom. 8:26–27). He thus eliminates the distance between us and God, creating in us the same relation he has with the Father and the Son.[19] Prayer and worship are thus explorations of the character of the holy Trinity.

---

18. Ibid. 3.1.4 (Battles, vol. 1, p. 541).

19. See Dumitru Staniloae, *The Experience of God: Orthodox Dogmatic Theology*, vol. 1: *Revelation and Knowledge of the Triune God*, ed. and tr. Ioan Ionita and Robert Barringer (Brookline, Mass.: Holy Cross Orthodox, 1994), pp. 248–249.

John 4:23–24

The Samaritan woman's question concerns the proper place of worship, whether at Jerusalem (which the Jews insisted Yahweh required) or Mount Gerizim (where the Samaritans worshipped). Jesus supports Jerusalem, indicating that the Jews worshipped according to knowledge, while the Samaritans did not. Both the Bible and history support this. The Samaritans were a mixed race, formed from remnants of the ten northern tribes together with settlers from other nations brought in by the Assyrians after the destruction of the northern kingdom. Their religion was syncretistic, combining elements of the worship of Yahweh, based on the Samaritan Pentateuch, together with aspects of the ancestral religions of the various imported nations. However, Jesus says now the time has arrived, when the distinction between Israel and Samaria, between Jerusalem and Mount Gerizim, is superseded. True worshippers now worship the Father in spirit and in truth.

What does Jesus mean? This hardly means merely that a particular location is completely irrelevant, or that true worship can now occur anywhere, although that may be entailed in what he says. Nor is 'spirit' a reference to the human spirit, as if true worship were purely inward and externals of no consequence; such an interpretation is reminiscent of Descartes. Rather, we should remember the extensive teaching in the Fourth Gospel on the Holy Spirit, concentrated later in chapters 14–16. Every reference to *pneuma* (spirit) in this Gospel, bar probably two, points to the Holy Spirit. In this connection Jesus means that true worship is directed to the Father in the Holy Spirit. In the words of Basil the Great, referring *inter alia* to this passage:

> It is an extraordinary statement, but it is nonetheless true, that the Spirit is frequently spoken of as the *place* of them that are being sanctified . . . This is the special and peculiar place of true worship . . . In what place do we offer it? In the Holy Spirit . . . It follows that the Spirit is truly the place of the saints and the saint is the proper place for the Spirit, offering himself as he does for the indwelling of God, and called God's temple.[20]

Again, with reference to 'truth', do we have to look any further than John's record of Jesus as the embodiment of truth (14:6), as the true light coming into the world (1:9), 'full of grace and truth' (1:14), who as a result brought grace

---

20. Basil of Caesarea, *On the Holy Spirit* 26.62 (PG 32:184; tr. from *NPNF*² 8:38), emphasis added.

and truth into the world (1:17)? Jesus is pointing to himself, implying, as does Paul, that new covenant worship is trinitarian. We worship the Father in the Holy Spirit and in the fullness of truth, his incarnate Son.[21] In summary, Gregory of Nazianzus puts these passages in context with his comment 'This, then, is my position ... to worship God the Father, God the Son, and God the Holy Ghost, three persons, one Godhead, undivided in honour and glory and substance and kingdom.'[22]

Putting it another way, from the side of God, *the worship of the church is the communion of the holy Trinity with us his people*. We are inclined to view worship as what we do, but if we follow our argument, it is *first and foremost* something the triune God does; our actions are initiated and encompassed by his. The author of Hebrews refers to Christ's offering himself up unblemished to the Father 'in' or 'through eternal spirit' (Heb. 9:14, my tr.), which is a reference to the Holy Spirit.[23] Since our salvation is received in union with Christ, what is his by nature is ours by grace. Thus, in his self-offering to the Father, he offers us, his people, in him. We are thereby enabled to share in the relation he has with the Father. (Thus we can pray 'Our Father in heaven' – God is our Father by grace because he is first Jesus' Father by nature.) Jesus ascended to his Father and our Father, to his God and our God (John 20:17). By his cross, resurrection and ascension he brought us into the same relation he has with the Father. Thus Christ is, in reality, the one true worshipper,[24] our worship a participation in his. A focus on our worship, on what we do, is inherently Pelagian. Further, our worship is *by the Holy Spirit* in Christ. As John Thompson puts it, 'If one understands the New Testament and the view it gives of how we meet with and know God and worship him as triune, then worship is not primarily our act but, like our salvation, is God's gift before or as it is our task.'[25] This should reassure us, for as Owen reminds us, while 'the love of God is like himself, – equal, constant, not capable of augmentation or

21. See Athanasius, *Letters to Serapion on the Holy Spirit* 1.33 (PG 26:605–608), for a similar explanation.

22. Gregory Nazianzen, *Oration* 31.28 (PG 36:164–165; tr. from *NPNF²* 7:326–327).

23. Letham, *Holy Trinity*, pp. 66–67; F. F. Bruce, *Commentary on the Epistle to the Hebrews: The English Text with Introduction, Exposition and Notes* (London: Marshall, Morgan & Scott, 1964), p. 205.

24. A. M. Ramsay, *The Glory of God and the Transfiguration of Christ* (London: Longmans, 1949), pp. 91–100.

25. John Thompson, *Modern Trinitarian Perspectives* (New York: Oxford University Press, 1994), pp. 99–101.

diminution; our love is like ourselves, – unequal, increasing, waning, growing, declining'.[26]

The worship of the church is thus not only grounded on the mediation of Christ but takes place in union with and through his mediatorial work and continued intercession:

> Being still endued with the human shape, he moulds accordingly the form of his prayer, and asks as though he possessed it not . . . in Him, as the firstfruits of the race, the nature of man was wholly reformed into newness of life, and ascending, as it were, to its own first beginning was moulded anew into sanctification. . . . Christ called down upon us the ancient gift of humanity, that is, sanctification through the Spirit and communion in the Divine Nature.[27]

Behind this lies the incarnation (the Son of God did not simply indwell human nature but came *as man*, permanently assuming unabbreviated human nature – sin apart), the vicarious humanity of Christ (he took our place in every way – including in worship, since as man he owed it to the Father), his full and complete obedience to the Father by the Holy Spirit, and his continuing high priestly intercession.[28] Therefore, since Christian worship is determined, initiated and shaped by, and directed to, the holy Trinity, *we worship the three with one undivided act of adoration.*

John Owen comments that our communion with the Trinity rests on the union we have with Jesus Christ, for 'communion is the mutual communication of such good things as wherein the persons holding that communion are delighted, bottomed upon some union between them'. Thus our communion with God consists 'in his *communication of himself unto us, with our returnal unto him* . . . flowing from that *union* which in Jesus Christ we have with him'.[29]

What can be said, tentatively, about our worship of the three, remembering that the three coinhere, mutually indwell each other in the unity of the undivided Trinity? We recall the vital point made by Gregory of Nazianzus, 'No sooner

---

26. John Owen, *Of Communion with God the Father, Son, and Holy Ghost, Each Person Distinctly, in Love, Grace, and Consolation* (1657), reprinted in *The Works of John Owen*, ed. W. Goold, 16 vols. (Edinburgh: Banner of Truth, 1965–8), vol. 2, pp. 29–30.

27. Cyril of Alexandria, *St. John*, pp. 496, 536, 538.

28. See Robert Letham, *The Work of Christ* (Leicester: Inter-Varsity Press, 1993), pp. 106–123.

29. Owen, *Of Communion with God*, 2.8–9, emphases original.

do I conceive of the One than I am illumined by the splendour of the Three; no sooner do I distinguish them than I am carried back to the One.'[30]

It is often said that the only distinction of the persons is the ineffable eternal generation and procession. While this is so, the missions of the Son and the Spirit reflect the eternal relations. Only the Son became incarnate, not the Father or the Holy Spirit. Only the Holy Spirit came at Pentecost, not the Son or the Father. Only the Father, not the Holy Spirit, sent the Son. As I argued before, these economic activities point back to immanent relations.[31] There is something *appropriate* in the Son qua Son's becoming incarnate.[32] We may ask whether this irreducible distinctiveness lends sharpness to our worship.

The Bible indicates that the Father determined that his kingdom be established and advanced principally by the Son. In this sense it is the Son who occupies centre stage. This is entirely in accord with the purpose of the Father: ''Tis the Father's pleasure we should call him Lord.'[33] The Father sent the Son with the purpose that he receive the glory and praise for our deliverance. His exaltation following his resurrection, by which he is given 'the name which is above every name', is to the glory of God the Father, in pursuance of his eternal plan (Phil. 2:9–11, my tr.). In turn, the Son will, after the economy of salvation is complete, hand the kingdom back to the Father (1 Cor. 15:28). Again the Holy Spirit works anonymously in the background, not speaking of himself or bringing glory to himself but testifying of Christ, the Son. He hears the Son and witnesses to him. He works unseen. Gregory of Nyssa writes of

> a revolving circle of glory from like to like. The Son is glorified by the Spirit; the Father is glorified by the Son; again the Son has his glory from the Father; and the Only-begotten thus becomes the glory of the Spirit . . . In like manner . . . faith completes the circle, and glorifies the Son by means of the Spirit, and the Father by means of the Son.[34]

---

30. Gregory Nazianzen, *Oration on Holy Baptism* 40.41 (PG 36:417; tr. from *NPNF²* 7:375).

31. Gilles Emery, O. P., *The Trinity: An Introduction to Catholic Doctrine of the Triune God*, tr. Matthew Levering (Washington, D.C.: Catholic University of America Press, 2011), pp. 175–194.

32. Anselm, *De Fide Trinitatis et de Incarnatione Verbi* 3.27–37 (PL 158:276–284). See Jasper Hopkins and Herbert Richardson, ed. and tr., *Anselm of Canterbury* (Toronto: Edwin Mellen, 1975–6); Letham, *Holy Trinity*, pp. 222–223.

33. From the hymn 'At the Name of Jesus', written by Caroline Noel.

34. Gregory of Nyssa, *On the Holy Spirit* (tr. from *NPNF²* 5:324).

These distinct appropriations, whereby a particular work is attributed to one trinitarian person, are to be regarded in terms of the inseparable work of the Trinity, each of the three being engaged.

Thus we worship *in one undivided act of adoration* the three in their distinct persons and relations with one another. A living relationship with God requires that each of the persons be honoured and adored in the context of their revealed relations. The nature of our response in worship is to be shaped by the reality of the one we worship. We worship the Father, who chose us in Christ before the foundation of the world, who planned our salvation from eternity, who sent his Son into the world and gave him up for us. We worship the Son, in filial relation with the Father, who willingly 'for us and our salvation' was made flesh, who submitted himself to life in a fallen world, who trod a path of lowliness, temptation and suffering, leading to the cruel death of the cross. We worship him for his glorious resurrection, for his ascension to the right hand of the Father, for his continual intercession for us, and for his future return to judge the living and the dead, and to complete our salvation. As John says, 'our fellowship is with the Father, and with his Son Jesus Christ' (1 John 1:3a ESV). We worship the Holy Spirit, who gives life and breath to all, who grants us the gift of faith, who sustains us through the difficulties of life as Christians in a world set in hostility to God, and who testifies of the Son. And, as Gregory would urge us, we worship with *one* act of adoration the one undivided Trinity, for as we cast our minds and hearts before the three persons of the holy Trinity we at once are enlightened by the one. As Staniloae says, the three are 'wholly interior to one another'.[35]

No one has expressed this better than John Owen. He writes that 'the saints have distinct communion with the Father, and the Son, and the Holy Spirit (that is, distinctly with the Father, and distinctly with the Son, and distinctly with the Holy Spirit)'. This is evident in the distinct ways in which Scripture refers to the three persons, particularly in the communication of grace to us. In this the Father communicates grace by way of original authority, the Son by making out a purchased treasury and the Spirit by way of immediate efficacy.[36] However, as Owen is quick to point out, when we hold distinct communion with any one person, the other two persons are also included. We may have communion with one person principally, but the other two are included secondarily, 'for the person, as the person, of any one of them, is not the prime *object* of divine worship, but as it is *identified* with the nature or essence

---

35. Staniloae, *Experience of God*, p. 255.
36. Owen, *Of Communion with God* 2.9–17.

of God'. Whenever we have communion with any one person, there is an influence from every person in that act. Moreover, communion with God, Owen acknowledges, is broader than this, for we have communion with the whole deity as such.[37]

Does this not demonstrate our own ignorance? These are matters beyond us. It is like the old illustration of dipping a teacup into the ocean. Besides the vastness of the Atlantic, the water in our teacup is infinitesimal. But yet – the water in the teacup *is* the Atlantic ocean, in so far as it is a true sample. It is true we do not and cannot know the inner workings of the Trinity, so it may even be better to remain silent. But we do know what the Son is like. We know that

> being in the form of God, he did not count equality with God something to be
> exploited for his own advantage, but he emptied himself, taking the form of a
> servant, becoming in the likeness of men. And being found in form as a man,
> he humbled himself, becoming obedient to death, even the death of the cross.
> (Phil. 2:5–8, my tr.)

We know also that he created and sustains the laws of physics. We also know something of what the Holy Spirit is like, for we know that in the midst of the turmoil of everyday life love, joy, peace, patience, kindness, goodness, faithfulness, meekness and self-control are the fruit of the Spirit, hallmarks of his own character produced in us on a creaturely level. We know that the Father chose that his kingdom be initiated and advanced by the Son and the Spirit. We know, in Pannenberg's words, that

> as Jesus glorifies the Father and not himself . . . so the Spirit glorifies not himself
> but the Son, and in him the Father . . . The Father hands over his kingdom to the Son
> and receives it back from him. The Son is . . . obedient to [the Father] and he thereby
> glorifies him as the one God. The Spirit . . . fills the Son and glorifies him in his
> obedience to the Father.[38]

We also know, as Calvin put it, that the will of the Father differs not in the slightest from what he has revealed in his Word. And as we think of the three in their distinctness, we recall that they indwell each other in undivided union.

---

37. Ibid., pp. 18–19, emphases added.
38. Wolfhart Pannenberg, *Systematic Theology*, tr. Geoffrey W. Bromiley, 3 vols. (Grand Rapids: Eerdmans, 1991), vol. 1, pp. 315, 320.

In what way is God to be worshipped?

How is God to be worshipped?

The second commandment, in prohibiting the worshipping of man-made images, entails the point that we are to worship God in the image he has provided. The commandment goes beyond a simple condemnation of idolatry. In the Bible where a promise is made, a corresponding warning is implied, and vice versa. Hence the prohibition against human construction of images of false deities for worship should be understood as a requirement to worship in the image God has provided, Jesus Christ, the image of the invisible God (Col. 1:15; 2 Cor. 4:4; Heb. 1:3).

The third commandment forbids taking on our lips the name of the Lord in an empty, careless or irreverent manner. The reverse of this is that, positively, we are to worship in faith. Taking the whole sense of Scripture, this means that worship is to be in the Holy Spirit, who is the giver of faith.[39]

How far does the worship of today's church reflect a robust trinitarian faith?

According to Bulgakov:

> the dogma of the Holy Trinity is not only a doctrinal form, but a living Christian experience which is constantly developing; it is a fact of the Christian life. For life in Christ unites with the Holy Trinity, it gives a knowledge of the Father's love and the gifts of the Holy Spirit. There is no truly Christian life, apart from knowledge of the Trinity.[40]

However, since the great outburst of trinitarian theology in the fourth and fifth centuries that filtered through the Middle Ages, there has been a paucity of hymnology that is clearly trinitarian. Many favourites could equally be sung by Unitarians, orthodox Jews or Muslims: 'My God, How Wonderful Thou Art', 'Praise My Soul, the King of Heaven', 'Immortal, Invisible, God Only Wise', 'Praise to the Lord, the Almighty, the King of Creation'. We may bring to these texts trinitarian assumptions, but a trinitarian framework is not present in the hymns themselves. Since theology and worship are integrally connected,

---

39. See Basil of Caesarea, *Holy Spirit* 26.62 (PG 32:184; tr. from *NPNF²* 8:39); Athanasius, *Serapion* 1.33.2 (PG 26:605–608).

40. Sergius Bulgakov, *The Orthodox Church* (Maitland, Fla.: Three Hierarchs Seminary Press, 1935), p. 122.

as the fathers taught,[41] this is serious. Among the more recent informal hymns and choruses, 'There Is a Redeemer' makes an attempt in this direction but the refrain 'Thank you, O our Father, for giving us your Son, and *leaving your Spirit* till the work on earth is done' (my emphasis) misses the mark. The studied and stubborn opposition to fixed liturgies in much evangelicalism, with its descent into flippant informality, has accentuated this deficit.

The structure of church worship

In the worship of the church God takes the initiative
This is the invariable pattern in all God's ways and works. He is the Creator, bringing into existence all entities other than himself. The incarnation of the Son occurred without input or advice from any of his creatures. The redemption of the world by our Lord Jesus Christ was not the result of a committee decision. The Spirit was not sent at Pentecost in response to a request of a church session. In all these cases it was God who acted in sovereign freedom. The Father's determination is brought into effect through the Son by the Holy Spirit, yet all three are inseparably involved at each stage.

It is the part of the faithful to respond to the actions of God in faith. This human reply is by God's grace, brought about by the Holy Spirit through the Son and focusing as the goal on the Father. In the worship of the church, Christ the Son joins with and leads the congregation in its praise to the Father (Heb. 2:10–13).

This paradigm is in stark contrast to the various Pelagian forms of worship common today, where the focus is almost entirely on the worshipper. When the topic of worship is mentioned, immediate attention is normally directed to what we do, to the attitudes of the worshippers' hearts, to the sincerity or fervour we generate. Clearly, the worshippers must be living in communion with God and one another. If anything, there is a priority for reconciliation over worship; if we are living at odds with another, we must do all in our power to put the situation right and be reconciled before ever we join in the worship of God (Matt. 5:23–24; 1 Cor. 11:17–34). However, this is a prerequisite for worship; it is not worship itself.

---

41. Hilary of Poitiers claimed that God cannot be known except by devotion. Origen held that *theologia* and *eusebeia* (piety) mutually condition each other. Prosper of Aquitaine coined the seminal formula *legem credendi lex statuat supplicandi* (the rule of prayer establishes the rule of faith – and vice versa).

No, worship is above all a transcendent activity in which the holy Trinity is the agent. It is the meeting place between heaven and earth. In it the triune God grants us access to the worship around the throne of God in heaven. In union with Christ we are seated with him in heavenly places (Eph. 2:5–7). We have come to Mount Zion, to innumerable numbers of angels in festal gathering, to the saints of the Old and New Testament, and above all to Jesus the mediator of the new covenant (Heb. 12:18–24), a scene into which angels themselves long to look (1 Peter 1:12). The worship of the church is, in an astounding way, a dialogue in which the Trinity takes the lead.

God's words have priority

In the call to worship, the Father calls us in Christ his Son by the Holy Spirit to worship. This entails that the Trinity is present first, that God takes the initiative and that our part in worship is a response to his prior call. The habit of many evangelical churches in starting their services with chatty informality may accord with contemporary tastes but misses the point entirely.

It is well to understand that the words of the ordained minister are not uttered on his own authority. Called to the ministry by Christ, he is there solely on Christ's behest and so speaks for him. These words themselves are a declaration of grace, cosmic in their significance. Whereas by our deeds we warranted everlasting exclusion from the presence of the Lord, we are instead called near to communion and union in Christ. Distance is overcome, and we draw near through the blood of Christ. In this connection the confession of sins (preferably by the congregation as a whole) and the subsequent declaration of pardon (better, *absolution*)[42] seals this glorious reality.

---

42. The English language has suffered impoverishment in this matter. Many words have lost their force. There are three aspects to sin in this context. First is *the reality of sin*, committed in thought, word or deed, or in omission. Second comes *the objective guilt* that this entails. Third is *the penalty of sin*. 'Pardon' can be issued to one convicted of a crime but this does not of itself remove the reality of what has been done. The penalty is removed or curtailed but the guilt remains and the criminal action cannot be effaced. 'Remission' merely suspends part of the sentence but does nothing about the guilt or the deed. 'Forgiveness' is something notoriously difficult for us to give; as C. S. Lewis remarked, we may find ourselves needing to forgive seventy times seven for the same offence; C. S. Lewis, *Reflections on the Psalms* (London: Geoffrey Bles, 1958), pp. 24–25, who remarks, 'there is no use in talking as if forgiveness is easy . . . the work of forgiveness has to be done over and over again'. The point is that while God forgives, our understanding of forgiveness is easily

It follows that the reading of Scripture is of prime importance. It is the Word of the Lord himself, no less, speaking to the congregation of his people. In turn the proclamation of that Word carries his imprimatur. In Ephesians 2:17 Christ is said to have preached peace to the Gentiles at Ephesus: 'he came and preached peace to you who were far off and peace to those who were near' (ESV). Jesus never visited Ephesus; Paul refers to his own preaching in founding the church. In Paul's preaching Christ himself preaches. In Romans 10:14, where Paul insists on the urgency of preachers being sent to his compatriots, the Jews, the subjective genitive is to be preferred, yielding the clause 'how are they to believe him whom they have not heard?' (my tr.). In short, Christ is heard in the preaching of the gospel.[43] When the Word is truly preached, Christ is present.[44] That the preacher is sent indicates the ministerial nature of preaching; the preacher is subservient to the Word.[45] Other passages that address this theme are Luke 10:16, John 5:25–47 and 2 Corinthians 5:19–20.[46] Here the Father speaks in the Son in the words uttered by the Holy Spirit in holy Scripture.

In line with this Calvin regarded preaching as both a human and a divine activity, the Holy Spirit working in sovereignty through the words of the preacher.[47] As such, he states that 'God himself appears in our midst, and,

shaped by the problems we find ourselves facing with it. To my mind, the best word to use, the one that most encapsulates what happens before God, is 'absolution', from *absolvere*, meaning to acquit, justify, dispose of (*Oxford Latin Dictionary*, ed. P. G. W. Glare [Oxford: Clarendon, 1996]). It covers not only the penalty of sin but also its guilt and, more than that, creates the situation where the offence is effectively removed from all consideration on the part of God (Ps. 103:10–14; Mic. 7:18–19).

43. John Murray, *The Epistle to the Romans*, 2 vols., NICNT (Grand Rapids: Eerdmans, 1959–65), vol. 2, p. 58; C. E. B. Cranfield, *A Critical and Exegetical Commentary on the Epistle to the Romans*, 2 vols., ICC (Edinburgh: T&T Clark, 1975–9), vol. 2, pp. 533–534; Leon Morris, *The Epistle to the Romans*, PNTC (Grand Rapids: Eerdmans, 1988), pp. 389–390; James D. G. Dunn, *Romans 9–16*, WBC 38B (Dallas: Word, 1988), p. 620.

44. Hughes Oliphant Old, *The Reading and Preaching of the Scriptures in the Worship of the Christian Church*, vol. 1: *The Biblical Period* (Grand Rapids: Eerdmans, 1998), pp. 186–187.

45. Ibid., p. 184.

46. See my article 'The Necessity of Preaching', *Ordained Servant* (Oct.– Dec. 2013), http://www.opc.org/OS/Ordained_Servant_2013.pdf (accessed 24 Nov. 2015).

47. See the discussion by John H. Leith, 'Calvin's Doctrine of the Proclamation of the Word and Its Significance for Us Today', in Timothy George (ed.), *John Calvin and the Church: A Prism of Reform* (Louisville: Westminster John Knox, 1990), pp. 210–212.

as Author of this order, would have men recognize him as present in his institution.'[48]

In turn, in the sacraments the Father enables us to commune with the Son by the Holy Spirit. Baptism and the Supper, as means of grace, are the chief ways by which we are nurtured in union and communion with the Trinity.[49]

The benediction is not a pious wish, a form of prayer in which we address God. It is rather a declaration of a state of affairs that exists, established by the Father in the Son by the Holy Spirit. The minister, ordained to that task, pronounces the blessing, a blessing in the name of the holy Trinity, a blessing that is a glorious actuality. In doing so, he dismisses the congregation to serve the Lord in the callings to which they have severally been called.

The church speaks in response

As we saw above, the church's response to hearing God's Word is an act of faith, by the Holy Spirit through the Son to the Father.

Singing his praise

It is clear from what I have said that there is a need for trinitarian hymnology, newly composed or retrieved from the archives. As Benedict XVI insisted, church music must reflect transcendence, wonder, amazement and awe. This is in contrast to the alleged 'simplicity' of much Reformed worship, which at times may be a euphemism for staleness, and also to excitement generated in some circles by unrealistic expectations of sensational or unusual events. Instead, the most sensational event of all is that we are given access to the trinitarian life of God, the Spirit granting us audience with the Father in, through and with his eternal Son. In this we join with Christ in singing praise (Heb. 2:11–12). What could outstrip this?

Feeding on Christ

The Lord's Supper is the communion of the body and blood of Christ. We feed on him by faith. As bread and wine enter our system and become integrally part of us, so Christ and his people are one flesh, a union unbreakable by anything in the entire creation. In feeding on Christ by the Spirit – who unites us to him – we are given access to the Father and receive his life, signified at creation by

---

48. Calvin, *Institutes* 4.1.5 (Battles, vol. 2, p. 1017).

49. WSC 88; contra Owen, *Of Communion with God*, who focuses on individual worship, with the ministry of the church effectively as a back up.

the tree of life, realized and embodied in the Son, given by the Spirit of life who proceeds from the Father.

Receiving the blessing of the Holy Spirit by the Son in the name of the Father
The benediction is not a prayer, expressing a wish that such and such may be the case. It is a declaration of a state of blessing that the church has received, given in the name of the Father, the Son and the Holy Spirit. The church receives the benediction. Christ's last visible act was to raise his hands in blessing as he was taken up into heaven. This was to be the state of affairs that exists from then to his parousia. In union with him we have been raised and have ascended to the right hand of the Father. Man with God is on the throne. In the benediction we hear this reality.

How a trinitarian-focused worship may be taught

A judicious use of the church calendar
Advent, Crucifixion, Easter, Pentecost, Ascension are all trinitarian events and provide ample opportunity to teach the congregation. Abandonment of the church calendar leaves congregations hostage to the whims and idiosyncrasies of individual ministers. Its focus is on the great central themes of the faith and keeps the church anchored in these. The anti-liturgical movement that has driven an aversion to these great milestones is based on the fallacy that faith and spontaneity go together, form inevitably wedded to formalism. If this were so, it would be well that the ministers of the church avoided preparing sermons and that hymns be composed on the spot.

Preaching
Preaching is the high point of worship. Not only must the Trinity as such be preached, but *all* preaching must be shaped by the recognition that the God whose Word is proclaimed is triune. A trinitarian mindset must become as integral to the preacher as the air we breathe. As Peter Toon comments, 'preachers and teachers need so to communicate the Faith and so direct public worship that they really and truly give the impression that the Holy Trinity is God and God is the Holy Trinity'.[50] This will come only as preachers give explicit recognition in their prayers and sermons to God as triune, and so

---

50. Peter Toon, *Our Triune God: A Biblical Portrayal of the Trinity* (Wheaton: BridgePoint, 1996), p. 234.

encourage their congregations to think, pray and live in that light. Sinclair Ferguson remarked to me in an email that when Jesus gave his upper room discourse to disciples about to be plunged into grief and stress, he instructed them not on stress management techniques but on the Trinity.[51] The most practical preaching enables us to advance in our knowledge of the God who is three persons.

The sacraments

Baptism is into the name of the Father, the Son and the Holy Spirit. Each baptism provides a point for reinforcing the congregation's awareness of the Trinity. In turn, the Lord's Supper entails our feeding on Christ through faith by the Holy Spirit. The sacraments derive their significance from the Word. Careful and appropriate words of instruction can guide the church in this regard.

Prayers

Many of the great prayers of the Christian church are steeped in trinitarian teaching, Foremost among these is the great *Te Deum*. The Collects in *The Book of Common Prayer* express the church's relationship to the triune God; these prayers impress themselves on the memories of congregants. Not only do they provide a springboard for refreshing the prayers of individuals when they find it difficult to pray, but they also contain a nucleus of trinitarian expressions that can be internalized in the minds of the faithful. Another resource not to be despised but to be used with discernment is the ancient Liturgy of St Chrysostom.

Prayer is, *inter alia*, exploration of the holy Trinity. Christian experience is trinitarian, prayer very centrally included. One wonders, how much of the decline in appreciation of the Trinity is due to *exclusively* unguided extemporaneous prayer. At times of theological strength and spiritual vitality this may be fine, but when decline sets in there is nothing to check it. I am not suggesting that written liturgical prayer should be the exclusive, or even the main, diet of church worship. However, it can and does provide a backbone, a foundation, for the prayers of the church. If anyone wants biblical support for this claim, the book of Psalms will do; there we have written prayers and doxologies that have been prayed and sung down the ages.

In prayer we engage directly with our three-personed God, with 'our Trinity', to borrow from Gregory of Nazianzus. In the words of Lukas Vischer, 'in our calling upon him the mystery of the Trinity itself is actualized. So we pray with

---

51. See Letham, *Holy Trinity*, p. 375.

Christ and in the power of the Spirit when we call on God his Father as *our* Father.'[52] Dimitru Staniloae adds that the intratrinitarian love is the foundation of our salvation, 'the extension to conscious creatures of the relations that obtain between the divine persons'. Through his incarnation the Son introduces us to filial communion with the Father, while through the Spirit we pray to the Father or speak with him as sons. In prayer the Spirit draws us into his own prayer, creating between us and the Father, through grace, the same relation he has with the Father and the Son by nature. The incarnate Son as man expressed his filial love of the Father as an obedient love, while the Father was affirming his love to us as Father. For his part the Holy Spirit sanctified and pervaded the Son's humanity, making it fit to participate in the love the Son has for the Father. Thus we are drawn through the Holy Spirit into the relationship the Son has with the Father. We are raised 'into communion with the persons of the Holy Trinity'.[53]

This should affect the way we treat people

Worship and reconciliation go together. Christian worship focused on the holy Trinity and controlled by the Trinity, on the undivided Trinity in which the three indwell each other in love, seeking the interests of the other cannot but promote the unity of the body of Christ. Worship entails the whole person submitting to, becoming conformed to, the one worshipped (Pss 115; 135; 2 Cor. 3:18). This is the one exception – the one thing to which worship is, in the short term, to be subordinate. If reconciliation is needed, that must come first (Matt. 5:24).

Glory to you, our God; glory to you.

O heavenly King, the Comforter, Spirit of Truth, who is in all places and fills all things; Treasury of good things and Giver of life: Come and take up your abode in us, and cleanse us from every stain; and save our souls, O Good One.

O Holy God, Holy Mighty, Holy Immortal One, have mercy upon us.

O Holy God, Holy Mighty, Holy Immortal One, have mercy upon us.

O Holy God, Holy Mighty, Holy Immortal One, have mercy upon us.

Glory to the Father, and to the Son, and to the Holy Spirit, now and ever, and unto ages of ages.

O all-holy Trinity, have mercy upon us. O Lord, wash away our sins. O Master, pardon our transgressions. O Holy One, visit and heal our infirmities, for your Name's sake.

---

52. Lukas Vischer (ed.), *Spirit of God, Spirit of Christ: Ecumenical Reflections on the Filioque Controversy* (London: SPCK, 1981), p. 10, emphasis original.

53. Staniloae, *Experience of God*, pp. 248–249.

Lord, have mercy.
Lord, have mercy.
Lord, have mercy.
Glory to the Father, and to the Son, and to the Holy Spirit, now and ever, unto ages of ages.
   Amen.[54]

---

54. The all-night vigil service, the third hour in Isabel Florence Hapgood, *Service Book of the Holy Orthodox-Catholic Apostolic Church*, 3rd ed. (Brooklyn, N.Y.: Syrian Antiochene Orthodox Archdiocese of New York and all North America, 1956), p. 43 (language modernized).

14. THE TRINITY AND PREACHING

Michael Reeves

Preaching, for the Christian, is an irreducibly trinitarian activity. As such, Christian preaching will always be richer, more faithful and more powerful when it is *deliberately* and *self-consciously* trinitarian. Now by definition no Christian could deny the trinitarian nature of biblical preaching: after all, to be a Christian involves believing that the only true God is the triune God. Yet it has not always been made easy for preachers to see the connection. Surprisingly little has been written on the Trinity and preaching, and standard textbooks on preaching tend not to give much – if any – time to explaining how the Trinity should inform the preacher's task. Trinitarianism can thus be assumed by the preacher and can thus be a sidelined irrelevance.

But what has the nature of God to do with preaching? We could all agree that 'trinitarian preaching' is a Good Thing, and yet the connection between the Trinity and preaching could seem so practically frail that we dismiss it as a subject fit only for the cloister. The place to start is surely with the basic Christian affirmation that God is the ground of all being. His identity and nature constitute the logic of the gospel, and of every Christian belief. In that sense, far from being a tangential nicety, the triune nature of God must shape our preaching if we are to ensure even its basic Christian identity. What I hope we will then come to see in this chapter is that, by deliberately building our understanding of preaching on the triune nature of God, preachers will find decidedly *practical* help.

The God who speaks

For the bulk of this chapter I will be turning to John Calvin as an exemplar of a preacher who saw and acted upon the intimate connection between the Trinity and preaching. His presence, I hope, will not only bring cohesion and wisdom, but will also serve to prove that the connection is a mainstream and historic one, and thus no novelty.

We start, however, with Martin Luther. When Luther came to comment on John 16:13 ('whatever [the Spirit] hears he will speak'), he made the following bold observation: 'here', he wrote, 'Christ refers to a conversation carried on in the Godhead, a conversation in which no creatures participate. He sets up a pulpit both for the speaker and for the listener. He makes the Father the Preacher and the Holy Spirit the Listener.'[1] It is as if, with the triune God, there is in eternity a pulpit! The first sermon – the first proclamation of the Word – was not in Acts 2, or Genesis 3, or even Genesis 1. God the Father is an eternal preacher, ever speaking out his Word; and the Holy Spirit has eternally been listening. Before any creatures were brought into being, the Holy Spirit was enjoying the ultimate sermon – a sermon he now shares with us. In the triune God there is an eternal conversation into which we have been brought.

Luther couched it in his own inimitably striking way, but the point is incontestable and basic for Christians: God is not silent or speechless; the living God is a God who speaks. That could sound a yawn-inducing claim, but the claim is not that he just *happens* to speak. Other gods, from Allah to Zeus, and from Baal to Yama, are all said by their worshippers to have spoken. That is not at all the point. In the triune god we find a God who *cannot be Wordless*. 'In the beginning was the Word, and the Word was with God, and the Word was God. He was in the beginning with God' (John 1:1–2).[2] Before all things, before anything was 'made through him' (John 1:3; cf. Col. 1:17), God had a Word to speak. The Word was God. Here is a God who does not *happen* to speak; by his very nature he *is* a speaking God.

Human preachers, then, are not the hirelings of a God incapable or unwilling to do his own publicity or teaching (as if God entertains himself with angel songs while his servants go out on the stump). Preaching is a natural expression of this God's identity. The Spirit who speaks what he has heard enables

---

1. *LW*, vol. 24, p. 364.

2. English translations are taken from the ESV.

preachers to join in with God's own proclamation of his Son. To preach Christ
is to participate in the life of God.

God communicates himself

Since the Word *is* God, when God speaks he communicates nothing less than
his very self. That is why in the Old Testament God's Word can be described
as the very creative power of God (Gen. 1:3; Ps. 33:6), the means by which he
reveals himself (Amos 3:1), the means of God's healing and deliverance (Ps.
107:20; Isa. 55:1). That is why, when the Word of God goes out, the very glory
of God shines out: 'For God, who said, "Let light shine out of darkness," has
shone in our hearts to give the light of the knowledge of the glory of God in
the face of Jesus Christ' (2 Cor. 4:6). A similar point is made in Hebrews 1,
where God's speaking to us by his Son is tightly connected to the Son's being
'the radiance of the glory of God and the exact imprint of his nature' (v. 3). As
Athanasius argued at some length in *Against the Heathen* 3.2, *because* the Word is
God, light, life, logic and being abound in his presence: apart from the Word
all is darkness, formlessness and unbeing (see Jer. 4:22–23). Because the
Word is God, it effectively creates, saves and reveals. It does what it says.

It means that, in speaking, God holds out more than (though not less than)
information and propositions. The Word of God brings the very presence of
God. When the Word of God comes to us, it is God himself, in all his life-giving
glory, who comes to be with us.

This is entirely different to how it is with the words of other gods. Dagon
or Quetzalcóatl might deign to speak, but their words would at most only tell
you something *about* them. Allah might be thought an exception to this rule: he
does, after all, have an *eternal* word beside him in heaven, the Qur'an. But it is a
book Allah could do without. Allah depends on nothing. He *has* a word, but
this word is not God. He is not *by nature* a God who speaks. And this word, the
Qur'an, cannot therefore bring the very presence of Allah with it. It simply tells
us *about* Allah, the character he claims for himself, and what he wants from us.
When Allah gives his Qur'an, he gives something other than himself: a deposit
of information and record of his will.

And the fact that the word of Dagon is not Dagon and the word of Allah
is not Allah means that those words cannot be as deeply revealing as the Word
who *is* God. The Word who is God cannot but display to us the very being of
the Father, for that is who he is. The words of other gods need not say much
about them. In fact, they could be more misleading than truly revealing. Allah,
for example, describes himself in the Qur'an as 'the best of deceivers', leading

men astray when he chooses.[3] That cannot be with Jesus, the divine Word. Since he is God, with him a direct and unmediated encounter with God happens. He is no pale reflection of God: in seeing him we see the Father who sent him (John 14:9), for he is perfect 'image of the invisible God' (Col. 1:15). In him God meets with us.

All of this should be great encouragement to the preacher. Without God's Word we simply would not know God. 'No one has ever seen God; the only God, who is at the Father's side, he has made him known' (John 1:18; cf. Matt. 11:27). It is because God is triune – that is, because the Father has this Word who is himself God, of his very essence – that we can confidently say that through the Word *we know God*.

This is a truth that needs to be heard loudly and clearly, especially in post-Christian Europe, where the situation is generally so disheartening. Faced with reams of horrifying statistics about church decline, a wearying negativity or defeatism can set in. Focused on the sheer immensity of the uphill battle before us, we can eventually develop a siege mentality. Losing the confidence to step out with the old Word of God, we circle the wagons and lose the confidence to step out into the world. Or we look elsewhere for the solution. But because of who God is preachers can know that they are not mere teachers of an unfashionable message, nor salesmen of one religious product: preachers herald the Word who is God. This is the very Word that – in the darkness – brought light, life and creation itself into being, the Word that now brings the new creation into being. The Word entrusted to the preacher is the very power of God who does not return empty, who will one day drive all darkness away for good.

God communicates in a trinitarian way

We have seen, then, that the triune God is a speaking God, a God who communicates himself when he utters his Word. Now, this communication is necessarily and completely trinitarian. Martin Luther brought out part of what

---

3. Surah 3:54; 4:88; 8:30; 14:4; 16:93. The nature of faith in Allah is naturally affected by this, as the first Caliph of Islam, Abu Bakr, showed in his response to an assurance that he would have a place in paradise: '"By Allah!" he said, "I would not rest assured and feel safe from the deception of Allah, even if I had one foot in paradise"' (Khalid Muhammad Khalid, *Successors of the Messenger*, tr. Muhammad Mahdi al-Sharif [Beirut: Dar al-Kotob al-Ilmiyah, 2005], bk. 1, p. 99).

this means in his comments on John 16:13, that the Father speaks, the eternal Word is spoken and the Spirit hears this Word – and then passes it on to us. That very act of the Spirit – hearing and speaking – is in fact a wholly trinitarian act, for the Father and the Son send the Spirit to do that work of speaking (John 15:26). The apostle Peter put it like this:

> Concerning this salvation, the prophets who prophesied about the grace that was to be yours searched and enquired carefully, enquiring what person or time *the Spirit* of Christ in them was indicating when *he* predicted the sufferings of Christ and the subsequent glories. It was revealed to them that they were serving not themselves but you, in the things that have now been announced to you through those who preached the good news to you *by the Holy Spirit* sent from heaven, things into which angels long to look. (1 Peter 1:10–12)

That is, through the Spirit God breathes out the Scriptures (2 Tim. 3:16) so that in them the 'word of Christ', Christ the Word, may be known (Rom. 10:17; Col. 3:16).

It is worth noting the vital point here, that the Word spoken by the Father and the message made known by the Spirit of truth are one and the same. What the Father holds out is his Word; what the Spirit testifies to is the Son. The Father sends the Spirit to make known his Word – the Word through whom the Father himself can be known (John 1:18; cf. 2 Tim. 3:15).

There is more to be said, though, about the trinitarian nature of God's self-communication. Not only is the Spirit sent to make the Son known (and, through him, to make the Father known); the Word goes out from the Father *in the power of the Spirit*. The sending forth of the Word is inseparable from the Spirit. 'By *the word* of the LORD the heavens were made', we read in Psalm 33:6, 'and by *the breath* [or 'Spirit'] of his mouth all their host.' The psalmist is clearly alluding to Genesis 1, when the Word of God is spoken into the darkness only as the Spirit hovers over the waters to bear it forth.

God always speaks, that is, in the power of his Spirit. His self-communication is a Spirit-enabled and Spirit-illumined speech. It is something that is both comforting and humbling for the preacher: God's Word does not go out powerless, but the power in which it goes out is not the power of the human preacher.

Sharing in the Father's proclamation of his word

Seeing how God himself speaks gives a fundamental framework to any theology of preaching. God the Father is the prime preacher, who speaks his Word and so communicates himself in the power of the Spirit. That is the trinitarian foundation on which the content, form and intent of truly Christian preaching must be built.

The first thing this means is that, since God in his speaking does not *merely* give information *about* himself, but actually gives *himself*, so the Christian preacher can know that he is about much more than the transferral of information. Jean-Jacques von Allmen expressed it like this:

> God is not so much the object as the true source of Christian preaching. Preaching is thus speech *by* God rather than speech *about* God . . . The Holy Spirit, indeed, has as His chief ministry to make effective today – with all that that implies – what Jesus Christ said and did, and also what He will say and do. Christian preaching cannot therefore be understood apart from the doctrine of the Trinity: on the basis of the past work of His Son, and in the perspective of the work He is yet to do, God the Father gives us today, through the Holy Spirit, faith in the salvation which has been accomplished and hope in the salvation yet to be revealed.[4]

Allmen was seeking to express what he saw as a standard Reformed view, and by way of illustration we can compare what we might call a 'Zwinglian' and a 'Calvinist' view of preaching.

The Zurich Reformer Ulrich Zwingli taught that in the Lord's Supper Christ's body is not present in any sense, but only *symbolized*. For him the Lord's Supper was a mere *memorial* pointing to a truth located elsewhere. If we take that logic into preaching, then in the same way, the point of the sermon, like the Supper, is to serve as a *memorial* to God's Word. God's Word is called freshly to mind, but no more.

Such a theology of preaching (whether or not Zwingli would expressly have owned the extension of his logic) stands in stark contrast to that articulated by his successor, Heinrich Bullinger, and championed by John Calvin in Geneva. When writing the Second Helvetic Confession, Bullinger boldly stated that 'The Preaching of the Word of God *Is* the Word of God.'[5] This requires a little clarification to avoid confusion. Bullinger never meant to imply that the words of a preacher somehow have the same standing and authority as Scripture. Scripture never bows to the preacher; the preacher must bow to Scripture, his preaching

---

4. Jean-Jacques von Allmen, *Preaching and Congregation*, tr. B. L. Nichols (Richmond, Va.: John Knox, 1962), pp. 7–8, emphases original.

5. The Constitution of the Presbyterian Church (USA), pt. 1, *Book of Confessions* (Louisville: Office of the General Assembly, 1999), 5.004, my emphasis.

depending on the Word of God in its supreme authority. The word preached from the pulpit is authoritative only in so far as it is a faithful proclamation of the Word of God found in Scripture; yet in so far as it is faithful, the people hear the very Word of God. Thus the Christian faithful can be told in Hebrews to remember their leaders 'who spoke to you the word of God' (Heb. 13:7).

T. H. L. Parker has argued at some length in his book *Calvin's Preaching* that what Bullinger articulated so succinctly was deeply decisive for Calvin's own preaching ministry.[6] He starts by asking why Calvin was so painstakingly committed, year after year, to expositional preaching. He answers that Calvin believed that through such preaching the very creative voice and Word of God would be heard. Not simply remembered or memorialized, but *heard*:

> If the preacher faithfully hands on what he himself has learned in the school of God, then God himself 'presides' (CO 53.264[8]), he is 'in the midst' (CO 53.264[8]), as if you were showing himself visibly (CO 53.264[18]) or face-to-face (CO 53.264[18]), and his people are 'joined' to him (CO 53.264[8]). Our Lord Jesus Christ is present (CO 53.264[8]) and the Church is united with him (CO 53.264[8]). The pulpit is 'the throne of God, from where he wills to govern our souls' (CO 53.520[40]).[7]

Calvin is worth hearing more directly and at length on this. Preaching on 1 Timothy 3:2 (that an overseer must be 'able to teach'), he declares:

> St Paul does not mean that one should just make a parade here or that a man should show off so that everyone applauds him and says 'Oh! well spoken! Oh! what a breadth of learning! Oh! what a subtle mind!' All that is beside the point ... When a man has climbed up into the pulpit, is it so that he may be seen from afar, and that he may be pre-eminent? Not at all. *It is that God may speak to us by the mouth of a man. And he does us that favour of presenting himself there* and wishes a mortal man to be his messenger.[8]

The Reformer was fully aware of the downright audacity of this (often repeated) claim. Elsewhere he therefore sought to substantiate it:

---

6. T. H. L. Parker, *Calvin's Preaching* (Edinburgh: T&T Clark, 1992), pp. 1–53. In his previous work *The Oracles of God* (London: Lutterworth, 1947), pp. 45–64, Parker also argues for how robustly trinitarian Calvin was in his theology of preaching.

7. Ibid., p. 26.

8. *Ioannis Calvini opera quae supersunt omnia*, ed. G. Baum, E. Cunitz and E. Reuss, Corpus Reformatorum 29–87 (Brunswick: Schwetschke, 1863–1900), 53.266, my emphasis.

When a man is the envoy of his prince and has complete authority to do what is committed to his charge, he will so to say borrow the prince's name. He will say, 'We are doing this; we instruct; we have commanded; we want that done.' Now, when he speaks like this, he is not intending to take anything from his master. So it is with God's servants. . . . It is said that the ministers are sent to enlighten the blind, to deliver the captives, to forgive sins, to convert hearts. What! these are things which belong to God alone . . . For there is nothing more properly his own than to pardon sins; he also reserves to himself the converting of the heart. Now, nevertheless it is the case that he imparts all these qualifications to those whom he appoints to convey his word and declares to them that he does not separate himself from them, but rather shows that he uses them as his hands and his instruments.[9]

Though not explicitly stated here, Calvin's argument builds on a concealed trinitarian substructure. That is, because God does not simply talk *about* himself, but communicates himself in his Word, so the proclamation of his Word by human preachers means the holding out of God himself in all his glory and grace. Considering Calvin's thoughts on 2 Corinthians 5:20, T. H. L. Parker summarizes:

It has become quite clear that with 'the school of God' we are not thinking of preaching as a purely educative exercise, and with 'ambassadors for Christ' we are not to consider only a repetition of instructions . . . What is daily preached in Geneva, Calvin is saying, is that God is gracious, that Jesus Christ has made the satisfaction for our sin. But when this message is preached, its reality is present and (how could it therefore be otherwise?) effective. It was not simply declared that God is a gracious God; in his Word God was being gracious in St Pierre and La Madeleine and St Gervais in May 1555. It was not only declared that Christ died for our sins, but before the eyes of the Genevans as of the Galatians fifteen hundred years earlier Jesus Christ was evidently set forth, crucified among them (Gal. 3.1). This is the language of revelation.[10]

Preaching, as God does, in a trinitarian way

The fact that God is triune, and always speaks in a trinitarian way, should inform both the *content* and the *intent* of Christian preaching.

---

9. Ibid. 26.66–67.
10. Parker, *Calvin's Preaching*, p. 29.

In terms of content – and I start at rock bottom here – the fact that God is triune must mean that Christian preachers preach the Trinity. And on more than one-off specials like Trinity Sunday. If this is who God is, then to preach the Trinity is not to indulge in esoterica, but to distinguish the living God from idols. As Calvin put it:

> God also designates himself by another special mark to distinguish himself more precisely from idols. For he so proclaims himself the sole God as to offer himself to be contemplated clearly in three persons. Unless we grasp these, only the bare and empty name of God flits about in our brains, to the exclusion of the true God.[11]

This means it simply will not do for Christian preachers to mouth a vague or general theism. How, then, will the glory of the living God be distinguished from the glory of all others? A faithful servant of this God will be eager to speak in trinitarian language as often and as clearly as possible, knowing our natural propensity to squash God into our own fallen perception.

'Preaching the Trinity' really (unfortunately) requires a little explanation. All too easily that could be taken to mean that, every now and again, the preacher departs from his usual expository ministry and puzzles his congregation with the question of how three can be one. Out with the verse-by-verse that week; in with talk about triangles and 3-in-1 hair shampoo. But the Trinity is not an addendum to the gospel of Jesus, a side room for those ready to move on: the triune God *is* the God of the gospel. To preach the Trinity is simply to preach the Father who is made known by his Son Jesus Christ in the power of the Spirit. It is, in fact, *no more* than to preach Jesus Christ, who is the Son of God anointed with the Holy Spirit. Note the trinitarianism of the simple summons to faith in Jesus found in John's Gospel: 'these are written so that you may believe that Jesus is the Christ, the Son of God, and that by believing you may have life in his name' (John 20:31). Perhaps part of the difficulty is all the technical theological jargon associated with the Trinity: extrabiblical words that can give the impression that the Trinity is an extrabiblical doctrine. But those words – *homoousion, hypostasis*, essence, and so on – were formulated specifically to *protect* what the church saw in Scripture, not *add* to it. To preach the Trinity is to herald the God made known in Scripture.

---

11. John Calvin, *Institutes of the Christian Religion*, ed. John T. McNeill, tr. Ford Lewis Battles, 2 vols., LCC 20 (Louisville: Westminster John Knox, 1960), 1.13.2 (vol. 1, p. 120). Hereafter 'Battles'.

To move up a level: preaching the Trinity involves more than merely slipping the words 'Father, Son and Spirit' into every sermon. Such tokenism equally betrays a belief in the peripherality of the Trinity. If people are to know the gospel of the triune God, then the very syntax and structure of that gospel must be clearly seen to be trinitarian. Take John Calvin again, as an example of this done well. In the first real outline of his theology, his preface to Olivétan's New Testament (1535), he gives the following succinctly trinitarian summary of the gospel: 'Scripture is also called gospel, that is, new and joyful news, because in it is declared that Christ, the sole true and eternal Son of the living God, was made man, to make us children of God his Father, by adoption.'[12]

The very structure of Calvin's *Institutes* (final 1559 edition) follows an explicitly trinitarian shape.

Book One, on 'The Knowledge of God the Creator', is concerned especially with the Father and explains how, through Scripture, we may know the triune God. 'In scripture, from the creation onward, we are taught one essence of God, which contains three persons' (the title of ch. 13). Book One also explains our plight as a fallen race: in 'this ruin of mankind *no one now experiences God either as Father* or as Author of salvation, or favorable in any way, until Christ the Mediator comes forward to reconcile him to us'.[13] Calvin thus not only spoke of God in expressly trinitarian terms, but the very nature of the human problem was also conceived by him in trinitarian terms: sinners cannot now experience God as Father.

Book Two, on 'The Knowledge of God the Redeemer in Christ', is concerned especially with the Son and how he brings us 'to God our Author and Maker, from whom we have been estranged, in order that he may again begin to be our Father'.[14] Here Calvin makes plain the trinitarian logic and framework of redemption: the Son comes from the Father to share with us his sonship:

> His task was so to restore us to God's grace as to make of the children of men, children of God; of the heirs of Gehennna, heirs of the Heavenly Kingdom. Who could have done this had not the self-same Son of God become the Son of man, and had not so taken what was ours as to impart what was his to us, and to make what was his by nature ours by grace?[15]

---

12. 'Preface to Olivétan's New Testament', in *Calvin: Commentaries*, ed. Joseph Haroutunian, LCC 23 (Philadelphia: Westminster, 1958), p. 64.

13. *Institutes* 1.2.1 (Battles, vol. 1, p. 40, emphasis mine).

14. Ibid. 2.6.1 (Battles, vol. 1, p. 341).

15. Ibid. 12.2 (Battles, vol. 1, p. 465).

Calvin saw that it is insufficient to conceive or speak of salvation as simply being about 'reconciliation with God'. While true, such language on its own fails to grasp the full wonder of the Son's redemption. It is only when Christ's work is viewed in its full trinitarian magnificence that we can grasp how 'the only Son of God . . . has adopted us as his brothers'.[16] Only then can the Christian know real confidence before the Most High, love him and dare to call him 'Father'.

Book Three, on 'The Way in Which We Receive the Grace of Christ', is concerned with the Spirit's application of the Son's redemption to believers. Calvin asks, 'How do we receive those benefits which the Father bestowed on his only-begotten Son – not for Christ's own private use, but that he might enrich poor and needy men?' He answers, by 'the secret energy of the Spirit, by which we come to enjoy Christ and all his benefits'.[17] In fact, he argues, it would be right to say that the first title of the Spirit is

> the 'Spirit of adoption' because he is the witness to us of the free benevolence of God with which God the Father has embraced us in his beloved only-begotten son to become a Father to us; and he encourages us to have trust in prayer. In fact, he supplies the very words so that we may fearlessly cry, 'Abba, Father!' [Rom. 8:15; Gal. 4:6].[18]

'Spirit of adoption' being the first title of the Spirit, Calvin could not have made more plain the primal and determinative significance of the triune being of God for salvation and the Christian life.

Book Four, on 'The External Means or Aids by Which God Invites Us Into the Society of Christ and Holds Us Therein', is concerned especially with the church. Having already covered the creative and redemptive work of Father, Son and Spirit in Books One to Three, Calvin takes his explanation of baptism as an opportunity to summarize the trinitarian shape of the Christian faith:

> All the gifts of God proffered in baptism are found in Christ alone. Yet this cannot take place unless he who baptizes in Christ invokes also the names of the Father and the Spirit. For we are cleansed by his blood because our merciful Father, wishing to receive us into grace in accordance with his incomparable kindness, has set this Mediator among us to gain favor for us in his sight. But we obtain regeneration by Christ's death and resurrection only if we are sanctified by the Spirit and imbued with

---

16. Ibid. (Battles, vol. 1, pp. 465–466).
17. Ibid. 3.1.1 (Battles, vol. 1, p. 537).
18. Ibid. 1.3 (Battles, vol. 1, p. 540).

a new and spiritual nature. For this reason we obtain and, so to speak, clearly discern in the Father the cause, in the Son the matter, and in the Spirit the effect, of our purgation and our regeneration.[19]

It was not at all a question of unnecessarily wedging trinitarianism in, though. Calvin held that baptism belongs at the very beginning of our faith because of how our faith is trinitarian to the core. Elsewhere he writes:

> There are good reasons why *the Father, the Son, and the Holy Spirit,* are expressly mentioned; for there is no other way in which the efficacy of *baptism* can be experienced than when we begin with the unmerited mercy of *the Father,* who reconciles us to himself by the only begotten *Son;* next, Christ comes forward with the sacrifice of his death; and at length, *the Holy Spirit* is likewise added, by whom he washes and regenerates us, (Tit. iii.5,) and, in short, makes us partakers of his benefits. Thus we perceive that God cannot be truly known, unless our faith distinctly conceive of Three Persons in one essence; and that the fruit and efficacy of *baptism* proceed from God *the Father* adopting us through his *Son,* and, after having cleansed us from the pollutions of the flesh through *the Spirit:* creating us anew to righteousness.[20]

Sharing the divine emphasis

The One held out by the Father, and the One to whom the Spirit of truth testifies, is the eternal Son who comes 'from the Father, full of grace and truth' (John 1:14). He is the truth and glory of God; in him the grace of God is found. That is why the law finds its fulfilment in him (Rom. 10:4), and why the prophets, the apostles and all the Scriptures testify about him (Luke 24:27, 44–46; John 5:39–40, 46).

Calvin argued this point at some length in his preface to Olivétan's New Testament. Indeed, he wrote:

> it is not only the Father, the Son, the Holy Spirit, the angels, the prophets and apostles that bear witness to Jesus Christ . . . all the elements and all the creatures have given

---

19. Ibid. 4.15.6 (Battles, vol. 2, p. 1308).

20. John Calvin, *Commentary on Harmony of the Evangelists,* tr. William Pringle, 3 vols. (repr. Grand Rapids: Baker, 2003), vol. 3, p. 387 (on Matt. 28:19), emphases mine.

Jesus Christ the glory ... There has been nothing in heaven or on earth which has not witnessed that Jesus Christ is God, Lord and Master, and the great Ambassador of the Father sent here below to accomplish the salvation of mankind.[21]

Jesus Christ is 'the beginning, the middle, and the end of our salvation ... It follows that every good thing we could think or desire is to be found in this same Jesus Christ alone.'[22] What all that means is this:

This is what we should in short seek in the whole of Scripture: truly to know Jesus Christ, and the infinite riches that are comprised in him and are offered to us by him from God the Father. If one were to sift thoroughly the Law and the Prophets, he would not find a single word which would not draw and bring us to him. And for a fact, since all the treasures of wisdom and understanding are hidden in him, there is not the least question of having, or turning toward, another goal; not unless we would deliberately turn aside from the light of truth, to lose ourselves in the darkness of lies. Therefore, rightly does Saint Paul say in another passage that he would know nothing except Jesus Christ, and him crucified.[23]

For the preacher, the application is straightforward: if the desire of the Father, the work of the Spirit and the purpose of Scripture is to make Jesus known, so too the preacher must seek to 'draw and bring us to him'. For the preacher there cannot be 'the least question of having, or turning toward, another goal'. And no preacher need worry that that necessarily means leap-frogging or manhandling his scriptural text: the ultimate purpose of his text *is* to testify in some way to Christ.

To know Christ is what we were made for; it is the essence of life and wisdom – the life and wisdom of the Father now shared with us in the Spirit:

What more would we ask for, as spiritual doctrine for our souls, than to know God, to be converted to him, and to have his glorious image imprinted in us, so that we may partake of his righteousness, to become heirs of his Kingdom and to possess it in the end in full? But the truth is that from the beginning God has given himself, and at present gives himself more fully, that we may contemplate him in the face of his Christ. It is therefore not lawful that we turn away and become diverted even in the smallest degree by this or that. On the contrary, our minds ought to come to a

21. 'Preface to Olivétan's New Testament', pp. 65–66.
22. Ibid., p. 69.
23. Ibid., p. 70.

halt at the point where we learn in Scripture to know Jesus Christ and him alone, so that we may be directly led by him to the Father who contains in himself all perfection.[24]

It would be wise at this point if we got more specific. For a 'Christ' could be preached who is not the eternally beloved of the Father or the subject of the Spirit's testimony. The 'Christ' set forth could be a good man and no more; he could be a godlet, or a God with no Father. Such distortions of Christ would utterly distort the gospel proclaimed.

First of all, if the Father did not eternally love the Son 'before the foundation of the world' (John 17:24), then we have no basis on which to say that eternally God *is* love (1 John 4:8). From what, then, would any grace and mercy spring in him? And why should we love him?

Second, without belief that God the Father has an eternal Son, of his very being, whom he sent to be our Saviour, we are left with a creature who simply would not have the right to allow us to be known as the sons of God. Perhaps we would be left with a man, powerless to do any more than inspire us to win our own way to God. Take these famous words from Charles Gore as he considered Nestorianism (the idea that Jesus was a man *in close relationship with* the Son, a man *helped along* by God's grace):

> Inadequate conceptions of Christ's person go hand in hand with inadequate conceptions of what human nature wants. The Nestorian conception of Christ . . . qualifies Christ for being an example of what man can do, and into what wonderful union with God he can be assumed *if he is holy enough*; but Christ remains one man among many, shut in within the limits of a single human personality, and influencing man only from the outside. He can be a Redeemer of man if man can be saved from outside by bright example, but not otherwise. The Nestorian Christ is logically associated with the Pelagian man . . . *The Nestorian Christ is the fitting Saviour of the Pelagian man.*[25]

In other words, the triunity of God fundamentally affects how we conceive both the person and the work of Christ. Since the Son is God himself, one with his Father, we clearly need and have a divine Saviour. The fact that God would step in to our rescue shows the gravity of our need: evidently, by ourselves, even if we were assisted, we could not save ourselves. And the fact that God himself

---

24. Ibid.

25. Charles Gore, 'Our Lord's Human Example', *CQR* 16 (1883), p. 298, my emphases.

has come to our rescue shows we have a gospel of grace. A helpless humanity, a gracious God and a sufficient Saviour: such must be the preached emphases of a trinitarian gospel.

Sharing the divine intent

The triune God has a particular intent in communicating: he speaks and makes himself known through his Word in order that we may enter into the divine life. In his high priestly prayer Jesus says:

> O righteous Father, even though the world does not know you, I know you, and these know that you have sent me. I made known to them your name, and I will continue to make it known, *that the love with which you have loved me may be in them, and I in them.* (John 17:25–26)

The Son comes to us from the Father to share with us his life of knowing the Father, being loved by the Father and loving the Father in return. In that way we who are made in God's image are conformed to him by the Spirit, loving the Father as the Son does and loving the Son as the Father does. It means that the knowledge of himself that God shares is not a bare cognition. We may say that the triune God who is love is not truly known where he is not truly loved.

This was of signal importance to John Calvin as he fought the Roman Catholic notion of an 'unformed', 'implicit' faith that accepts church teaching without any movement of the heart towards trust in God or filial love and fear of him:[26]

> We are called to a knowledge of God: not that knowledge which, content with that empty speculation, merely flits in the brain, but that which will be sound and fruitful if we duly perceive it, and if it takes root in the heart.[27]

---

26. *Institutes* 3.2.8 (Battles, vol. 1, pp. 551–552).

27. Ibid. 1.5.9 (Battles, vol. 1, p. 61). Following Rom. 10:10, Calvin held that 'the seat of faith is not in the head, but in the heart. Yet I would not contend about the part of the body in which faith is located: but as the word *heart* is often taken for a serious and sincere feeling, I would say that faith is a firm and effectual confidence, and not a bare notion only' (John Calvin, *Commentaries on the Epistle of Paul the Apostle to the Romans*, ed. and tr. John Owen [repr. Grand Rapids: Baker, 2003], p. 393 [on Rom. 10:10]).

Calvin considered this so vital that he dedicated the second chapter of his *Institutes* to the claim that 'piety', 'trust' and 'reverence' are requisite components of any true knowledge of God. 'We shall not say that, properly speaking, God is known where there is no religion or piety.'[28] He believed this to be the case because of the sheer glory and goodness of God: such a God cannot be known without being adored. 'How', he asked,

> can the mind be aroused to taste the divine goodness without at the same time being wholly kindled to love God in return? For truly, that abundant sweetness which God has stored up for those who fear him cannot be known without at the same time powerfully moving us.[29]

For the preacher it means that a sermon cannot be confused with a simple lecture. The preacher has a greater responsibility (a responsibility that demands a deeper integrity): God shares knowledge of himself in order that we may be *affected*, that we may be 'wholly kindled to love God', just as the Father loves the Son and the Son loves the Father. Preaching should foster sincere worship. And Calvin was clear that such heartfelt worship is precisely what is most essentially and practically transformative for the Christian, what is most productive of true obedience. That is because love for God enables true love for neighbour (1 John 4:7–21). The first table of the law (concerning worship) is the foundation for the second (concerning love for neighbour), and only in that order can the law be fulfilled.[30]

Conclusion

As Luther put it, God the Father is an eternal preacher, and thus preaching finds its ultimate rationale and shape in the very nature of God. The Trinity therefore underpins the highest view of preaching, and practically preserves it from being

---

28. *Institutes* 1.2.1 (Battles, vol. 1, p. 39).

29. Ibid. 3.2.41 (Battles, vol. 1, p. 589). Edward Dowey observed that, whether 'discussing the encounter with God in creation or Scripture, Calvin always uses the term "knowledge" in conjunction with the love or hatred, mercy or wrath of God, as well as man's total response in trust or fear, obedience or disobedience' (Edward A. Dowey Jr., *The Knowledge of God in Calvin's Theology* [Grand Rapids: Eerdmans, 1994], p. 24).

30. *Institutes* 2.8.11 (Battles, vol. 1, pp. 367–368).

confused with mere lecturing, moralizing or entertaining. When by the Spirit a preacher holds out God's Word, he proclaims more than a message: he participates in the divine life, wielding the very power of God to raise dead sinners to enjoy the loving life of God.

INDEX OF SCRIPTURE REFERENCES